Blindness and Reorientation

Blindness and Reorientation

Problems in Plato's Republic

C. D. C. Reeve

OXFORD
UNIVERSITY PRESS

OXFORD

UNIVERSITY PRESS

Oxford University Press is a department of the University of Oxford.
It furthers the University's objective of excellence in research, scholarship,
and education by publishing worldwide.

Oxford   New York
Auckland   Cape Town   Dar es Salaam   Hong Kong   Karachi
Kuala Lumpur   Madrid   Melbourne   Mexico City   Nairobi
New Delhi   Shanghai   Taipei   Toronto

With offices in
Argentina   Austria   Brazil   Chile   Czech Republic   France   Greece
Guatemala   Hungary   Italy   Japan   Poland   Portugal   Singapore
South Korea   Switzerland   Thailand   Turkey   Ukraine   Vietnam

Oxford is a registered trademark of
Oxford University Press in the UK and in certain other countries.

Published in the United States of America by
Oxford University Press
198 Madison Avenue, New York, NY 10016

© Oxford University Press 2013

Library of Congress Cataloging-in-Publication Data
Reeve, C. D. C., 1948–
Blindness and reorientation : problems in Plato's Republic / C.D.C. Reeve.
p. cm.
ISBN 978–0–19–993443–0
1. Plato. Republic.   I. Title. JC71.P6R42
2013321'.07—dc23
2012015002

1 3 5 7 9 8 6 4 2
Printed in the United States of America
on acid-free paper

For Siri

CONTENTS

PREFACE

In the closing lines of the *Phaedo*, Socrates is described as "a man who, we would say, was the best of all those we've experienced, and, generally, the wisest and most just" (118a16–17). More than anyone, he embodied the true philosophical spirit for Plato. It is to a Socrates "made fine and new" (314c1–4), indeed, that the author of the (almost certainly spurious) *Second Letter* attributes all of Plato's writings. Yet the apparently unreformed Socrates we meet in the *Apology*, who is arguably closest to the historical figure, seems to be motivated as much by pious obedience to the god Apollo as by the sheer love of wisdom itself. His target is hubris. His method is elenctic examination pursued in private conversation. His message is the pessimistic one that the god alone is wise, whereas human wisdom consists in the hard-won recognition of what this implies about oneself. Like the "sophist of noble lineage" (*Sph.* 231b8), he seems to educate exclusively by purging those who falsely think they know of their conceit of wisdom, not by putting positive knowledge or wisdom into them. He is a midwife, not a begetter of children. Moreover, he is catholic in his examination. Anyone—man or woman, slave or free—is a suitable target for his deflationary therapy. A professional teacher and Sophist like Thrasymachus is a candidate, but so, too, is an ordinary young man like Polemarchus or an old one like Cephalus.

Paiderasteia, or boy-love between an older man (*erastēs*) and an adolescent boy (*erōmenos*), was an accepted practice in Socratic Athens. As Greek comedy makes plain and common sense suggests, sex was common in such relationships, with the boy playing the passive role. Once he reached manhood, however, that had to change. On pain of losing his citizen rights, he could no longer be a passive sexual partner. Instead, he was expected to marry, have children, and became an *erastēs* in his turn. Though erotic in nature, the relationship was conceived as primarily educative. By associating with someone who was already a man, a boy learned *aretē*—virtue or excellence. He learned how to be a man himself. We might think here of rites of passage in primitive warrior societies, some of which also involve sexual contact between men and boys. It is often suggested, indeed, that Greek *paiderasteia* had its roots in a warrior past.

Adding to the complexity of an already complex situation is the dimension of romance. Various factors in ancient Greece contrived to keep romance out of courtship and marriage, especially among the upper classes: marriages were typically arranged for social or economic reasons; brides were often much younger than their spouses; women were sequestered in the household, excluded from the public world in which men worked out their destinies. As a result, it was often relationships between men and boys that took the form of romance, with its rituals of pursuit and avoidance, the giving of love gifts, and the writing of love songs and poems. The world of Plato's dialogues—especially those in which Socrates converses with beautiful boys and acknowledges his attraction to them—is the world of such romance. "You can't measure anything by me," he says at one point, "I'm simply a blank measuring tape when it comes to beautiful boys— practically anyone of that age seems beautiful to me" (*Chrm.* 154b8–10). In the *Symposium* and to some extent in the *Phaedrus*, philosophy seems to be special to this world, implying, apparently, that only a lover of boys can be a true Platonic philosopher.

The Socrates who is at home in this world, and whose elenctic conversations often take place within it, is the focus of chapter 1 ("Human Wisdom"). The problem he presents for a reader of the *Republic* is this: why isn't he adequate for its argumentative purposes? Why, having apparently refuted Thrasymachus in *Republic* 1, must he be transformed in *Republic* 2–10 from a negative critic into a positive theorist, with complex views on knowledge, reality, the human soul, and moral virtue, who famously argues that women—and not just paiderastic males—can be philosophers, even philosopher-kings? This question is at the center of chapter 2 ("Alcibiades and the Socratic Craft of Love") and is returned to in chapter 6 ("From Beauty to Goodness"), where some of Socrates' philosophical limitations are diagnosed, and their relationship to the project of the *Republic* is characterized. Prominent in these chapters and a topic in almost every other is the notion of a *technē* or craft as representing the sort of ethical wisdom that Socrates sought but never found, and its transformation, too, in Plato's hands.

As reformed by Plato, Socrates is apparently less sanguine on two fronts than his unreformed self, more sanguine on a third. Unless we have a certain psychological nature, unless we have a soul in which reason, with its inherent love of wisdom, goodness, and truth, can come to rule the appetites and emotions, elenctic examination, especially when we are young, is more likely to be corruptive than salvational. Here is the reformed Socrates vividly making this very point to Glaucon, repeatedly using the verb *elegchein* ("refute" or "examine")—the root of our noun "elenchus"—to drive it home:

> I take it that we hold from childhood convictions about what things are just and fine; we are brought up with them as with our parents, we obey and honor them....And there are also other practices, opposite to those, which possess pleasures that flatter our soul and attract it to themselves, but which do not persuade people who are at all moderate, who continue to honor and obey the convictions of their fathers....What happens, then, when someone of that sort is met by the question, "What is the fine?" and, when he answers what he has heard from the traditional lawgiver, the argument refutes (*exelegchē[i]*) him, and by refuting (*elegchōn*) him often and in many ways reduces him to the belief that the fine is no more fine than shameful, and the same with the just, the good, and the things he honored most....Then when he no longer regards them as honorable or as his own kin, the way he did before, and cannot discover the true ones...he will be taken, I suppose, to have changed from being law-abiding to being lawless....I mean, I don't suppose it has escaped your notice that when young people get their first taste of argument, they misuse it as if it were a game to play, always using it for disputation. They imitate those who have refuted (*exelegchontas*) them by refuting (*elegchousi*) others themselves, and, like puppies, enjoy dragging and tearing with argument anyone within reach....Then, when they have refuted (*elegxōsin*) many themselves and been refuted (*elegchthōsi*) by many, they quickly fall into vehemently disbelieving everything they believed before. (*R.* 7, 538c6–539c2)

Natural gifts of the requisite sort are not enough to save us from such a fate. We also need the right sort of early upbringing and training—the right habits—and the right subsequent education in music (*mousikē*) and physical training (*gumnastikē*), the mathematical sciences, dialectic (a descendant of the Socratic elenchus), and practical politics. The nature and effects of this education are discussed in various chapters but primarily in chapter 7 ("Education and the Acquisition of Knowledge"). Nonetheless, if we do have the right natural gifts and do receive the right upbringing and education, something approximating the wisdom of the gods can apparently be ours.

One consequence of this revision is that Socrates' *daimonion*, which was his own peculiar gift and represented the special care of Apollo for him, becomes the daimon in all of us—the rational element in our souls. Chapter 5 ("Souls, Soul-Parts, and Persons") discusses the tripartite psychology presupposed by this revision of Socrates' outlook and philosophical methods. It is the centerpiece of *Republic* 4, and a lynchpin of the *Republic's* overall argument.

Insofar as human beings are ruled by their rational part, insofar as they are rational, they pursue whatever they pursue for the sake of *eudaimonia*—"happiness," as it is usually translated. Since this consists in having good things be theirs throughout their lives, they need a reliable paradigm to serve as their standard or measure of goodness. This the Platonic form of the good—the good itself—alone provides. It is discussed in chapter 8 ("Craft, Dialectic, and the Form of the Good"). As a good—indeed an ideal of goodness—the form of the good is itself loved in the way such a thing can be loved: by being known or contemplated. Knowing the good is thus the pinnacle of happiness, and the philosophical life, which is centered on it, is the best human one. The good also casts its illuminating glow on all the things it determines as really good, or as choiceworthy because of themselves. Included among these, the *Republic* argues, are the virtues—wisdom, justice, courage, and temperance.

In the *Crito*, Socrates distinguishes himself and those persuaded by his arguments from other people by reference to their attitude to justice (49c10–d9). Philosophers value justice so much more highly than any fruits of injustice, he claims, that they would rather suffer injustice than do it. In the *Republic*, Plato's brothers, Glaucon and Adeimantus, challenge him to show that being just really does further happiness better than being unjust. The nature of this challenge is discussed in chapter 4 ("Glaucon's Thrasymachean Challenge"). The vexed question of whether Socrates succeeds in meeting it in the crucial case of the philosopher-kings is the topic of chapter 9 ("The Happiness of the Philosopher-Kings"). The Thrasymachean provenance of Glaucon's challenge connects both these chapters to chapter 3 ("Cephalus, Odysseus, and the Importance of Experience"), which discusses the *Republic's* opening and closing scenes, the significance of its cast of characters, and the relevance of experience to the form-focused wisdom of the philosopher-kings.

Though specialist scholars of Plato should find something for themselves in these pages, I have had them less in view than all those readers of Plato who have been inspired enough by the *Republic* to want to understand it better. So, though I deal with many of the deepest interpretative and philosophical problems that specialists have raised, I usually do so by developing materials contained within the work itself, not by directly confronting opposing views, unless it seems particularly profitable to work through these. My aim is to lead readers deeper into the *Republic*, sometimes by traveling through some surrounding Platonic territory, such as the *Apology*, *Meno*, *Phaedo*, and *Symposium*, which probably predate the

Republic, and *Phaedrus,* which probably antedates it slightly, sometimes (though less often) by venturing further afield into such late dialogues as the *Timaeus, Philebus,* and *Laws.* The abbreviated titles of these and other ancient works occasionally used in references are explained in the Index of Passages.

Years ago, a reviewer of my *Philosopher-Kings: The Argument of Plato's Republic* (Princeton University Press, 1988; reissued, Hackett, 2006), mentioned the love of the *Republic* that was palpable in it and commented on the blindness as well as the insight that love can bring. The love has, if anything, intensified over the intervening years—years in which I have revised one translation of the *Republic* and produced another. With luck it is the insight that has grown, not the blindness.

ACKNOWLEDGMENTS

The chapters of this book revise, redeploy, or (in the case of chapter 5) reproduce views first explored in the following essays and papers: Chapter 1: "Socrates the Apollonian?" *Reason and Religion in Socratic Philosophy*, ed. Nicholas D. Smith and Paul B. Woodruff (Oxford: Oxford University Press, 2000), pp. 24–39. Chapter 2: "Telling the Truth about Love: Plato's *Symposium*," *Proceedings of the Boston Area Colloquium in Ancient Philosophy* 8 (1992): 89–114, and "A Study in Violets: Alcibiades in the *Symposium*," in *Plato's Symposium: Issues in Interpretation and Reception*, ed. J. H. Lesher, Debra Nails, and Frisbee C. C. Sheffield (Cambridge, Mass.: Harvard University Press, 2006), pp. 124–146. Chapter 3: "Philosophy, Craft, and Experience in the *Republic*," *Southern Journal of Philosophy* 63 (2005): 1–21. Chapter 4: "Glaucon's Challenge and Thrasymacheanism," *Oxford Studies in Ancient Philosophy* 34 (2008): 69–103. Chapter 5: "Soul, Soul-Parts, and Persons in Plato," in *Reason and Analysis: Essays in Honor of David Keyt*, ed. Georgios Anagnostopolous and Fred D. Miller Jr. (Dordrecht: Springer, 2013). Chapter 6: "Plato on Begetting in Beauty," in *Platon, Symposion*, ed. Christoph Horn (Berlin: Akademie Verlag, 2011), pp. 159–189. Chapter 7: "Blindness and Reorientation: Education and the Acquisition of Knowledge in the *Republic*," in *The Cambridge Critical Guide to the Republic*, ed. Mark L. McPherran (Cambridge: Cambridge University Press, 2010), pp. 209–228. Chapter 8: "The Role of *Technē* in Plato's Construction of Philosophy," *Proceedings of the Boston Area Colloquium in Ancient Philosophy* 16 (2000): 207–222, and "Plato's Metaphysics of Morals," *Oxford Studies in Ancient Philosophy* 25 (2003): 39–58. Chapter 9: "Goat-Stags, Philosopher-Kings, and Eudaimonism in the *Republic*," *Proceedings of the Boston Area Colloquium in Ancient Philosophy* 22 (2006): 185–209.

Translations of Plato—often silently modified—should be credited as follows: *Apology, Euthyphro*: my *The Trials of Socrates* (Indianapolis: Hackett, 2002), pp. 3–61. *Lysis*: Stanley Lombardo, *Plato: Complete Works*, ed. John M. Cooper (Indianapolis: Hackett, 1997), pp. 687–707. *Phaedrus*: C. J.

Rowe, *Plato: Phaedrus* (Warminster: Aris and Phillips, 1986). *Philebus*: Dorothea Frede, *Plato: Philebus* (Indianapolis: Hackett, 1993). *Republic*: my *Plato: Republic* (Indianapolis: Hackett, 2004). *Sophist*: Nicholas P. White, *Plato: Sophist* (Indianapolis: Hackett, 1993). *Symposium*: C. J. Rowe, *Plato: Symposium* (Warminster: Aris and Phillips, 1998). *Timaeus*: Donald J. Zeyl, *Plato: Timaeus* (Indianapolis: Hackett, 2000).

I am grateful to the publishers involved for allowing me to make use of these materials.

For comments, criticisms, and other sorts of important help I thank Julia Annas, Ruby Blondell, Christopher Bobonich, John Cooper, Pierre Destrée, David Keyt, Richard Kraut, Katy Meadows, David O'Connor, Mark McPherran, Constance Meinwald, David Sedley, and Nicholas Smith.

A study leave in spring 2009, a W. N. Reynolds research leave in fall 2009, and an Espy Family Fellowship in spring 2010 provided the leisure needed to complete this book. To the University of North Carolina at Chapel Hill, Geoff Sayre-McCord, (now ex-) Chair of its Philosophy Department, the donors of these leaves and fellowships, and those who administer them, I extend my thanks. I extend them, too, to ΔKE, the first fraternity in the United States to endow a professorial chair, and to UNC for awarding it to me. The generous research funds that the endowment makes available each year have greatly aided my work.

CHAPTER 1

ᴄᴧᴐ

Human Wisdom

About the historical Socrates it has been said that we know only that we know nothing. One thing we do know, though, is that he was put on trial in 399 BC, at the age of seventy, found guilty on a capital charge, and sentenced to death by hemlock poisoning. Plato's *Apology* presents itself as his speech of defense, and is frequently adverted to in other dialogues—including the *Republic*. Whatever conclusion we come to about its historical accuracy, it will be hard to disagree with the great Victorian historian of Greece George Grote in thinking that no one "can conceive fairly the character of Sokratēs who does not enter into the spirit of that impressive discourse."[1] It is with the spirit of the *Apology* in another sense that we will be concerned, however, namely, with the spirit or daimon that haunts it, and with the relationship between Socratic wisdom and the god Apollo that it implies.

Socrates' Daimonic Sign and Its Provenance

Although Socrates does not refer to Apollo by name in the *Apology*, he uses the phrase "the god" twenty-six times, twenty-three as a referring expression with a determinate reference.[2] Twenty times it refers to "the god in Delphi," whom Socrates elsewhere does name, speaking of "Apollo in his

---

1. George Grote, *A History of Greece*, vol. 7 (London: John Murray, 1888), p. 94.
2. 19a6, 20e8, 21b3, e5, 22a4, 23a5, b5, b7, c1, 26e3*, 28c5*, e4, 29b6*, d4, 30a5, 6, e1, 3, 6, 31a7, 8, 33c5, 35d7, 37e6, 40b1, 42a5. Those marked with an asterisk are nonreferring (predicative) uses.

temple at Delphi" (*Prt.* 343b1–2; also *R.* 4, 427b2–3). The three remaining occurrences require brief investigation:

> [1] Even so, let the matter proceed as the god may wish, but I must obey the law and make my defense. (19a5–7)
>
> [2] The usual prophetic sign of my *daimonion* was always very frequent in all of the time before this and held me back even on small matters, if I was about to do something that was not right. But now, as you can see for yourselves, that I was faced with what someone might think to be the greatest of evils, the sign of the god did not hold me back. (40a4–b2)
>
> [3] Now it is time to go, I to die and you to live; which of us goes to a better thing is uncertain to everyone except the god. (42a2–5)

Because the god in (3) is the only being with certain knowledge about the comparative goodness or badness of Socrates' death, (2) and (3) are clearly connected. Yet, having experienced the silence of his *daimonion*, Socrates acquires derivative certainty on a closely related topic: "It is certain that it is now better for me to be dead and to leave my troubles behind. Because of this the sign did not hold me back" (41d3–6). It seems safe to infer that the same god is referred to in both passages. But the only god represented as having any interest at all in Socrates' trial is the one whose wish Socrates is able to discern when, at the end of the trial, he comes to understand what the silence of his *daimonion* signifies about his death. Hence that god must be the one referred to in (2) and (3).

Twenty times "the god" refers to Apollo. When, on three other occasions, it refers to a single god who may or may not be Apollo, common sense suggests that the reference must be to Apollo, too. Hence "the sign of the god" in (2) must be the sign of Apollo. With a little more work, we may specify its provenance with greater precision. Throughout the *Apology*, the neuter plural *daimonia* is consistently used to mean *daimonia pragmata* or daimonic activities (27c1), which are daimonic precisely because they are the activities of substantive daimons: "if I believe in daimonic activities (*daimonia*), then surely there is a great necessity that I also believe in daimons (*daimonas*)" (27c5–9).

Daimons, Socrates says, are either gods or the children of gods (27c10–d3). Meletus readily agrees. So the view can hardly be controversial or idiosyncratic; it must reflect conventional wisdom. Now look at (2). The phrases "the sign of the god" and "the usual prophetic sign of my *daimonion*" are used interchangeably in it. But the latter phrase, we know, is to be understood as involving reference to the activities of a substantive daimon. Hence the daimon responsible for Socrates' *daimonion* is either Apollo himself or his child or children acting as his spokesperson. The Apollonian provenance of the *daimonion* is therefore an intimate one. It is also long-lived. For Socrates is explicit that the *daimonion* has been a part of his life since he was a child: "a daimonion comes to me. . . . This began when I was a child" (31c8–d3; also *Thg.* 128d2–3). No wonder Socrates takes the pronouncement of the Delphic oracle so seriously as to spend the rest of his life under its spell. No wonder—if it is even remotely appropriate to speak in this way—that Apollo provides the oracle in the first place.

Doxa, Praxis, and the Real Apollo

One might well buy all of this, yet claim that it fails to get to the heart of the matter. For just as many people call themselves Christians with doubtful warrant, so not all apparent or self-styled followers of Apollo need be the genuine article:

> To the ordinary juror Apollo is many things besides "the lord whose oracle is at Delphi," whom the city consults before every important undertaking. He is, for example, god of the plague and of the lyre; music, disease, but also medicine, are among the fields in which he is active. In myth he is a rapist, killer of children, and the flayer of Marsyas. . . . Our juror could well be in doubt that the rigorously moral divinity to which Plato's Socrates keeps referring is the old Apollo he has known since childhood or a newly made god of Socrates' own.[3]

The underlying idea is plain enough. Socrates' Apollo—wise, virtuous, truthful—is so different from the Apollo of tradition that to an ordinary juror he would seem to be a Socratic invention.

Large issues are joined here that encourage large and for the most part familiar responses. There is no canonical theology in Greek religion, no revelation, no founding prophet, no sacred scripture. The works of Homer and Hesiod, sometimes referred to as "the Bible of the Greeks," are not really the equivalent of our Bible. They were not supported by a church or clergy and did not have to be believed on pain of heterodoxy or excommunication—terms of doubtful application in Greek religion.[4] There is not even

---

3. Myles Burnyeat, "Cracking the Socrates Case," *New York Review of Books* 35.5 (March 31, 1988): 18.

4. Walter Burkert, *Greek Religion* (Cambridge, Mass.: Harvard University Press, 1985), p. 8.

a term in Greek with quite the same meaning as "religion." Besides, by the time of Socrates' trial, it is possible to speak of a "collapse of the authority of the poets and the myth administered by them" and of "the creation of a typical enlightened attitude of the average educated man towards religion," which represented the poet's myths, literally interpreted, as "untrue and impious."[5] It is significant that even "such a zealot as Euthyphro expresses neither horror nor surprise" when Socrates refuses to believe the traditional accounts of Zeus castrating his own father (*Euthphr.* 6a6–9).[6] The services, rites, and rituals sanctioned by tradition—in a word, *praxis*—are what have been described as "the nucleus of the relationship between 'religion' and 'faith' in the Greek world."[7]

It is for this reason that Socrates can comfortably combine a radical critique of the characterizations of the gods given by Homer and Hesiod with strong support of traditional Delphian authority and the religious practices it commands:

> For the Delphic Apollo there remain the greatest, finest, and first of legislations.... [Those about] the establishing of temples and sacrifices, and other forms of service to gods, daimons, and heroes; the burial of the dead, and the services that ensure the favor of those who have gone to the other world. For we, of course, have no knowledge of these things, and so, when we are founding a city, we won't take anyone else's advice, if we have any sense, or employ any interpreter, except our ancestral one. And, in fact, this god—as he delivers his interpretations from his seat at the navel of the earth—is the ancestral guide on these matters for the whole human race. (*R.* 4, 427b2–c4)

Aristotle is no different in this regard: "as for the buildings assigned to the gods, ... it is fitting for them to be located together on a suitable site—except in the case of temples assigned a separate location by the law or the Delphic Oracle" (*Pol.* 7.12, 1331a26–28).

Since Socrates seems to have been entirely and publicly conventional in his religious practices (*Euthd.* 302c4–303a1; Xenophon, *Ap.* 11–12), it is anything but clear that an ordinary late fifth-century juror would think that just because his Apollo fails to fit the traditional (but increasingly suspect) stereotype, he must be an invention. What matters most is whether Socrates participates in the services, rites, and rituals sanctioned

---

5. Burkert, *Greek Religion*, pp. 119–125.
6. A. E. Taylor, *Varia Socratica* (Oxford: James Parker, 1911), p. 16 n. 1.
7. Mario Vegetti, "The Greeks and Their Gods," in *The Greeks*, ed. Jean-Pierre Vernant (Chicago: University of Chicago Press, 1995), p. 256.

by tradition as Apollonian. What he says or believes is much less significant (*Euthphr.* 3c6–d1).

The overshadowing of *doxa* by *praxis* of faith by the services, rites, and rituals sanctioned by tradition is a fundamental fact of Greek religion. Yet if we make the shadow too dark, so that *doxa* is altogether occluded by *praxis*, we are in danger of making Meletus' indictment of Socrates seem completely unintelligible. The relevant clause is this: "Socrates commits injustice by *ou nomizōn* the gods that the city *nomizei*."[8] Taken at face value, it is a charge of heterodoxy, not heteropraxy, so that what seems to be at issue is what Socrates believes, not what he does. The classic commentary on the *Apology* argues that it should not be taken in that way. *Ou nomizōn*, it claims, means "'not acknowledging' by giving them the worship prescribed by *nomos*. . . . The charge is one of nonconformity in religious practice, not of unorthodoxy in religious belief."[9] If this were right, Socrates' religious beliefs would be irrelevant to Meletus' charges and would have seemed so to the jurors.

The fatal flaw in the proposal is revealed by the fact that throughout the *Apology* (26b8–d5, 29a1–4, 32d2–5) *nomizein theous* is used in the sense of *nomizein theous einai*.[10] Since *einai* means "to be" or "to exist," the phrase cannot mean what the proposal says it does. Yet it would be wrong to conclude that the correct translation of *nomizein* must therefore be "believe." Witness Socrates' closing words to the jury just before they give their verdict:

> Clearly, if I persuaded you and forced you by begging [you to find me innocent], after you had sworn the [juror's] oath, I would be teaching you not to *hēgeisthai theous einai* and in defending myself I would be accusing myself of *theous ou nomizō*. But that's far from being the case: *nomizō* them, men of Athens, as none of my accusers does. (35c5–d7)

If Socrates makes a begging defense, he accuses himself of *theous ou nomizō* and teaches the jurors not to *hēgeisthai theous einai*. By eschewing such a defense, he shows himself to *nomizein* the gods, while his accusers, by unjustly bringing him to trial, show that they do not *nomizein* them. Manifestly, the point at issue here is not one of according the gods the worship prescribed by *nomos* or convention, but neither is it one of belief pure

8. Diogenes Laertius, *Lives of Eminent Philosophers* (Cambridge, Mass.: Harvard University Press, 1925), 2.40, p. 171.

9. John Burnet, *Plato: Euthyphro, Apology, and Crito* (Oxford: Clarendon Press, 1924), p. 104.

10. J. Tate, "Greek for 'Atheism,'" *Classical Review* 50 (1936): 3–5, and "More Greek for 'Atheism,'" *Classical Review* 51 (1937): 3–6.

and simple: if the jurors were persuaded to violate their oaths, they would not thereby come to disbelieve in the existence of gods. What is at issue is, rather, behaving in ways that show or fail to show proper acknowledgment of the gods' existence. Acknowledging gods (*nomizein theous*), although primarily a matter of giving them the worship prescribed by convention, through participating in the services, rites, and rituals sanctioned by tradition, thus encompasses all behavior that shows proper acknowledgment of their existence (*nomizein theous einai*). Meletus is neither accusing Socrates of doing the ancient equivalent of failing to go to church on Sunday nor of heterodoxy, but of failing to be god-fearing, of behaving in ways that do not properly acknowledge the existence of the city's gods.

Faced with Meletus' charge so understood, the jurors will be concerned about whether he behaves in ways that acknowledge the existence of Apollo. This is a broader issue, certainly, than the one we considered earlier. It cannot be answered solely by appeal to Socrates' religious practices. It allows what is done outside the traditional services, rites, and rituals, outside the purview of religion narrowly construed, to carry weight, but it still makes *praxis*, not *doxa*, the principal focus. This may help explain why, despite Socrates' radical revision of the traditional stereotype of Apollo, 220 jurors out of 500 found him innocent of Meletus' charges (36a5).

Socrates and Delphi

Though this response is generally persuasive, it is not the only one worth exploring. For even if we concede that Socrates is not a traditional Apollonian pure and simple, his Apollo is still not an invention, and he is still a traditional Apollonian *of a sort*. His Apollo is, as he claims, "the god in Delphi," and he is himself recognizably and profoundly Delphian. To be convinced of this, we need to understand something about Delphi and something about Socratic ethics.

"Through the cultic prescriptions emanating from Delphi, the outlines of a universal morality overriding tradition and group interests may be discerned for the first time among the Greeks."[11] The inscriptions on the temple walls well convey the spirit of this morality: know thyself; nothing in excess; observe the limit; bow before the divine; fear authority; glory not in strength. The cardinal sin they all warn against is that of hubris, of thinking that one is more than a mere mortal; indeed,

11. Burkert, *Greek Religion*, p. 148.

one inscription explicitly admonishes us to hate it. The many reported oracular responses denigrating famous men and praising modest and unknown ones manifest the same spirit. The happiest man is not Gyges, ruler of Lydia, but Aglaus of Psophis, an obscure Arcadian, who has never left his tiny farm. Chilon the Spartan and Anacharsis the Scythian are both famous for wisdom, but Myson of Oeta, a humble peasant living in a backward part of Greece, is "provided with sounder wits than either of them."[12] When Socrates' follower Chaerephon asks the Delphic oracle, "Is anyone wiser than Socrates?" and gets the famously negative response, it is on this list, as we shall see, that the response should be inscribed.

Very much at the center of his ethics is the contrast Socrates draws between the more-than-human wisdom claimed by the Sophists and his own human wisdom (20d6–e3). The former, as we shall see in greater detail later on, is the sort of *technē*, the sort of expert craft-like knowledge of what is good or bad for human beings, that guarantees happiness to its possessor (20a5–c1). Human wisdom is quite different. It consists primarily in the recognition, achieved though elenctic questioning, that one does not possess such expert knowledge. But it also seems to have some positive content. For repeated questioning, living the examined life, Socrates claims, should convince a person that propositions he is unwilling to deny or abandon entail such Socratic principles as that it is better to suffer injustice than to do it, that *akrasia* or weakness of will is impossible, and that virtue is the most important contributor to happiness. Thus someone who really and sincerely believes these principles should care more for virtue than for anything else (29d2–b4).

The problem is that even though these principles may be tied down by arguments of iron and adamant (*Grg.* 508e6–509a4), they might still be false. How can Socrates claim (*Ap.* 36c3–d1), then, that by getting people to believe them, and to reshape their values and lives accordingly, he is "conferring the greatest benefit"? How can he claim that he makes the Athenians genuinely happy (36d9–e1)? Doesn't he only benefit and make happy provided the propositions he persuades his interlocutors to believe are true?

Socrates' thought seems to be something like this: Examination persuades an interlocutor to accept various ethical principles in part because they are elenchus-resistant or defensible in the face of elenctic questioning. Repeated examination, living the examined life, helps him to recognize that none of these principles amounts to more than merely human

12. These stories are collected in H. W. Parke and D. E. W. Wormell, *The Delphic Oracle I* (Oxford: Blackwell, 1956), pp. 378–392.

wisdom. This enables him to avoid the hubris of thinking that they amount to craft knowledge. So even if his principles are false, such examination brings him something of enormous value. First, it enables him to avoid "the most blameworthy ignorance" of thinking he has such knowledge of virtue when he does not (29b1–2). Second, it enables him to avoid the blameworthy vice to which such ignorance often gives rise—for Socrates does recognize that there is such vice (25d5–26a7). Because examination confers these rare benefits, it is the greatest good for a human being, and Socrates confers "the greatest benefit" on the Athenians and makes them really happy by examining them. For without craft knowledge, the closest we human beings can come to virtue (which is identical to that wisdom) and happiness (which virtue alone produces) is to avoid blameworthy ignorance and blameworthy vice. But if we manage this and achieve human wisdom, we also achieve human virtue, since if wisdom is virtue, human wisdom must surely be human virtue.

The temptation to hubris and blameworthy ignorance is perennial. Even in the next life it continues to plague us (40e4–41b7). That is why the elenchus never loses its value. It is always our best safeguard against culpable ignorance and vice: "How could you think," Socrates asks, "that I would refute you for any reason other than the one for which I would refute myself, fearing lest I might inadvertently think I know something when I don't know it?" (*Chrm.* 166c7–d2). The examined life is the best human life, no matter how long it lasts. Prolonged without end, it would bring us the greatest happiness of which we are capable—inconceivable happiness (*Ap.* 41b5–c7).[13]

We can now see why Socrates rates his Apollo-inspired mission to Athens so highly and how deeply Delphian his ethics is. At its core we find the same cardinal sin, namely, the hubris of thinking that one is a god possessed of divine wisdom, when one is merely a human being. That is the true meaning of the Delphic oracle, as Socrates finally comes to understand it:

> It looks as though, gentlemen, it is really the god who is wise, and in his oracle he is saying that human wisdom is worth little or nothing. In speaking of Socrates here before you and in making use of my name, he appears to be taking me as an example, as if to say, That one of you, humans, is wisest who, like Socrates, knows that in truth he is worth nothing where wisdom is concerned. (23a5–b4; also *Hp. Ma.* 289b3–5)

13. This sketch of Socratic ethics is elaborated and defended in my *Socrates in the Apology* (Indianapolis: Hackett, 1989).

Though Socrates may not be an Apollonian pure and simple, he does seem to be recognizably Delphian, recognizably someone the oracle might want to commend as it did Myson of Oeta.

But isn't there something we have overlooked? Apollo's oracle at Delphi is precisely that—an *oracle*. So if Socrates is truly Delphian, he must take Apollo as a source of something genuinely oracular or prophetic, genuinely mantic. To find out whether he does this, we need to look again at his *daimonion*, not at its provenance this time, but at its role in his life. In the *Apology*, Socrates represents daimonic intervention as both very frequent and of enormous ethical significance:

> The usual sign of my *daimonion* was always very frequent in all the time before this and held me back even on small matters, if I was about to do something that was not right. But now, as you can see for yourselves, that I was faced with what someone might think to be the greatest of evils, the sign of the god did not hold me back. (40a4–b2)

Yet, as all readers of Plato notice soon enough, the absence of such intervention is a conspicuous feature, so to speak, of his other dialogues. Indeed, there are only three cases altogether, two of which are cases of nonintervention:

> Son of Cleinias, I think it must surprise you that I, the very first of your lovers,...have not spoken one word to you for so many years. The reason for this is not something human, but a certain daimonic opposition....However, it now opposes me no longer, so I have come to you, as you see; and I have good hope that it will not oppose me again in the future. (*Alc.* 103a1–b2)

> As the gods would have it, I happened to be sitting alone in the dressing room, where you saw me. I was just planning to get up and leave. But as soon as I did, my accustomed daimonic sign came to me, so I sat down again. After a little while these two men Euthydemus and Dionysodorus came in, accompanied by what appeared to be quite a number of their students. (*Euthd.* 272e1–273a2)

> My friend, just as I was about to cross the river, the familiar divine sign came to me which, whenever it occurs, holds me back from something I am about to do. I thought I heard a voice coming from this very spot, forbidding me to leave until I made atonement for some offense against the gods....I recognize my offense clearly now. (*Phdr.* 242b7–c6)

If we had just these passages to go on, we might conclude that the Socrates of Plato's other dialogues—even the apparently unreformed

Socrates—is not the one portrayed in the *Apology*. For they seem to provide no evidence of the sort of systematic role for the *daimonion* in Socrates' life that the *Apology* both describes and relies on.

While this is certainly true, one memorable text suggests a quite different way of looking at things:

> Hippias, my friend, you're a lucky man, because you know which activities a man should practice....But I'm apparently held back by a *daimonia tis tuchē*, so that I wander around always puzzled. If I make a display of how stuck I am to you wise men, I get mud-splattered by your speeches when I display it. You all say what you said, that I am spending my time on things that are silly and small and worthless. But when I'm persuaded by you and say what you say, that it's much the most excellent thing to be able to present a speech well and in fine fashion, and get things done in court or any other gathering, I hear every insult under the sun from that man (among others around here) who has always been refuting me. He happens to be a close relative of mine, and he lives in the same house. So when I go home to my own place and he hears me saying those things, he asks me if I'm not ashamed that I dare discuss fine activities, when I've been so plainly refuted about the fine (*to kalon*) and it is clear that I don't even know at all what the fine itself is. (304b7–d8)

What has obscured its relevance is the key phrase, *daimonia tis tuchē*. One commentary suggests that *daimonion* has "the sense *infaustus* ['ill-omened']," although it notes that such a use "is not paralleled in Plato."[14] The meaning would then be: "some accursed fortune," "my crazy luck," or "some supernatural bad luck."[15] But the phrase can also mean "the act (or doing) of a daimon."[16] And Socrates is surely exploiting this double meaning, ironically suggesting that his *daimonion* is a misfortune, when it is anything but. For what, in the Socratic scale of evils, could be less right than "the most blameworthy ignorance" (*Ap.* 29b1–2) of thinking you know which "activities a man should practice," when you don't? If the *daimonion* holds him back "even on small matters" when he was about to do something wrong, it must hold him back here. Since nothing is more

14. Dorothy Tarrant, *The Hippias Major Attributed to Plato* (Cambridge: Cambridge University Press, 1928), p. 86.

15. H. N. Fowler, *Plato* IV (Cambridge, Mass.: Harvard University Press, 1926); Paul Woodruff, *Plato: Hippias Major* (Indianapolis: Hackett, 1982); Robin Waterfield, *Hippias Major*, in *Early Socratic Dialogues*, ed. Trevor J. Saunders (Harmondsworth: Penguin, 1987).

16. Compare *theia tis sumbē(i) tuchē(i)* (*R.* 9, 592a8). It may even be that by parity with *anagkaia tuchē* ("the activities of necessity"), which is a paraphrase for *Anagkē* ("Necessity"), *daimonia tuchē* ("the activities of a daimon") is simply a paraphrase for *daimonion*.

characteristic of Socrates or a more frequent occurrence in his life as a philosopher than his examination-induced puzzlement or *aporia* about ethical matters, such daimonic intervention of this sort must have been quite frequent indeed.

It might seem that by duplicating the function of such elenctic examination, the *daimonion* has come to look less like the oracular voice of Apollo and more like Socrates' own critical rationality.[17] If this view were correct, the *daimonion*'s status as genuinely prophetic, and Socrates' status as a genuine Delphian, would be jeopardized. Yet scarcely any of the examples we looked at can plausibly be taken as ironized references of the sort it requires.[18] This is particularly true of the apparently innocuous example from the *Euthydemus*, where the *daimonion*'s intervention has an odor of prophecy almost as strong as in the *Theages* (128d1–129d8).[19] For how could reason or elenctic argument have led Socrates to know that it would be good for him to remain in the changing room (or that it would be wrong of him to leave), when he had no idea at the time of who would eventually join him there in conversation? Only a rationalist bias could prevent us from seeing in this case a justification for Socrates' description of his sign as "prophetic" (*Ap.* 40a4)—a justification for our earlier characterization of it as the voice of Apollo, god of prophecy.

Craft, Reason, and Religion

Although the case for rationalizing the *daimonion* is weak, it embodies something that is both important and true. In the *Apology*, Socrates contrasts what is achieved through wisdom with what is achieved through inspiration, prophecy, and oracles: "I soon realized that the poets do not make what they make by means of wisdom, but by some natural talent and

---

17. See, for example, Martha C. Nussbaum, "Commentary on Edmunds," *Proceedings of the Boston Area Colloquium in Ancient Philosophy* 1 (1985): 234–235.

18. See Mark McPherran, "Socratic Reason and Socratic Revelation," *Journal of the History of Philosophy* 29 (1991): 371 n. 58.

19. Most modern scholars are skeptical about the authenticity of this dialogue. A recent editor argues that it was written c. 400 BC by a member of Plato's Academy. See Mark Joyal, *The Platonic Theages* (Stuttgart: Franz Steiner Verlag, 2000), pp. 121–157. Were it by Plato, we would need to add four more cases of daimonic intervention to the three we looked at, all of them prophetic in nature. In each, the *daimonion* urges Socrates to prevent someone else from doing something—Charmides from training for the Nemean Games, Timarchus from killing Nicias the son of Heroscamandrus, numerous Athenians from participating in the attack on Sicily (415–413 BC), and Sallo from joining an expedition to Ephesus and Ionia. In each, those who turn a deaf ear to his warning end up suffering for it.

by inspiration, like prophets and those who deliver oracles" (22b8–c3). In the *Ion*, he draws a parallel contrast in terms not of wisdom but of craft knowledge and understanding:

> All the good epic poets compose all those fine poems not out of craft-knowledge but through being inspired and possessed.... For a poet is an airy thing, winged and holy, and he is not able to make poetry until he becomes inspired and goes out of his mind and his understanding is no longer in him. (533e5–b6)

Both texts suggest that prophecy is something essentially nonrational. A related message is conveyed in the *Laches*:

> It seems to your friend and me that, where the various subjects of which there is knowledge (*epistēmē*) are concerned, it is never one thing to know how something that happened in the past happened, another to know how things that are happening in the present happen, and another to know how things that have not yet happened might come to happen in the finest way, but it is the same knowledge throughout. For example... in military affairs I am sure you yourselves will bear me out that it is generalship that makes the finest provision, particularly for the future, and does not expect that it should be the servant of prophecy but that it should be its ruler, because it has a finer knowledge of what is happening or is about to happen in war. That is why the law requires not that the prophet rule the general, but that the general rule the prophet. (198d1–199a3)

If we have craft knowledge in a given area, we have little need of prophecy. Such knowledge drives out prophecy, apparently, as surely as it drives out the need for luck. Again, the nonrational nature of prophecy seems assured.

What Socrates goes on to say in the *Ion*, however, shows that matters are not quite so straightforward as these other texts suggest:

> Because it isn't by means of craft-knowledge that they make poems and compose all those fine things about their subjects (as you do about Homer), but by means of a divine gift, each poet is able to compose in fine fashion only that for which the Muse has aroused him: one can compose dithyrambs, another encomia, another epics, and another still iambics, but each is useless for the other types of poetry. For it isn't by means of craft-knowledge that they compose those verses, but by means of divine power, since if they knew by means of craft how to compose in fine fashion on one kind of theme, they would know how to speak on all. That's why the god takes their understanding away from them when he uses them as his servants, as he does godly prophets and those

who deliver oracles, so that we who hear should know that *they* are not the ones who compose those verses that are of such great value, for their understanding is not within them: the god himself is the one who speaks, and he himself gives voice through them to us. (534b7–d4; compare *Smp.* 223d1–5)

Human poets do not compose out of craft knowledge, but the god who speaks through all of them and who can compose dithyrambs, encomia, epics, and iambics, clearly does. His knowledge of poetic composition, like his knowledge of good and evil, is beyond mortal grasp and capacity, but it is craft knowledge nonetheless, not something dark or nonrational. Thus what is nonrational from the human point of view, what exceeds human reason, does not fall outside the realm of reason altogether.

When the *daimonion* holds Socrates back if he is about to do something that isn't right, it manifests craft knowledge of good and evil. When Socrates defers to it and abandons his own preintervention best judgment about what to do, this is not a case of human reason deferring to the nonrational, but of human reason deferring to greater reason. The gods are wiser than we are and "it is bad and shameful" to disobey someone better than ourselves, be he god or man" (*Ap.* 29b6–7). The very fact that the gods interfere in human affairs at all, whether in sending the *daimonion* to Socrates, oracles to the Pythia at Delphi, or Socrates himself to Athens, is a manifestation of divine reason. For since the gods are both superlatively wise and virtuous, all their actions are expressions of their virtue and wisdom. We may not be able to understand fully why they do what they do. We may not even be able to give fully satisfactory accounts of the virtues they share with us. But we may be sure that they always act rationally and virtuously, never arbitrarily or viciously, that they are the source only of good things (*Euthphr.* 14e11–a2; *R.* 1, 335b2–e6; 2, 379b1–c7), and that neither they nor daimons lie (*Ap.* 21b6–7; *R.* 2, 382e6).

Because divine wisdom, as manifested in the prohibitions of Socrates' *daimonion* and elsewhere, is not human wisdom, nothing in what we have said undermines Socrates' status as a genuine Delphian, who takes oracles and other prophetic signs seriously as such. Socrates trusts the *daimonion* because he takes it to be a manifestation of divine wisdom, but the information he receives from it is not in every case information he could have acquired by the unaided use of his own human wisdom. We have seen this to be so in the *Euthydemus*, but it is equally so in the *Apology*. Socrates has reasons of his own to believe that the unexamined life is not worth living, but he has no such reasons to believe that it "is certain that it is now better for me to be dead and to leave my troubles behind" (41d3–6).

For such certainty, as we saw, is available only to Apollo, and (derivatively) to those he favors.

So much in Socratic theology that initially seems nonrational has turned out to be rational (although not always rational in a way that is accessible to human reason) that the less clearly rational elements are easy to overlook. Socrates never questions the existence of gods, or the traditional view that they are supremely wise and knowledgeable.[20] He shows no reservations about polytheism, even though his views about the harmony of the gods seem to threaten its foundations. He accepts the traditional pantheon of gods, although he rejects much in the traditional accounts of its members. This mixture of apparently uncritical acceptance of some things with thoroughgoing criticism of others is perhaps only to be expected, given the nature of the elenchus. For elenctic arguments must rely on premises that prove acceptable to the people Socrates examines. Since Socrates never meets an interlocutor who defends atheism, he is never provoked to examine this part of his life. If he had doubts of his own, he might have worked them into elenctic examinations as he does his views on friendship in the *Lysis*. That he doesn't do so would be testimony of his failure to lead the thoroughly examined life, if it were not more eloquent testimony of his profoundly religious cast of mind and of the omnipresence of the *daimonion*, assuring him of Apollo's existence and concern both for himself and for the Athens he served.

Human reason and divine reason are as strongly contrasted by Socrates as any two things are, even though both are answerable to the same objective standards of justice and virtue. There is much that we can discover for ourselves. The ordinary handicrafts, which provide us with "knowledge of many fine things" (22d2), are examples. When it comes to really worthwhile wisdom, though, what share we get of it must come from oracles, dreams, and daimons. By ourselves, we are capable only of elenchus-based human wisdom in these areas. And even there it helps to have a *daimonion* to hold us back from too readily giving our assent.

Socrates in Transition

All well and good, it might be retorted, but if Socrates really is an Apollonian of some sort, if he really is the Delphian we have taken him to be, if his *daimonion* has such a reassuringly Apollonian pedigree, why did Meletus bring him to trial for impiety, charging him with not acknowledging "the

---

20. For example, Homer, *Od.* 4. 379, 20. 75–76; Hesiod, *Op.* 267; *Thg.* 886–900.

gods the city acknowledges but other new daimonic activities" (24b8–c1)? And why did the jury find him guilty of Meletus' charges? These questions have weight, but they are lighter on careful inspection than when—as is more often the case—they are left hanging.

In the *Euthyphro*, on his way to the preliminary hearing of the charges against him, Socrates characterizes Meletus as accusing him of inventing "new gods while not believing in the old ones" (3b1–4). Euthyphro responds by connecting this charge to the *daimonion*: "That is because you say that the divine sign keeps coming to you." This is the closest Plato's dialogues come to representing the *daimonion* as something sufficiently anathema to traditional Athenian religion to warrant prosecution. Yet Euthyphro, a self-proclaimed expert on religious matters, immediately veers away from seeing it in that light: "He has written this indictment against you as one who innovates in the things that concern the gods, and he comes to court to misrepresent your conduct, because he knows that it is easy to misrepresent this sort of thing to the masses" (3b6–9). In other words, he does not believe that the *daimonion* could be the basis of an impiety charge unless it were misrepresented. Moreover, Socrates himself seems to accept this diagnosis. For he positively trumpets the *daimonion* at his trial as if it were the most harmless thing in the world—a defense against a charge of impiety rather than a basis for one.

Socrates recognizes that few if any besides himself have had a *daimonion* to keep them out of politics (*R*. 6, 496a11–e2), but he never suggests that the *daimonion* itself is significantly different in status from the many other traditionally acceptable ways, such as dreams and oracles, in which "divine providence ever ordered a human being to practice anything at all" (*Ap.* 33c6–7). Given that the god he takes himself to be serving is the Delphic Apollo, one of the city's most powerful gods, that the *daimonion* has the Delphic provenance we have uncovered for it, and that his own ethical views are so quintessentially Delphian, Socrates is surely justified in behaving as he does. Perhaps, some of the 220 jurors who found him not guilty were also influenced by these sorts of considerations. Whether they were or not, we should be. It is important, too, that Euthyphro does think that the *daimonion* is the sort of thing that can be easily misrepresented to the masses as something meriting a charge of impious religious innovation. This makes it difficult for us to be confident about just what its appearance in a writ of impiety tells us about Socrates. It follows, at a minimum, that we must be very cautious in what inferences we draw from the wording of Meletus' writ and from the jury's impressively ambivalent response to it.

Even when we do give all these considerations full weight, it may still be difficult for us not to feel that Meletus—especially as initially represented in the *Euthyphro* and in his written indictment—is on to something about Socrates, that he has prophetically if inchoately sensed the threat to Greek religion that his rationalism poses. Some of the jurors who found Socrates guilty perhaps also sensed this. But the major source of this feeling is surely hindsight. Like Nietzsche in *The Birth of Tragedy* (§12), we know what happens afterward, and so tend to see Socrates in somewhat apocalyptic terms as "an altogether newborn daimon," an embodiment of the spirit of science that destroyed myth, and with it the traditional Greek religion based on myth. Consequently, we find it easier than we should to go beyond the secure evidence we have and attribute to some of Socrates' own contemporaries a prescient recognition of this threat. Perhaps we are not entirely wrong to do this. But if Socrates were the first of something new in this way, it would be scarcely surprising if he were not also the last of something much older—a transitional figure, in other words.

Once what is prophetic from the human point of view is seen as merely craft knowledge from the divine one, moreover, a road that might seem closed off becomes open. For if divine wisdom just is craft knowledge of some sort, it is something to which we can at least aspire. We needn't settle for the modest—albeit difficult to achieve—human wisdom Socrates thinks may be the best we can achieve. Though we may not be able to become gods, we can at least become god *like*:

> If a man has become wholly engaged in his appetites or love of victory and takes great pains to further them, all his beliefs must become merely mortal. And so far as it is at all possible he will become thoroughly mortal, and not fall short of it even to the least degree, seeing that he has strengthened these all along. On the other hand, if someone has seriously devoted himself to the love of learning and to truly wise thoughts, if he has exercised these aspects of himself above all, then there is absolutely no way his thinking can fail to be immortal and divine. And to the degree that human nature can partake of immortality, he can in no way fail to achieve this. (*Ti.* 90b1–c4)

The *daimonion* that was once special to Socrates can then be transformed into something present in all of us:

> Concerning the kind of soul found in us that has the most control, we must think the following: God has given it to each of us as a daimon, the thing we say has its home in the topmost part of our body, and raises us up away from the earth toward what is akin to us in the heavens, as though we were a heavenly

plant, not an earthly one, as we rightly put it. For it is from the heavens, the place from which our soul was first born, that the divine suspends our head, that is, our root, and so keeps our whole body upright. (*Ti.* 90a2–b1)

In some sense, we can all become godlike philosophers—provided we can overcome the other loves we have that tie us to the merely human world. To achieve Socrates' human wisdom we needed only—*only*—to live the elenctically examined life. To achieve godlike wisdom, we need the sorts of political and scientific resources described in the *Republic*.

CHAPTER 2

❧

Alcibiades and the Socratic Craft of Love

Charged with having profaned the sacred and secret rites of the cult of Demeter and Persephone instituted in the city of Eleusis (the so-called Eleusinian Mysteries) and suspect in connection with the mutilation of the Herms (statues of the god Hermes used as boundary markers throughout Athens), Alcibiades, the most brilliant of the Athenian generals, defected to Sparta, where he greatly contributed to the defeat of democratic Athens at Sparta's oligarchic hands.[1] Critias, a relative of Plato, was also implicated in the mutilation of the Herms. He was possible author of the atheistical play *Sisyphus* and one of the bloodiest of the notorious Thirty Tyrants, the oligarchy installed in Athens in 404 BC by the victorious Spartans. In the eight months of their reign, they executed some fifteen hundred and banished some five thousand of their countrymen. Socrates was the companion and supposed teacher of both men. "You put Socrates to death," Aeschines says to the Athenians in one of his speeches, "because he was shown to have educated Critias." In another, he writes, "When your purpose was to accuse Socrates, as if you wished to praise him, you gave him Alcibiades as a pupil."[2]

In the Platonic dialogue named for Alcibiades, Socrates is portrayed as the lover who endeavors to set him on the road to virtue by disabusing him of the arrogant self-confidence that his good looks, family connections, and intelligence have given him. Previously, the *daimonion* prevented Socrates from conversing with him (*Alc.* 103a4–5); now it has given him the all clear (106a1). By the end of his elenctic examination, Alcibiades seems

---

1. See Thucydides, 6–8.
2. Aeschines, *Against Timarchus*, 173; *Busiris*, 5.

convinced that he lacks the virtue a free man and good political leader must possess, and that he should try to acquire it with Socrates' help. They will have to change roles, he says, since he will be the pursuing lover, while Socrates will be playing the role of the pursued boy—a theme developed in the *Symposium*. Socrates replies, using a vivid image to convey what his love will then have achieved: "Then my love (*erōs*) for you, my well-born friend, will be just like a stork[3]: after hatching a winged love in you, it will be cared for in return." Alcibiades understands immediately that the love Socrates wants to hatch in him is a love for justice and virtue: "Yes, that's right. I'll start to cultivate justice in myself right now" (135d7–e5).

Though everything seems propitious, and Apollo seems to have given his sign, the dialogue ends on a note of caution that Socrates himself is made to sound: "I should like to believe that you will persevere, but I'm afraid— not because I distrust your nature, but because I know how powerful the city is—I'm afraid that it might overcome both you and me" (135e6–8). The power of the city is pitted, in these closing words, against that of the elenctic Socrates. In the event, it does prove stronger: Alcibiades does not persevere. The problem of how to educate young people in virtue thus emerges as a political problem—a problem not so much for the hero of the elenchus, and for private one-on-one conversations, as for philosopher-kings and public education. In the *Symposium*, where Alcibiades is a major player, we see why he doesn't persevere. We see how even his sense of what Socrates might do for him—of who or what Socrates is—has been distorted by social and political forces.

Agalmata of Virtue

Someone "very drunk and shouting loudly" is asking where Agathon is, and "demanding to be taken to Agathon" (*Smp.* 212d5–7). Alcibiades, the "most beautiful and the tallest man around" (*Alc.* 104a5), has arrived in the *Symposium*, crowned with "a thick wreath of ivy and violets, and with a mass of ribbons on his head" (*Smp.* 212e1–2). The speech he subsequently gives is as riveting and dramatic as his entrance. It is the truth about Socrates, he insists, and he invites its subject to corroborate what he says: "if I ever say anything that isn't true, break in on me then and there, if you like, and say it's untrue, because I won't deliberately say anything

---

3. Nicolas Denyer, *Plato: Alcibiades* (Cambridge: Cambridge University Press, 2001), p. 247, explains: "Popular ornithology held that once storks had brought their offspring to an age at which they could fly, roles were then reversed, and the offspring tended their parents."

that's not true" (214e10–215a2). At the same time, Alcibiades admits that it isn't easy for someone as drunk as he is to present things "fluently and in the proper order (*euporōs kai ephexēs*)" (215a3). Given the importance of *euporia*, its opposite *aporia* (the puzzled state induced by Socratic elenctic questioning), and the idea of correct order in the dialogue, we are duly warned to interpret the speech with care.

"I declare," he says, "that Socrates is most like those silenuses sitting in the statuary shops, the ones the craftsmen manufacture, with pipes or flutes, but when opened in the middle, they turn out to have *agalmata* of gods inside them" (215a7–b3). Unfortunately, no examples of these have survived, "nor are there any references to such a type of statue except in late passages dependent on this one."[4] François Rabelais, writing in AD 1534, thought they were actually painted boxes: "a silenus, in ancient days, was a little box, of the kind we see today in apothecaries' shops, painted on the outside with such gay, comical figures as harpies and satyrs."[5]

With *agalmata*, we are apparently on less shaky ground. An *agalma* (from the verb *agallein*, meaning to glorify or honor something) was typically a figurative statue in honor of a god or—and more often in Plato—a figurative statue of any sort: the puppets that cast their shadows on the walls of the cave are *agalmata* (R. 7, 517d7).[6] It is things like this that Alcibiades initially seems to have in mind. As a silenus contained statues of gods, so Socrates, too, contained things relevantly similar to them. These were so beautiful and attractive, moreover, that Alcibiades wanted them for himself and tells us how he imagined getting them:

> As far as his appearance goes—isn't it silenus-like. It certainly is. His outside covering is like a carved silenus, but inside, when he is opened, gentlemen and drinking companions, you just couldn't imagine how he teems (*gemei*) with temperance within.... He is sly and dishonest (*eirōneuomenos*) and spends his whole life continually playing with people. I don't know whether anyone else has seen the *agalmata* inside when he is in earnest and he is opened up, but I saw them once, and they seemed so divine and golden to me, so outstandingly beautiful and amazing, that I had to do, in short, whatever Socrates told me to do. Thinking that he was earnestly attracted by the way I looked at my age, I thought it was a real piece of luck and amazingly fortunate for me, because I was in a position

4. Kenneth J. Dover, *Plato: Symposium* (Cambridge: Cambridge University Press, 1980), p. 166.

5. François Rabelais, *Gargantua and Pantagruel* (London: Penguin, 1955), p. 37.

6. The other occurrences in the dialogues are: *Chrm.* 154c8; *Criti.* 110b5, 116d7, e4; *Epin.* 983e6, 984a4, 5; *Lg.* 5, 738c6; 11, 931a1, a6, d6, e6; 12, 956b1; *Men.* 97d6; *Phdr.* 230b8, 251a6, 252d7; *Phlb.* 38d10; *Pr.* 322a5; *Ti.* 37c7.

to hear from Socrates everything he knew if I granted him my favors. For I was amazingly proud of the way I looked. (216d4–217a6)

It will matter that the exchange Alcibiades proposes is his sexual favors in return for Socrates' golden *agalmata*.

A third passage tells us that these *agalmata* were *agalmata* of virtue, and that they were also to be found inside Socrates' accounts or arguments:

As for the sort of man this one is, so strange is he, both himself and his accounts, one couldn't come even close to finding anyone like him if one looked, whether among people nowadays or among those in the past, unless perhaps if one were to compare him to the figures I'm talking about—not to anyone human, but to silenuses and satyrs, both him and his accounts. In fact this was something I left out at the beginning: his accounts, too, are like the silenuses that open up. For if one were willing to listen to Socrates' accounts, they'd appear quite ridiculous at first, such are the terms and expressions in which they're clothed, like some mischief-making satyr's skin. For he talks about pack asses, and things like blacksmiths, for example, and cobblers and tanners....[7] But if one were to see them opened up, and got inside them—then first of all one will find that they are the only accounts one hears with any sense in them, and then that they're the most godlike and contain within them the most *agalmata* of virtue, and that they have the greatest reach—or, rather, that they extend to everything that it is appropriate for a man who intends to be fine and good to consider. (221e1–222a6)

The less shaky ground *agalmata* seemed to provide now seems somewhat less secure. For while Socrates could contain statue-like entities, it is much less clear how his accounts could do this.

Finally, in something Alcibiades reports Socrates as saying, *agalmata* again seem to be involved:

My dear Alcibiades, you must really be a person of no mean quality, if indeed what you say about me is actually true, and there is in me some power that could make you a better man; it would be an inconceivable beauty that you were observing in me, and one altogether superior to your own fine looks. If, then, because you see it, you're trying to enter into partnership with me and exchange beauty for beauty, you are trying to do better than me in no small way. On the contrary, you are trying to get hold of truly beautiful things in return for only apparently beautiful ones, and truly are trying to trade bronze for gold. (218d7–219a1)

7. Alcibiades is referring to the crafts and craftsmen that figure in so many of Socrates' arguments.

Yet Socrates shows no inclination to endorse the view that he himself really possesses these truly beautiful things. A cautious "if indeed what you say about me is actually true" is as far as he will go.

When Socrates arrives at the party, Agathon greets him by saying: "Come here, Socrates, and lie down beside me, so that I can also have the benefit of touching that piece of wisdom of yours, the piece that came to you on the porch" (175c7–d1). The simile with which Socrates responds amplifies the sexual overtones of the verbs "lie down" (*katakeisthai*) and "touch" (*haptein*)[8]:

> It would be good, Agathon, if wisdom were the sort of thing that flowed from the fuller of us into the emptier, if only we touch each other, as water flows through a woolen thread from a fuller into an emptier cup. If wisdom is like that too, then I put a high value on lying down beside you, because I think it is I who'll be filled from you with quantities of beautiful wisdom. (175d4–e2)

Alcibiades' use of the verb *gemein* ("teems") at 216d7 is consonant with this picture and so provides support for it. For though it usually just means "to be filled with," which is also its most common meaning in Plato, *kuein* ("pregnant") is one of its synonyms, making "teems" a particularly apposite translation. But if Socrates is being imagined as pregnant with *agalmata* of virtue, the latter are themselves being imagined as embryo-like entities. Since these are genuinely similar to figurative statues, *agalmata* is an appropriate and evocative term for Alcibiades to apply to them.

The portrayal of Socrates as a male pregnant with embryonic virtue is one with deep roots in Greek thinking about sexual reproduction. In Aeschylus, for example, Apollo claims that a female serves only as an incubator for an embryo produced exclusively by a male:

> She who is called the child's mother is not
> Its begetter, but the nurse of the newly sown conception.
> The begetter is the male, and she as a stranger for a stranger
> Preserves the offspring. (*Eu.* 658–661)[9]

A similar theory was advanced by the pre-Socratic philosopher Anaxagoras of Clazomenae, who may well have been Aeschylus' source.[10]

---

8. See *Lg.* 8, 840a4; Aristotle, *Pol.* 7.16, 1335b40.
9. Hugh Lloyd-Jones, *Aeschylus: Oresteia* (London: Duckworth, 1979).
10. Alan H. Sommerstein, *Aeschylus: Eumenides* (Cambridge: Cambridge University Press, 1989), p. 206.

In a later generation, Diogenes of Apollonia and others also accepted some version of it. It is with this tradition that Diotima earlier allies herself when she portrays reproduction as involving pregnant males seeking females in whom to beget, and boy-love as involving a type of psychic pregnancy analogous to it:

> Those, then, she said, who are pregnant in their bodies turn their attention more toward women, and their love is directed in this way, securing immortality, a memory of themselves, and happiness, as they think, for themselves for all time to come through children; whereas those who are pregnant in their souls—for in fact, she said, there are those who are pregnant in their souls still more than in their bodies, with things it is fitting for the soul to conceive and to bring to birth. What then are these things that are fitting? Wisdom and the rest of virtue; of which all the poets are, of course, procreators, along with all those craftsmen who are said to be inventive. But by far the greatest and most beautiful kind of wisdom is the setting in order of the affairs of cities and households, which is called temperance and justice. When someone is pregnant with these things in his soul, from youth on, by divine gift, and with the coming of the right age, desires to give birth and procreate, then I imagine he too goes round looking for the beauty in which he might procreate; for he will never do so in the ugly. So he warms to beautiful bodies rather than to ugly ones, because he is pregnant, and if he encounters a soul that is beautiful and well-born and naturally well-endowed, his welcome for the combination—beautiful body *and* soul—is warmer still, and to this person he is immediately resourceful when it comes to producing accounts concerned with virtue, and what sort of thing the good man must be concerned with, and tries to educate him. (208e2–209c1)

It is these accounts that make "young men into better men" (210c1–3; compare 218e1–2).

In this respect, too, Alcibiades' portrait unwittingly (he was not present when she spoke) employs some of the same ideas as Diotima's. For when, as an out-of-order afterthought ("this was something I left out at the beginning"), he locates *agalmata* inside Socrates' accounts, he seems to be referring back to an earlier thought in which philosophical discussion rather than sexual contact is the mode of their transmission: "Well, as for me, bitten as I've been by something more painful, and in the most painful place one can be bitten—because it's in my heart, or my soul, or whatever one's supposed to call it, that I've been stricken and bitten by the arguments that philosophy brings with her, which bite into you more fiercely than a snake, whenever they fasten onto a young man's soul that isn't without some natural endowment" (218a3–7).

Alcibiades at the *Adōnia*

In the critique of writing at the end of the *Phaedrus*, Socrates claims that a written account, like the "offspring of a painting," stands there "as if alive." Yet it cannot answer questions or attune itself to the needs of different audiences, and "when it is ill-treated and unjustly abused, it always needs its father to help it; for it is incapable of defending or helping itself" (275d4–e5). Its legitimate brother, which is "the living and animate account possessed by the man who knows, of which a written account would rightly be called a kind of phantom image," is much better and more capable in all these departments (276a1–9). Then comes a telling contrast:

> The sensible farmer who had some seeds he cared about and wanted to bear fruit—would he sow them in earnest during the summer in some garden of Adonis, and delight in watching it become beautiful within eight days, or would he do that for playful purposes on a feast-day, when he did it at all; whereas for the purposes about which he was in earnest, wouldn't he make use of the craft of farming and sow them in appropriate soil, being content if what he sowed reached maturity in the eighth month? (276b1–8)

Then, an equally telling analogy. A man who has seeds of "knowledge about what is just, and what is beautiful, and what is good" will have "no less sensible an attitude toward his seeds than the farmer" (276c3–5). Thus, when others "resort to other sorts of playful amusements, watering themselves with symposia," he will amuse himself by writing "accounts concerned with justice and the other virtues," so as to "lay up a store of reminders both for himself, when 'he reaches a forgetful old age,' and for anyone who is following the same track, and he will be pleased as he watches their tender growth" (276d1–e3). But when "he is in earnest about them," he instead "makes use of the craft of dialectic, and taking a fitting soul plants and sows in it accounts accompanied by knowledge, which are able to help themselves and the man who planted them, and are not without fruit but contain a seed, from which others grow in other soils, capable of rendering it forever immortal, and making the one who has it as happy as it is possible for a man to be" (276e5–277a4). Living accounts (*logoi*) are now explicitly likened to seeds (*spermata*)—something on which the Stoics, with their *spermatikoi logoi* (seminal principles), will capitalize. The educative ideology of *paiderasteia* thus becomes fused with its erotic reality. It is this fusion that explains why Alcibiades can with equal ease locate *agalmata* of virtue in both Socrates and his accounts. We might think again of the image of the stork eggs employed in the *Alcibiades*.

Though Alcibiades is not mentioned by name in this section of the *Phaedrus*, he is hiding in the shadows of Adonis' garden. As part of the *Adōnia*, the feast celebrating the love affair of Aphrodite and Adonis, and mourning the latter's early death, women sowed "seed at midsummer in broken pots and placed these on the rooftops, so that germination was rapidly followed by withering."[11] These were Adonis' gardens. Three things connect them with Alcibiades. The first is the fact that the seeds Socrates sowed in him withered quickly: "whenever I leave him, I'm giving into my desire for the honor that comes from the masses... [and] I'm off and away from him like a runaway slave" (*Smp.* 216b4–6). The second is that Alcibiades was suspected of involvement in the mutilation of the Herms—statues of the god Hermes—and in the profanation of the Eleusinian Mysteries, both of which occurred in midsummer, right around the *Adōnia*. The use of the technical term "uninitiated (*bebēlos*)" (218b6) suggests that Plato had the profanation in mind. His use of the odd term *agalma* may be intended to memorialize the mutilation of the Herms, too. The third and most striking is entirely intertextual. In the *Symposium*, Alcibiades claims that Socrates, while always playing with people about matters of virtue, was in earnest with him about them (216d4–217a6). The *Phaedrus*, in which play and earnestness about such matters are obsessively contrasted, has obvious bearing on his claim. Someone who had "pieces of knowledge of what *is* just, fine, and good" (276c3–4) or "accounts accompanied by knowledge" (276d7), it explains, would never, except for playful purposes, sow them in a garden of Adonis like Alcibiades, whose planting-season (adolescence) was long past by the time Socrates began talking philosophy with him (compare *Alc.* 131c5–d8).

What generally happens to those who see him in elenctic action, Socrates tells us, is that they falsely infer that he is wise about the subjects on which he examines others (*Ap.* 23a3–5), that he does contain the relevant pieces of knowledge. When Alcibiades describes him as "sly and dishonest (*eirōneuomenos*)," and as "continually playing with people" (*Smp.* 216e4–5), he shows himself to have made exactly this inference. He must believe, then, that Socrates is a disingenuous *eirōn*—an ironist, as we say. So he must also believe, as other people do, that something like knowledge-conferring *agalmata* exist in Socrates to account for his elenctic competence. "I was in a position to hear from Socrates everything he knew," he says, "if I granted him my favors" (217a4–5). When Socrates tacitly accepts this description by not objecting, what he tacitly accepts,

---

11. *The Oxford Classical Dictionary*, 3rd ed. (Oxford: Oxford University Press, 1996), p. 12.

as we saw, is conditional: "*if* I have *agalmata* in me, of the sort that provide me with knowledge of virtue, then I am sly and dishonest and am continually playing with people." But that he has such knowledge of virtue, whether deriving from *agalmata* or not, is something he always denies. Thus Alcibiades' sense of privilege—"I don't know whether anyone else has seen the *agalmata* inside when he is in earnest and he is opened up, but I saw them once"—stands diagnosed as a common illusion.

Ta Erōtika

Though hesitant to claim that he has any knowledge of virtue, Socrates does make an apparently grand epistemic claim in the *Symposium*. "I claim not to know about anything," he insouciantly says, "except *ta erōtika*" (177d8–9; also *Thg.* 128b1–6). Literally translated, *ta erōtika* are "the things of love." But just as *ta phusika* is the science of physics and *ta politika* the craft or science of politics, so *ta erōtika* is also the art or craft of love— the one given to Socrates in the *Phaedrus* by Eros himself: "Do not in anger take away or maim," Socrates says to him, "the craft of love (*tēn erōtikēn technēn*) that you gave me" (257a3–9). What, we wonder, is this craft, and how can a man who has no worthwhile wisdom possibly possess it?

In the *Lysis* we find an appealing answer. Hippothales, like a true Socratic, loves Lysis, a beautiful boy, and philosophical conversation (203b6–204a3). But what he does to win Lysis' love is sing eulogies to him, and that, Socrates argues, no master of the craft of love would ever do:

> If you make a conquest of a boy like this, then everything you've said and sung turns out to eulogize yourself as victor in having won such a boyfriend. But if he gets away, then the greater your praise of his beauty and goodness, the more you will seem to have lost and the more you will be ridiculed. That is why someone who is wise in the craft of love (*ta erōtika*) doesn't praise his beloved until he has him: he fears how the future may turn out. And besides, these beautiful boys get swelled heads if anyone praises them and start to think they're really somebody. (205e2–206a4)

Persuaded, Hippothales turns to Socrates: "What different advice can you give me about what someone should say or do to get his prospective boyfriend to love him" (206c1–3)? Unlike in the *Symposium*, where he is laconic, Socrates goes into detail: "if you're willing to have him talk with me, I might be able to give you a demonstration of how to carry on a discussion with him" (206c4–6). An elenctic examination of Lysis quickly ensues.

"This is how you should talk to your boyfriends, Hippothales," Socrates says when the examination is finished, "making them humble and drawing in their sails, instead of swelling them up and spoiling them, as you do" (210e2–5). What he goes on to say about philosophy, however, shows elenctic discussion to be much more than merely chastening (compare *Smp.* 204a1–b5):

> Those who are already wise no longer love wisdom [or practice philosophy] (*philoso-phein*), whether they are gods or men. Neither do those who are so ignorant that they are bad, for no bad and stupid person loves wisdom. There remains only those who have this bad thing, ignorance, but have not yet been made ignorant and stupid by it. They are conscious of not knowing what they don't know. (*Ly.* 218a2–b1)

By showing Lysis that he isn't already wise, by getting him to recognize that he doesn't know, Socrates is setting him on the right road to love—the one that leads to the love of wisdom, and so to the beautiful itself.

In the *Symposium*, this way of understanding Socrates' knowledge of *ta erōtika* is encoded in a piece of nontrivial wordplay. The noun *erōs* (verb: *eran*) and the verb *erōtan* ("to ask questions") have cases or parts that are homophonic and homographic. "Allow me to ask Agathon a few more little questions" (*Smp.* 199b8–10), Socrates says to Phaedrus. "You have my permission," Phaedrus replies, "ask away (*erōta*)" (199c1). A few lines later Socrates says to Agathon: "try to say what the case is about love (*erōta*), too" (199e6). It is as if Phaedrus has told Socrates to love away and Socrates has told Agathon to ask him questions. Elsewhere, a basis for the wordplay is provided by a fictitious etymology:

> The name "hero" (*hērōs*) is only a slightly altered form of the word "love" (*erōs*)—the very thing from which the heroes sprang. And either this is the reason they were called "heroes" or else because they were Sophists, clever speechmakers and dialecticians, skilled at questioning (*erōtan*). (*Cra.* 398c5–e5)[12]

Thus when Socrates recalls his confident claim to know *ta erōtika* (*Smp.* 198d1–2), he explains what he meant by drawing a contrast between the sort of encomia to love given by the other symposiasts and the one that he knows how to give:

> It seems, you see, that what was proposed was that each of us should *appear* to be offering an encomium to Love, not that he should actually offer him one. It's

---

12. At *Phdr.* 261b6–d9, Socrates mentions "manuals on rhetoric" by the Homeric heroes Nestor, Odysseus, and Palamedes, "which they composed at Troy when they had nothing to do." The parallels between Gorgias, *Defense of Palamedes*, and Socrates' own speech of defense in the *Apology* have often been noticed. See my *Socrates in the Apology*, pp. 7–8.

for that reason, I imagine, that you rake up everything you can think of saying and attribute it to Love, declaring him of such a character and responsible for so many things that he will *appear* as beautiful and good as possible—evidently, to the ignorant sort of people (not, surely, to those with knowledge)....I'm not prepared to give another encomium in that way; I wouldn't have the capacity to give it. However, if you like, I *am* willing to say what is really true, on my own terms, and not on those of your speeches, because by your standards I'd be a laughingstock. So, Phaedrus, see whether you want this kind of speech too— whether you want the truth to be told about Love, and in whatever words and arrangement of expressions happen to occur to me. (198e4–b5)

The closing sentence recalls the opening of the *Apology*, where a similar contrast is drawn in similar terms: "from me you'll hear the whole truth, but not, by Zeus, men of Athens, expressed in elegant language like theirs, arranged in fine words and phrases. Instead, what you hear will be spoken extemporaneously in whatever words come to mind, and let none of you expect me to do otherwise—for I put my trust in the justice of what I say" (17b7–c3). There as here it heralds an elenctic examination: of Meletus in the one case, of Agathon in the other.

"A thing that desires, desires what it lacks," the *Lysis* tells us (221d7–e2). The *Symposium* delivers the same message yet more stridently: "what is *not* available, what is *not* present to him, what one does *not* have, what he himself is *not*, and what he is lacking—these are the sorts of things that are objects of desire and Eros" (200e2–5). The elenchus is important to love in part because it reveals the presence of these lacks or emptinesses— emptinesses that, because they were concealed or occluded by the false conceit of knowledge, were erotically inert. The revelation of a hunger thereby becomes a sort of feeding: "When a man has his mouth so full of food that he is prevented from eating, and is likely to starve in consequence, does feeding him consist in stuffing still more food in his mouth or does it consist in taking some of it away, so that he can begin to eat?"[13]

Even when a philosopher has climbed Diotima's ladder to the top and has seen the form of the beautiful, what he has in him for his beloved boy isn't what would fill up his emptinesses but what would activate them, turning them into effective motives to philosophical inquiry. No Platonic philosopher, one might say, no matter how wise and knowledgeable, can ever be more than a Socrates to another person: one must see the forms for oneself.

---

13. Søren Kierkegaard, *Concluding Unscientific Postscript* (Princeton: Princeton University Press, 1941), p. 245n. I owe notice of this passage to Jonathan Lear, *Therapeutic Action: An Earnest Plea for Irony* (New York: Other Press, 2004), pp. 106–107.

For this reason, too, *agalmata* is a peculiarly appropriate term to use for what such a philosopher does have in him. For an *agalma* originally had no "relation whatsoever to the idea of resemblance or imitation, of figural representation in the strict sense." Instead, it was something the aim of which was "to construct a bridge, as it were," that would reach "toward the divine." Yet "at the same time and in the same figure," it had to "mark its distance from that domain in relation to the human world." It had to make the divine power present, yet emphasize "what is inaccessible and mysterious in divinity, its alien quality, its otherness."[14] Like what is in a Platonic philosopher for another person, *agalmata* are a bridge to something else—an image for what is itself necessarily beyond images (212a4–5).

The idea of *agalmata* as a bridge between human and divine reminds us of Diotima's characterization of Eros as a daimon—a being that is "between the mortal and the immortal" (202d11–e1). "Always poor, far from delicate and beautiful... hard, dirty, barefoot, ... always with lack as his companion," yet also "a schemer after the beautiful and good, courageous, impetuous, and intense, always weaving new devices, both passionate for wisdom and resourceful in looking for it, loving wisdom through all his life," Eros sounds remarkably like Socrates himself (203c6–d8), whom Alcibiades describes as a "genuine daimon" (219b7–c1). But this implies that Socrates is, in the relevant respect, also remarkably like an *agalma*, and it like him. So, though Alcibiades claims to have seen *agalmata* of virtue inside Socrates before he tried to seduce him, it is noteworthy that in the penultimate section of his speech, it is the figure of Socrates as a model of virtue that is front and center. Whether in resisting Alcibiades' beautiful body or on campaign at Potidea or Delium, *he* is the paradigm of wisdom, temperance, fortitude, and courage (219d3–221c1).

Aporia and *Euporia*

The phrase *euporei logōn peri aretēs* ("resourceful when it comes to producing accounts concerned with virtue"), applied by Diotima to the pregnant and properly philosophical lover of boys (209b8), finds a parallel in last words about Socrates, which are also his last words in the dialogue:

> It's happening again just as it always does.... When Socrates is around, it's impossible for anyone else to get their share of beauties. So now see how resourcefully

14. Jean-Pierre Vernant, *Mortals and Immortals* (Princeton: Princeton University Press, 1991), pp. 152–153.

(*euporōs*) he's found a persuasive argument to make this fellow here [Agathon]
lie down beside *him*. (223a6–9)

They are words carefully prepared for: "Wasn't I being prophetic," Socrates
says, "when I said just now that Agathon would speak amazingly well, and
leave me at a loss (*aporēsoimi*)." "As for the idea that you would be at a loss
(*aporēsein*)," Eryximachus replies, "I don't think so." "Just how am I not
going to be at a loss (*aporein*)," Socrates responds, using the verb for the
third time, "after so beautiful and multifarious a speech as that?" (198a5–
b3). In Diotima's story of Poros and Penia, we discover how potentially
deceptive the words are:

> Because he is the son of Poros and Penia, Eros's situation is like this:...his
> nature is neither that of an immortal, nor that of a mortal, but on the same
> day, now he flourishes and lives, when he finds resources (*euporēsē[i]*), and now
> he dies, but then comes back to life again, because of his father's nature, though
> what resources he gets (*porizomenon*) are always flowing away, so that Eros is
> never at a loss (*aporei*) at any moment, nor rich, and again is in the middle
> between wisdom and ignorance. For this is how things stand: no god loves wis-
> dom [practices philosophy], or desires to become wise (for gods *are* wise); nor, if
> anyone else is wise, does he love wisdom. Nor, on the other hand, do the igno-
> rant love wisdom or desire to become wise; it's just this that makes ignorance
> so damaging, that someone who isn't a beautiful and good person, or a wise
> one, nevertheless seems to himself to be quite good enough. The person who
> doesn't think he needs something certainly won't desire what he doesn't think
> he lacks. (203c5–204a7)

Just as Socrates turns Athenian *paiderasteia* upside down by playing the
part of the pursued boy rather than of the pursuing older lover (222b3–4),
by means of his skill in asking questions, he turns *aporia* into *euporia*,
emptiness into a resource.

The way Alcibiades experiences the *aporia* Socrates induces in him, however, is quite different:

> I lay down under the short cloak that he—this person here—had over him,
> threw my arms around this daimonic and amazing man, and lay there all
> night long. You won't tell me I'm saying anything untrue here either, Socrates.
> Well, when I'd done all that, this man completely resisted me, disdained me,
> and laughed at and insulted my beauty—and it was just in that respect that
> I thought I was something, gentlemen of the jury; for it's up to you to judge
> Socrates' arrogance. You have my word for it, by the gods, and by the goddesses

too: I got up in the morning having slept with Socrates in a way not the slightest
bit more out of the ordinary than if I'd been sleeping with my father or elder
brother. What state of mind do you think I was in after that? On the one hand
I thought I'd been humiliated, on the other I admired the man for his nature,
his temperance and courage, because I'd come across a person with the sort of
wisdom and capacity of endurance I thought I'd never encounter. The result was
that I couldn't be angry—how could I?—and deprive myself of being with this
man, and yet I wasn't resourceful enough (*ēuporoun*) to win him over. For I knew
perfectly well he was far more invulnerable to money than Ajax was to iron
weapons, and as for the single thing I thought I'd catch him with [my beauty],
he'd already evaded me. So I was at a loss (*ēporoun*), and I went around in a state
of enslavement to this man unlike anyone's to anyone else. (219b6–e5)

What should be experienced as a resource is here experienced as a genuine
loss, recoupable only by gaining possession, through seduction or bribery,
of Socrates himself, and the *agalmata*-based wisdom he is imagined to contain. The idea that Socrates' love could be enjoyed only through joining him
in leading the philosophically examined life seems hopelessly far away.

An important passage in *Republic* 6 suggests that this negative interpretation of Alcibiades is very much Plato's own. In it he is explaining why
philosophers have an undeservedly bad reputation and what the real effect
is on their souls of contemplating forms:

The harshness of the masses towards philosophy is caused by those outsiders who
do not belong and who have burst in like a band of revelers (*epeiskekōmakotas*),
abusing one another, indulging their love of quarreling, and always arguing
about human beings—something that is least appropriate in philosophy.... For
surely, someone whose mind is truly directed towards the things that *are* has-
n't got the leisure to look down at human affairs, and be filled with malice and
hatred as a result of entering into their disputes. Instead, as he looks at and contemplates things that are orderly and always the same, that neither do injustice
to one another nor suffer it, being all in a rational order, he imitates them and
tries to become as like them as he can. Or do you think there is any way to prevent someone from associating with something he admires without imitating
it?... Then the philosopher, by associating with what is orderly (*kosmiōi*) and
divine becomes as divine and orderly as a human being can. Though, mind you,
there is always plenty of slander (*diabolē*) around. (500b1–d2)

Alcibiades accuses Socrates of abusing him (*Smp.* 213d2) and gives a
speech entirely about human beings, which is therefore as anti the philosopher Socrates as possible. No wonder it is represented by the latter

as slanderous in intent: "as if you didn't say everything for this reason, just to sow slander (*diaballein*) between me and Agathon" (222c7–d1; also 222d6). Finally, there is the "mass of revelers (*kōmastas*)" that shows up at the end of the dialogue (223b1–2) and, finding Agathon's doors as "open" (223b3) as Alcibiades thought he had found Socrates, bursts in and destroys all "order (*kosmō[i]*)" (223b4–5). The echoes are too insistent to be accidental.

Order and Disruption

The order the revelers literally destroy is that established by Eryximachus in his role as master of ceremonies—"I think each of us, beginning to the right (*epi dexia*), should give a speech—the most beautiful he can manage—in praise of Eros" (177d1–2). When Alcibiades arrives late at the party, Eryximachus tries to impose this order on him, too:

> Before you came in, we decided that each of us in turn, beginning to the right (*epi dexia*), should give a speech about Eros, the most beautiful he could manage, by way of an encomium to him. Well, all the rest of us have given ours; since you haven't given yours and you've finished your drink, the right thing is for you to do it now, and when you've given it, to give any instruction to Socrates you like—and he can then do the same with the man to the right (*epi dexia*), and so on with the rest. (214b9–c5)

As we have seen, Alcibiades does not follow the rule, since he speaks not about Eros, but a human being (214d2–10)—albeit one who is like Eros. Later, when Aristodemus wakes up, he finds order restored: "the only ones still awake were Agathon, Aristophanes, and Socrates, drinking from a large cup, and passing it to the right (*epi dexia*)" (223c4–5). Alcibiades and the mass of revelers—and the disorder they represent—seem to have gone.

As prominent in the *Symposium* as the fourfold repetition of *epi dexia*, and as deeply associated with Alcibiades, is the fourfold repetition of *exaiphnēs* ("all of a sudden"): *exaiphnēs*, the true lover catches sight of the beautiful itself (210e4–5); *exaiphnēs*, Alcibiades arrives at Agathon's house (212c6); *exaiphnēs*, Socrates turns up in Alcibiades' life (213c1); *exaiphnēs*, the mass of revelers burst in (223b2–6). What suddenly turns up in each case is a candidate object of love: the beautiful itself for the philosopher's love; Alcibiades for that of Socrates; Socrates for that of Alcibiades. As for the mass (*pampollous*) of revelers—it is what successfully competes with Socrates for Alcibiades' love, since it is to "the honors of the masses (*tōn pollōn*)" that Alcibiades caves in when not by Socrates' side (216b4–6).

For what suddenly turns up—for what lands the *coup de foudre*—to be truly beautiful, it has to come at the right place in an order that is first and foremost an education-induced order in the lover's own soul. This is something on which Diotima is insistent:

> The person who turns to this matter correctly must begin, when he is young, to turn to beautiful bodies; and first, if the one leading him leads him correctly, he must fall in love with a single body....I tell you that whoever is led by his teacher thus far in the craft of love, and contemplates the various beautiful things in the correct order (*ephexēs*)[15] and in the correct way, will come now toward the final goal of the craft of love, and will suddenly catch sight of a beauty amazing in its nature—the very beauty, in fact, Socrates, that all his previous toils were for. (210a4–e5)

And the importance of proper order doesn't end there. To stay in touch with the beautiful itself, the psychological order thus acquired must be sustained. Like Socrates' own fabled orderliness it must be of a sort that neither wine nor sexual desire nor extremes of hot or cold nor lack of sleep nor normal human weakness can disrupt.

With one clear exception, Eryximachus' order is followed from before the arrival of Alcibiades until all those present have spoken (214c2). The clear exception is Aristophanes.[16] He should have spoken after Pausanias, but he got the hiccups and so yielded his turn to Eryximachus, who praises orderly, harmonious, pious, temperate love, while condemning "the Pandemotic Eros of the many-tuned Muse Polyhymnia."[17] Comedy, which Aristophanes represents, is thus presented as a backward turn, a step in

---

15. *Ephexēs* is the word Alcibiades uses to characterize what his description of Socrates will *not* manifest.

16. The unclear case is Aristodemus, the narrator, who, because he is lying next to Eryximachus (175a3–5), should presumably have spoken after him, had Aristophanes not taken his turn.

17. Note *kosmios* at 187a5, d5, 188a3, c3, 189a3.

18. In the *Timaeus*, the "movement of the Same" is made to "revolve to the right (*epi dexia*)" (36c5–6) by the demiurge responsible for the creation of the cosmos. And, as in the *Phaedrus*, where good or philosophical love is identified with the parts of madness "on the right-hand side (*dexia[i]*)" of one of the definitional divisions (266a3–b1) of which Socrates proclaims himself a lover (266b3–4), this movement, too, is associated with philosophy: "whenever an argument concerns an object of reason, and the circle of the Same runs well (*euporos*) and reveals it, the necessary result is understanding and knowledge" (*Ti.* 37c1–3).

as antiphilosophical a direction as the "satyr play—or rather silenus play" of Alcibiades (222d3–4).[18]

Alcibiades' portrait of Socrates is the theatrical apogee of the *Symposium*. That we find it so is a measure of how interesting we find Socrates as a person and "human affairs" more generally—how much we like laughter, intoxication, disorder, disruption. Yet the *Symposium* diagnoses that interest as dangerously unphilosophical—as potentially an interest in the wrong things. It isn't *Socrates* we should be interested in, but philosophy and the forms. Alcibiades' speech is filled with human interest. But as neither *euporōs* nor *ephexēs* nor *epi dexia*, it is the work of an unreliable narrator—the product of a life that, torn between shame and the desire for the honor of the masses (216b3–6), self-confessedly does not run well (*ēporoun*, 219e3). Yet in part because of the conceptual density of the term *agalmata* and the skill with which Plato exploits it, there is a reading of the speech in which the image it presents of Socrates is uncannily correct. Socrates and his accounts do have *agalmata* of virtue in them, just not ones that, like a randy lover's embryo-containing semen, are there for the easy taking. To get hold of them, you must change your life.

CHAPTER 3

◦✧◦

Cephalus, Odysseus, and the Importance of Experience

The *Republic* begins with a verb: *katebēn*—"I went down"—Socrates says, describing his journey from Athens proper to the harbor town of Piraeus. "You don't often come down to the Piraeus to see us," Cephalus tells him (1, 328c6–7). Echoes of this descent are heard later on—the final one toward the end of the work. The soul of a person who has spent the afterlife being rewarded in the heavens "comes down" to choose the life it will lead during its next incarnation on earth (10, 614d7). If the soul is of someone who has "come from the heavens, having lived its previous life in an orderly constitution, sharing in virtue through habit but without philosophy," it chooses its next life "without adequately examining everything," and ends up as the soul of a tyrant, "fated to eat his own children among other evils" (10, 619b2–d1). The soul of Odysseus, by contrast, takes care in making its choice, and so chooses well (10, 619d3–5, 620c3–d2). In this regard, it is like the soul of the philosopher, which, because it has "the ability and the knowledge needed to distinguish a good life from a bad," also makes a wise choice (10, 618b6–619b1, 619d7–e5). The question is: What accounts for this similarity? What enables Odysseus to choose so well?

Rhetoric versus Philosophy

In the *Apology*, Socrates glories in his catholicity. Though he is particularly eager to help Athenian citizens, he is willing to examine anyone he meets "young or old, alien or fellow citizen" (30a2–4; also 23b5–6). This aspect of his philosophizing is reflected in the *Republic*'s cast of characters.[1] Cephalus is old; the others young men (1, 328d5). He and his sons, Polemarchus, Lysias, and Euthydemus, come from Syracuse, and live as resident aliens (so-called metics) in Piraeus. Thrasymachus is also a foreigner, from Chalcedon, at the mouth of the Black Sea (modern Turkey). So of the ten people present, half are foreigners, and it is exclusively with them (Cephalus, Polemarchus, and Thrasymachus) that Socrates converses in *Republic* 1—the book that most resembles a Socratic or elenctic dialogue.

Such catholicity is attractive to us. The examined life, we think, should be open to anyone who wants to lead it. Philosophy shouldn't be an ethnically or culturally closed shop. Yet Socrates, who used to be willing to question anyone, eventually argues that Kallipolis must be a thoroughly Greek city (5, 470e4–6)—presumably because love of learning is itself a peculiarly Greek natural asset (4, 435b7–436a1). Moreover, he is critical of democracies like Athens, because their love of freedom and equality leads them to treat metics and foreigners as the equals of citizens (8, 562e9–563a1). It is important to notice, therefore, that the replacement of the aporetic and largely negative Socrates by the reformed, constructive Socrates isn't the only replacement to occur after *Republic* 1. Socrates' foreign interlocutors also get replaced by Athenian citizens—Athenian citizens who also happen to be related to Plato.

Cephalus says that as "the other pleasures—the bodily ones—wither away," his "appetites for speeches and their pleasures grow stronger" (1, 328d2–4). He gives quite a long speech himself as if to prove his point. And that speech—which is on age, wealth, and poverty—associates him very strongly with Thrasymachus (1, 329a1–330a7). No one is better than "the mighty Chalcedonian," we learn in the *Phaedrus*, at "the art of making speeches bewailing the evils of poverty and old age" (267c7–9).

Polemarchus and Thrasymachus are associated by their names, which are near synonyms (both mean something like "war-leader" or "war-starter"), but also, more significantly, by their views about justice. Socrates claims that Polemarchus' account of justice, as what benefits friends and harms enemies, was coined by "Periander, or Perdiccas, or Xerxes, or Ismenias of Thebes, or some other wealthy man who thought he had great power" (1, 336a5–7). His examples—all were infamous tyrants—and his phraseology find clear echoes in

---

1. See Debra Nails, *The People of Plato: A Prosopography of Plato and Other Socratics* (Indianapolis: Hackett, 2002).

Thrasymachus' account, where the "man of great power" also turns out to be a consummate tyrant (1, 344a1–c4). Since Polemarchus inherited his account of justice from Cephalus, the latter is for this reason, too, associated with Thrasymachus (1, 331d4–9).

Besides this more important textual evidence, there is also some external evidence for the centrality of Thrasymachus. He was a friend of the speaker of Lysias' speech *Against the Members of a Sunousia*, who may well have been Lysias himself. He is supported by Clitophon (1, 340a3–b8), and is also associated with him, as with Lysias, elsewhere (*Clit.* 406a1–4, 410c6–8; *Phdr.* 266c1–5, 269d6–8). He is mentioned by Aristotle in the same sentence as Niceratus (who is present but does not speak)—albeit one in which Thrasymachus is making a joke at the latter's expense (*Rh.* 3.11, 1413a7). Hence, if we exclude the shadowy figures of Euthydemus[2] and Charmantides (who also has a nonspeaking role), it is not much of an exaggeration to say that the cosmopolitan party of Thrasymachus is being pitted from the beginning against the Athenian—indeed, Platonic—party of Socrates.

The same impression is created by yet a third sort of affiliation between Thrasymachus and many of the others. Cephalus is a self-proclaimed lover of speeches; Charmantides—surely the son and not his elderly father—is a student and benefactor of the well-known rhetorician Isocrates; Clitophon is a Sophist; Lysias, a famous orator; Niceratus, a near-professional quality rhapsode; Thrasymachus, a Sophist and rhetorician. We are in for a replay, we might infer, of that favorite of Plato's: the philosopher (Socrates) versus his deceptive shadows or images (Sophists, orators, rhetoricians).

It would be foolish to claim this as the whole story, or even that there is a whole story for it to be. The political sympathies of the characters may also be important, since they seem to "cover the Athenian political spectrum."[3] Thrasymachus is a spokesman for tyranny; Glaucon and Adeimantus (and so, Plato) had close relatives among the Thirty Tyrants (Critias was their mother's cousin; Charmides their uncle); Socrates, as we saw, was believed to be the teacher of Critias and of Charmides; Polemarchus, Lysias, and Niceratus were among the Thirty's best-known victims.[4] Lysias was one of the staunchest defenders of the democracy that replaced the Thirty; Socrates was its best-known victim. What led the Thirty Tyrants to murder Polemarchus and drive Lysias into exile, moreover, was the wealth they

2. Not to be confused—as editors always warn us—with the Euthydemus of the eponymous Platonic dialogue.
3. Ruby Blondell, *The Play of Characters in Plato's Dialogues* (Cambridge: Cambridge University Press, 2002), pp. 167–168.
4. See Lysias, *Against Eratosthenes*, for the details.

inherited from Cephalus. Thus the money that brought him contentment and peace of mind made them targets of tyrannical greed. Since, unlike us, Cephalus did not know what fate awaited his sons, an element of tragic irony is added to the text by our knowledge.

Socratic conversations usually take place in the Athenian agora or in one of the wrestling schools or as in the case of the *Meno*, in an unspecified location. When Socrates leaves his usual haunts, as he does in the *Euthyphro*, for example, or in the *Phaedrus*, much is made of it within the dialogue itself. The setting of the *Republic* is unique in taking place both outside Athens (like *Phaedrus*) and in a private house (like *Protagoras* and *Symposium*). Yet, though Socrates is physically away from home, there is another sense in which he is on home turf: he is discussing the very thing he has spent his life thinking about, namely, the virtues. Adeimantus reminds him and us of this fact (2, 367d8–e1), as—though somewhat less pointedly—does Glaucon (2, 358d1–3, 7–8). That is why the *Republic* is free—Myth of Er excepted—of the sorts of disclaimers of personal responsibility Socrates usually issues when he ventures to discuss something else, like his etymologizing in the *Cratylus*, his knowledge of love in the *Symposium*, or his knowledge of rhetoric in the *Phaedrus*. This coupling of alien milieu with familiar subject matter groups the *Republic* uniquely with the *Protagoras*. Since we are in Callias' house to meet Protagoras, we might reasonably believe that we are in Cephalus' to meet Thrasymachus.

On balance, then, we should be more impressed by the Thrasymachean provenance of one set of the *Republic*'s cast of characters and the Platonic provenance of their opponents (if we may call them that) than by these other facts about them. In part this is because these other facts do not significantly affect what follows. Even their political histories, an occasional element of tragic irony aside, seem to be largely irrelevant to it. If we didn't know anything about these people beyond what Plato tells us, we wouldn't, as readers, be that much worse off. The pervasive influence of Thrasymachus, by contrast, is something we can establish on internal evidence alone, even if external evidence enriches our appreciation of it.

Cephalus

It is as a man of experience that Cephalus (the aged father of Polemarchus) is introduced to us as worthy of Socratic attention:

> I enjoy engaging in discussion with the very old. I think we should learn from
> them—since they are like people who have traveled a road that we too will

probably have to follow—what the road is like, whether rough and difficult or smooth and easy. And I would be particularly glad to find out from you what you think about it, since you have reached the point in life the poets call old age's threshold. Is it a difficult time of life? What have you to report about it? (1, 328d7–e7)

As a young man, he tells us in response, he was importuned by his appetites for "sex, drinking parties, feasts, and the other things that go along with them" (1, 329a6–7). Old age, which brings "peace and freedom from all such things," has left him feeling better off, glad to have escaped from such a "deranged and savage master" (1, 329d1).

What his long life has taught him—apparently because he has been temperate in his appetites (1, 329d3–4)—is that men's characters are the major influence on the quality of their lives, whether they are old or young: "If they are orderly and contented, old age, too, is only moderately onerous; if they aren't, both old age...and youth are hard to bear" (1, 329d2–6). Socrates finds what Cephalus has learned from his life congenial, as we might expect, but thinks the mass of people would not find it so. They would say that Cephalus bears his old age more easily than his friends simply because of his wealth (1, 329e1–2).

Cephalus agrees that wealth has a role to play, but not the one the masses accord it:

> There is something in their objection, though not as much as they think. Themistocles' retort is relevant here. When someone from Seriphus insulted him by saying that his high reputation was due to his city, not to himself, he replied that, had he been a Seriphian, he would not be famous; but nor would the other had he been an Athenian. The same account applies to those who are not rich and find old age hard to bear: a good person would not easily bear old age if it were coupled with poverty, but one who wasn't good would not be contented even if he were wealthy. (1, 329e6–330a6)

Even if you're Themistocles, you can't have fame (ease in old age) if you're from Seriphus (poor); but if you're the Seriphian, you can't have it even if you're from a very famous place, such as Athens (very rich). So, in the face of contrary public opinion, Cephalus continues to uphold the greater importance of character. For you have a good character, poverty makes old age only moderately onerous and not easy to bear, whereas a bad character, even when coupled with wealth, makes life hard to bear, contentment impossible.

The really significant contribution wealth makes to ease in old age is quite limited in scope. With death drawing near, a person becomes afraid of what will happen to him in Hades if he has been unjust. So he "begins to calculate and consider whether he has been unjust to anyone." If he sees that he has committed many injustices, he "often even awakes from sleep in terror, as children do." If he finds no injustices, he has "sweet good hope as his constant companion" (1, 330d4–331a2). Fair enough. But how does being wealthy help provide such hope? This is what Cephalus says:

> It is in this connection I would say the possession of wealth is most valuable, not for every man, but for a good and orderly one. Not cheating someone even unintentionally, not lying to him, not owing a sacrifice to some god or money to a person, and as a result departing for that other place in fear—the possession of wealth makes no small contribution to this. It has many other uses, too, but putting one thing against another, Socrates, I would say that for a man with any sense that is how wealth is most useful. (1, 331a10–b7)

The thought is oddly difficult to parse. It isn't, as is easy to suppose, that wealth enables an old person to pay his outstanding debts, but more a matter of wealth bringing peace of mind through some such reflection as this: "I'm a good and orderly person. Nonetheless, poverty can make life hard enough that even someone like me might cheat (whether intentionally or unintentionally), or lie to someone, or put off making a sacrifice or paying a debt. And that thought erodes contentment as death approaches. But I know that I have been wealthy enough throughout life that I am not likely to have done anything like that. So I am contented." This is a far cry, indeed, from what the masses think.

Since someone can fail to be wealthy without living in poverty, Cephalus need not be claiming that a "just life without *wealth* is hard to bear."[5] Modest means may, for all he says, be enough for contentment in the face of death. (Between Athens and Seriphus there are places of moderate fame.) Moreover, if such contentment is available only to someone who is good and orderly, he cannot be claiming or implying that justice is "inferior to wealth,"[6] or presenting it "as something that money can buy."[7] Surely, he is trying to do exactly the opposite.

Cephalus' use of the word *penia* ("poverty") reminds us of Socrates: I live in *penia(i) muria(i)* ("extreme poverty"), he tells the jurors at his

---

5. Terence Irwin, *Plato's Ethics* (Oxford: Oxford University Press, 1995), p. 170. Emphasis added.
6. Irwin, *Plato's Ethics*, p. 170.
7. Blondell, *The Play of Characters*, p. 171.

trial (*Ap.* 23c1).[8] A little later in *Republic* 1, the trial is proleptically memorialized. If Thrasymachus can produce a good definition of justice, what penalty would Socrates deserve to pay? That of the ignorant, he says, to "learn from the one who does know" (shades here of *Ap.* 25e5–a7). All well and good, Thrasymachus replies, but "in addition to learning, you must pay money." "I will," Socrates answers, "if I ever have any." As in the *Apology*, a son of Ariston steps in to pay on Socrates' behalf: there Plato, here Glaucon (1, 337d1–10). We are surely intended to notice this: by keeping Thrasymachus in the conversation, Glaucon gives Socrates an opportunity to pay a debt he owes (see 2, 366d7–e9). But are we intended to see Cephalus' remarks about character and wealth in a new light, as insensitively telling a poor man (Socrates) that it is "very hard for a poor man to be just throughout life"?[9] Socrates' own reaction, which betrays not hurt feelings but the very opposite, makes it difficult to be confident: "I admired him for saying that, and I wanted him to tell me more" (1, 329d7–e1).

On the whole, Socrates seems to like Cephalus. He contrasts him favorably with people who are excessively fond of money, and are "difficult even to be with, since they are unwilling to praise anything except money" (1, 330b8–c8). He commends the speech in which Cephalus identifies the chief benefit of wealth as "fine in every way" (1, 331c1). When Cephalus leaves, Socrates behaves in "an uncharacteristically humane way," and lets him go, "with his composure and dignity intact."[10]

Given Socrates' "notorious indifference to money, alluded to in this very book (337d, 338b)," should we "suspect some irony" in all of this?[11] Perhaps we should, but it is important to remember that Socrates' indifference is comparative, not absolute. "I do nothing else," he says to the jurors, "except go around trying to persuade you, both young and old alike,

---

8. Socrates was actually a member of the middle or hoplite class: as he also reminds the jurors, he fought for Athens as a hoplite at Potidea, Amphipolis, and Delium (*Ap.* 28e2–3). Moreover, he was able to spend his days in conversation, to support a wife and three children without having to work for a living, and to pay a substantial fine without doing himself any great harm (*Ap.* 38b5). Compared to many Athenians, he was anything but poor. In any case, he isn't to be cavalierly included in the class Cephalus is calling poor: people sufficiently without resources to be worried as death approaches that their poverty may have wittingly or unwittingly led them to commit injustice. Socrates, on his deathbed, will turn out to have been plenty rich enough to have no worries on that score. His one outstanding debt—the famous cock he owes to Asclepius—will be paid by Crito (*Phd.* 118a7–10).

9. Julia Annas, *An Introduction to Plato's Republic* (Oxford: Clarendon Press, 1981), p. 19.

10. John Beversluis, *Cross-Examining Socrates* (Cambridge: Cambridge University Press, 2000), p. 201.

11. Blondell, *The Play of Characters*, p. 171.

not to care about your bodies or your money *as intensely as* about how your soul may be in the best possible condition" (*Ap.* 30a7–b2). Virtue is more important than money, so you should care about it more. And that, one might think, is just what Cephalus already does, making him a suitable candidate for sincere Socratic compliment.

Even if our suspicions of irony were not for these reasons allayed, they should not be "confirmed with the development of Kallipolis, in which the virtuous person is supremely indifferent to material wealth (416a–417a)."[12] For though the virtuous guardians and rulers of Kallipolis are indifferent to wealth, they can afford to be, since their upkeep is provided by their city, as Socrates thinks his own should be by Athens (*Ap.* 36d1–37a1). Their indifference isn't to any degree of wealth, to put it that way, but, like Socrates' own, to more wealth than they need to be as virtuous and so as good at their job as possible (see 3, 416d7–e3; 4, 421d1–423c4). Hence their analogues outside Kallipolis— insofar as they have any—are those who obey the Socratic injunction to care more about virtue than wealth, not those who care nothing about wealth, not even about such modest amounts of it as are required to live the examined life. As we look to the "model of Kallipolis in the heavens," in hopes of establishing its constitution in our souls, we must "guard against disturbing anything there either with too much money *or with too little*" (9, 591d6–592b6).

Though Cephalus values good character and justice more than wealth, he has seemed to some readers to err by valuing them simply for their consequences, since he seems to be glad to have avoided injustice not because of its intrinsically bad effects on his soul but because that way he has less to worry about at the hands of the gods.[13] Though this is a view that will later come in for extended criticism, it is criticism that Adeimantus thinks equally applicable to—anyway the unreformed— Socrates himself, as well as to everyone else who has praised justice (2, 366d7–e9). So what looks like a flaw in Cephalus turns out to be something widely shared rather than something damning of him in particular.

The details Plato provides about Cephalus' old age with its attendant physical weakness—he needs all those cushions on his chair and hasn't the strength to travel to Athens to see Socrates—may seem no more than touches of realism in a portrait of someone who has been described

---

12. Blondell, *The Play of Characters*, pp. 171–172.
13. Irwin, *Plato's Ethics*, p. 170.

as "closer to being identifiably human than any other elderly person in Greek literature."[14] Nonetheless, they, too, have been seen as subtly disparaging—as "a trope for moral and intellectual inadequacy."[15] That Cephalus' physical weakness is at least in part a trope may be true. But for what? "When the appetites cease to stress and importune us," he says, it is then that we take an interest in "discussions." Philosophy, it might be inferred, is being represented simply as "a fitting hobby for those whose health and vigor is waning."[16] A backhanded compliment, apparently, especially if we take the ever-vigorous Socrates as our model of the philosopher, able to walk to and from Athens (ten miles or so) and stay up all night talking with the young men. Suppose we consider Theages, though, whose diseased body helped make him a philosopher (6, 496b6–c3). Or the philosophers in the *Phaedo*, whose philosophizing is a practice of separating soul from body, a practice of dying (67d4–68b6). Then we might see Cephalus' old age (his dying) as having helped him become—not a philosopher, I'm not claiming that—but *like* one.

Socrates' conversation with Cephalus ends suddenly, just as the conversation takes a genuinely philosophical elenctic turn:

> Speaking of that thing itself, justice, are we to say it is simply speaking the truth and paying whatever debts one has incurred? Or is it sometimes just to do these things, sometimes unjust? I mean this sort of thing, for example. Everyone would surely agree that if a man borrows weapons from a sane friend, and if the latter goes mad and asks for them back, his friend should not return them, and would not be just if he did. Nor should anyone be willing to tell the whole truth to someone in such a state. (1, 331c1–9)

Since Cephalus made his money as an arms manufacturer, Socrates' counterexample may be more pointed than it appears.[17] It may be inviting Cephalus to examine not just his views on justice, but his conscience—an invitation he is represented as unattractively refusing. The intact composure with which he leaves can now begin to look like something morally suspect. Yet it is noteworthy that the counterexample seems to work particularly badly if the weapon in question is a shield. Yet it was hoplite

14. R. Garland, *The Greek Way of Life: From Conception to Old Age* (Ithaca: Cornell University Press, 1990), p. 272.
15. Blondell, *The Play of Characters*, p. 169.
16. Blondell, *The Play of Characters*, p. 169.
17. As Mark Gifford argues in his "Dramatic Dialectic in *Republic* Book I," *Oxford Studies in Ancient Philosophy* 10 (Summer 2001): 35–106.

shields, not weapons generally, that Cephalus made.[18] Still, the counterexample does seem to have more point when made against a manufacturer
of some sort of weapons than it would against someone having nothing
to do with weapons at all. So it may be that though Plato does not explicitly tell us what Cephalus did for a living he intends it to cast him in a
negative—or at least equivocal—light.

Cephalus agrees that were he to define justice as Socrates suggests he
would run afoul of the deposited weapons counterexample (1, 331d1).
But before he can be further examined, Polemarchus interrupts, and
Cephalus hands over the discussion to him, "since it is time to look after
the sacrifices" (1, 331d6–7), and "with a laugh," off he goes, never to return
(1, 331d10). If we already see Cephalus in a negative light, we will likely
have our views confirmed by our final glimpse of him. He claims to have
a strong appetite for discussion, we will think, but how seriously can we
take that claim, given his behavior? It is a fair question, but not a decisive
one. "Have your conversation *with these young men*," he says, as if even as
he is introduced he is being portrayed as someone who won't be participating himself (1, 328d5). His mind, as he tells us, is squarely focused on
the afterlife (1, 330d4–e5). So we might see his departure as textually
prepared for and of a piece with what Plato shows us of his character. He
symbolically leaves the world of men for that of the gods, making his son
"heir to the discussion," as he will make him heir to all his possessions
(1, 331d6–e2), when symbol becomes reality.

For Socrates, famously, the "unexamined life isn't worth living for a
human being"—where a life is unexamined if the values central to it have
not been persistently submitted to elenctic scrutiny (*Ap.* 38a2–6; *Prt.*
333c7–9). A person's claim to care about justice more than money is thus
refuted if what he says about it collapses quickly when he is examined
(*Ap.* 29e3–30a2). Since this will be Cephalus' fate if he is examined, we
might plausibly conclude that we are intended to see him as "a limited and
complacent man."[19] If complacency is entailed by failing to engage in elenctic self-examination, Cephalus is surely complacent. Yet that entailment is
apparently something Plato encourages us to resist. Examination may be
one way to avoid complacency, but it is not the one to be recommended to
most people. Taken up by the young, for example, it can easily lead to ethical skepticism (7, 538c6–539c2). Examination is best restricted, therefore, to mature people whose habits have been shaped from childhood by

18. J. K. Davies, *Athenian Propertied Families* (Oxford: Clarendon Press, 1971),
p. 589.

19. Annas, *Introduction to Plato's Republic*, p. 19.

musical and gymnastic training and whose minds have been shaped by lengthy training in mathematics. One reason Plato saves Cephalus from elenctic refutation, in fact, might be to leave such claim to virtue as he has problematically intact.

An unbiased reader of what we have discovered so far about Plato's portrait of Cephalus should conclude not that it is an unfavorable portrait, or indeed a favorable one, but that it is an equivocal one—one on which even careful readers of the *Republic* have trouble reaching consensus. Just why it is so is another question to which we will need to return.

Odysseus

Cephalus appears within fifty lines of the beginning, Odysseus within fifty of the end.[20] Since beginnings and endings are important, we might suspect on structural grounds that the two are intended to go together in some significant way.

Odysseus' soul is about to be reincarnated. It has drawn the last lot and as a result has fewer lives to choose from than any other soul. Not a happy situation, apparently. Yet because his soul remembers its former sufferings, things turn out well. It rejects its earlier "love of honor" in favor of "the life of a private individual who did his own work" (10, 620c3–d2). Hence life-experience has enabled Odysseus to make a good choice, without the aid of philosophy or elenctic examination. Earlier, too, he is presented in a somewhat good light: the spirited element in his soul abides by the judgment of the rational one, even when there is strong temptation not to (3, 390d1–5; 4, 441b3–c2). This is evidence not only that he has "not been corrupted by bad upbringing" (4, 441a2–3), but also that he possesses some measure of the fortitude or endurance (3, 390d1) characteristic of Socrates (*Smp.* 219d7).

Nonetheless, the portrait of Odysseus might with some justice also be called equivocal. The episode in which he exhibits his fortitude, for example, is one in which he restrains his anger at his serving maids, so that he can more successfully massacre them and Penelope's suitors later on (Homer, *Od.* 20.1–55). Plato doesn't advert to this fact any more than he does to what Cephalus did for a living. Perhaps he wants us to focus

---

20. It is interesting that Odysseus, though referred to before (1, 334b1; 3, 390d1; 4, 441b3–c2), is not directly mentioned by name till then. But because the earlier references are to the Homeric Odysseus and not, for example, the Odysseus of tragedy, it must be to him that Book 10 also refers.

only on the restraint and not what it serves. The fact remains that what it serves is something unsavory.

The phrase "Diomedean compulsion" (6, 493d6) may also refer to an ethically unflattering episode involving Odysseus. After stealing the Palladium from Troy with the help of Diomedes, Odysseus tries to kill his comrade to gain all the glory for himself. Diomedes overpowers him, ties his hands, and compels him to return to the Greek camp with blows from the flat of his sword. Again, Plato doesn't spell out any of this. The phrase he uses may not have anything to do with Odysseus at all.[21] But if it does, it is a reminder that Odysseus, like Cephalus, has his dark side.

Odysseus has something like fortitude; Cephalus is in some sense temperate and orderly. Odysseus has renounced the love of honor, which characterized his life as a Homeric hero, and "gladly (*hasmenēn*)" chooses that of a private individual (10, 620d2); Cephalus has renounced the appetites for food, drink, and sex that characterized his life as a moneymaker, and, like Sophocles (whom he quotes with approval), is "very glad (*hasmenestata*) to have escaped from all that, like a slave who has escaped from a deranged and savage master" (1, 329c3–4). As Odysseus has a sort of experienced-based wisdom despite not having led the examined life, so does Cephalus: he doesn't blindly follow in his father's spendthrift ways or in his grandfather's miserly ones but charts a middle path of his own (compare 10, 619a5–b1); he doesn't parrot the views of his elderly friends (1, 329a1–8) or accept those of the masses or Thrasymachus about the benefits of wealth.

It is no doubt difficult to separate the contribution (degree of) virtue makes to life choices from the contribution made by experience. Yet there is some reason to think that in the Odysseus example, at least, Plato had the contribution of experience particularly in mind. In the *Phaedo*, the philosophical soul escapes the cycle of reincarnation altogether, while "those who have practiced popular and political virtue, which they call temperance and justice, and which developed by habit and practice but without philosophy or understanding," become bees, wasps, or ants, and then, in their next incarnation, decent human beings (82a10–c8). It is possible that the difference between the *Phaedo* and the *Republic* on this head amounts to a real difference in doctrine, with philosophy now gaining in importance at the expense of habitual virtue. In the former you merely become a sociable insect if you are ignorant of philosophy; in the latter you end up a tyrant who eats his children. But it is also possible that experience, not philosophy, is making the gain.

---

21. See James Adam, *The Republic of Plato*, vol. 2 (Cambridge: Cambridge University Press, 1969), p. 24.

The habitually virtuous choosers of *Republic* 10 have been brought up in "an orderly constitution (*tetagmenē[i] politeia[i]*)" (619c7). One thing we can be sure of is that this is the very sort of constitution had by Kallipolis. For the philosopher-king looks to the forms of the virtues as his model in sketching the plan of Kallipolis's constitution. Since these forms are "orderly (*tetagmena*) and always the same" (6,500c3), the constitution based on them must be so, too—or as close to it as possible. An expressed aim of this constitution, however, is to insulate its inhabitants from the experience of bad or evil things (3, 401b1–d3, 409a1–c1). And it is this aim, in particular, that seems to be the mark of its orderliness. How else are we to explain the fact that those brought up in an orderly constitution are guaranteed to be "untrained in sufferings" (10, 619d3)? The crucial difference between the habitually virtuous of the *Phaedo* and those of the *Republic*, then, is that the former are like Odysseus and Cephalus in that they do have experience of sufferings, while the latter do not. Thus habitual virtue coupled with such experience can accomplish some, at least, of what philosophical wisdom also accomplishes.

Theory and Practice

Socrates refers to the wisdom that Sophists claim to possess, but he lacks as a craft that can make people virtuous (*Ap.* 20a5–c1, d6–e3)—"the knowledge of good and evil" (*Chrm.* 174b11–c3). To it, he claims, all the virtues of character are somehow identical, with the result that it, and it alone, guarantees us happiness, *eudaimonia* (*Men.* 87d2–89a5). Since there seems to be nothing more to being virtuous than having this sort of knowledge, virtue seems to be an exclusively intellectual condition, independent of the condition of one's desire structure or will. Because the temperance of Cephalus and the fortitude of Odysseus involve having appetites or spirited desires that are responsive to reason, each is a problem for intellectualism. The one can be seen as pointing forward, the latter back, to the *Republic*'s anti-intellectualist account, according to which virtue requires a harmony in the soul between reason, spirit, and appetite.

At least since Aristotle, philosophers have drawn a distinction between theoretical and practical wisdom or knowledge. Socrates does not, as we say, *thematize* that distinction. He does not refer to it explicitly, or situate himself with respect to it. But if we had to decide where to put his ethical craft, we might be inclined to put it more on the theoretical side, even though a craft seems to be quintessentially a type of know-how. After all, Socrates focuses obsessively on what seem to be objects of theoretical knowledge—namely, definitions of virtues, expressible in language (*Chrm.* 158e7–159a7). Moreover, once we possess such definitions, he seems to imply, there is nothing more we need know either to apply it correctly in particular cases and circumstances (*Euthphr.* 6d9–e6) or—incontinence or weakness of will being impossible—to make ourselves and our actions accord with it (*Prt.* 352a8–358d4). Theoretical knowledge thus seems to have left little or no work for its distinctively practical partner to do.

Socrates as reformed by Plato is often justifiably represented as also being a fan of theory. Yet he is also quite explicit about theory's limitations. In order to count as a genuine craft, he argues in the *Phaedrus*, rhetoric would have to do three things: First, it would have to "describe the soul with complete rigor and enable us to see whether it is one and uniform in nature or, like the form of the body, multiform, like the shapes of bodies; for that's what we say it is to reveal the nature of something." Second, it would have to "make clear with which of its forms it is its nature to do what, or have what done to it by what." Third, having classified "the kinds of speeches and of soul, and the ways in which these are affected, it would go through all the causes, fitting each to each, and explaining what sort of soul's being subjected to what sorts of speeches necessarily results in one being convinced and the other not, giving the explanation in each case" (271a5–b5). Mere theoretical knowledge of how kinds of soul are affected by kinds of speeches, however, is not enough:

> After having grasped these things adequately, the student [of rhetoric] must observe them as they are in real life, and actually being put into practice, and be able to follow them sharply with his perception, or otherwise get no advantage, as yet, from the things he heard earlier when he was with his teacher. But when he both has adequate ability to say what sort of person is persuaded by what sorts of speeches, and is capable of telling himself when he sees a nearby person that this is the person and this the nature that were discussed before, now actually present in front of him, to whom he must apply these kinds of speeches in this way in order to persuade him of this kind of thing—when he possesses all this, and has also grasped the occasions for speaking and for holding back, and for speaking concisely, or piteously, or in an exaggerated fashion, or for giving any of the other kinds of speeches he has learned, recognizing the right and the wrong time for these, then, and only then, will he finally have mastered the craft well and completely. (271d7–272a8)

Theoretical knowledge alone doesn't make one a rhetorician. One also needs the sort of practical knowledge that comes only with experience gained outside school.

In *Republic* 10, the most important subject for us to know about is described as follows:

> Here [at the spindle of Necessity], a human being faces the greatest danger of all, and because of that each one must [1], to the neglect of all other subjects, take care above all else to be a seeker and student of that subject which will enable him to learn and discover who will give him the ability and the knowledge to distinguish a good life from a bad, so that he will always and in any circumstances choose the better one from among those that are possible. [2] He must calculate the effect of all the things we have mentioned just now, both jointly and severally, on the virtue of a life, so as to know what the good and bad effects of beauty are when it is mixed with wealth or poverty and this or that state of the soul; what the effects are of high and low birth, private life and ruling office, physical strength and weakness, ease and difficulty in learning, and all the things that are either naturally part of the soul or can be acquired by it, when they are mixed with one another. On the basis of all that he will be able, by considering the nature of the soul, to deduce (*syllogisamenon*) which life is better and which worse and choose accordingly, calling worse the one that will lead the soul to become more unjust, and better the one that leads it to become more just. Everything else he will ignore. For we have seen that this is the best way to choose, whether in life or death. (618b7–e4)

This subject can only be the ethical craft Socrates sought, whether described in his terms or not. (1) describes the Socratic search for the truly wise person; (2) describes what that wise person must know. Since what he must know is structurally identical to the craft of rhetoric, its need to be augmented by practical knowledge should also be recognized—and to some extent it is.

When the trainee philosopher-kings have been educated in science and dialectic, Socrates tells Glaucon, you "must make them go down into the cave again, and compel them to take command in matters of war and the other offices suitable for young people, so that they won't be inferior to the others in experience" (7, 539e2–5; also 5, 467a8, d6; 6, 484d6). This practical training in city management lasts fifteen years (7, 540a4)— three times longer than training in dialectic (7, 539e2). In *Republic* 9, we find experience listed along with knowledge and reason as sources of good judgment (582a4–5) and learn that the judgment of pleasures by the philosopher is authoritative, because only he has "gained his experience" of them "with the help of knowledge" (582d4–5). Then, in *Republic* 10, we learn that the "user of each thing has the most experience of it," and that it is he who has knowledge of what "the good and bad points are in actual use" of the thing he uses (601d8–602a1). Since philosophers have knowledge (5, 479e1–480a13), it is an easy inference that they must also have experience in using whatever it is they know the good and bad points of.

It is fair to say, all the same, that without the *Phaedrus* to help us, we might not have seen these texts as making the point that it makes so much more explicitly. But that should strengthen rather than weaken our confidence that the distinction between theory and practice is on Plato's mind in the *Republic*, eventually coming into sharp focus in *Phaedrus*, in a way that it is not in earlier dialogues. Besides reminding us of the nonintellectual components of virtue, Cephalus and Odysseus are emblematic of this development. That practice's gain has to some extent been theory's loss should not blind us to the fact that these losses and gains occur *within* the confines of craft.

Caves and Souls

A chasm (*chasma*) isn't quite a cave (*spēlaion*), but it is "cavelike (*spēlaiōdei*)" (7, 514a3), and down into a chasm Gyges goes (2, 359d5). There he finds a ring that confers invisibility on its wearer when the setting is turned inward. Cloaked in this invisibility, and so shielded from experiencing the consequences of his actions, a just man would, Glaucon argues, act in exactly the same way as an unjust one (2, 360b6–c3). Invisibility thus has the same effect as "the illusionist painting of virtue" that Adeimantus presents Thrasymachus and others as urging us to create around ourselves to "deceive those who come near," by hiding from them "the wise Archilochus' greedy and cunning fox" that we keep behind the painting (2, 365c3–6).

In the cave, too, there are shadows that conceal what lies behind them from the cave's prisoners. When the philosopher goes back down into the cave, and becomes accustomed to the dark, he sees this. But because cities and souls are structural analogues, the philosopher's political spelunking is also an adventure in depth psychology:

> Let's not become dazzled by looking at the tyrant—since he is just one man—or at the few who surround him. Instead, as is necessary, let's go in and study the [tyrannical] city as a whole and, when we have gone down and looked into every corner, only then present what we believe... [Similarly,] the only fit judge of [the comparative happiness of tyrant and philosopher king] is someone who can in thought go into a man's character and discern it—not someone who sees it from the outside, the way a child does, and is dazzled by the façade that tyrants adopt for the outside world, but someone who discerns it adequately. (9, 576d8–577a5)

The person who can discern it adequately is the one with intimate personal experience of tyrannical people, who has "lived in the same house as a tyrant and witnessed his behavior at home; who has seen how he deals with each member of his household, when he can best be observed stripped of his tragic costume" (9, 577a6–b1).[22] But it is the philosopher who, by drawing on tripartite psychological theory, can explain the tyrant's behavior (9, 577c1–580b7). Hence if we want to understand Cephalus and Odysseus as Plato does, that is the theory we must use to go down into their souls.

In his former life, Odysseus was an honor-lover. Consequently, his soul must have been ruled by its spirited part, and the spirited desires it contains (9, 581a9–b3). But because it recollected the sufferings caused by love of honor, it renounced these desires when making its new choice at the spindle of Necessity, and "went around for a long time looking for the life of a private individual who did his own work (*apragmonos*)" and, when it found one, "chose it gladly," saying that "it would have done the same even if it had drawn the first place lot" (10, 620c6–d2). That this choice represents an improvement in virtue can hardly be doubted. But what sort of improvement? The only one available in Platonic psychology is that in which the soul is ruled not by spirit, but in some sense by reason (9, 583a6–10). That, I think, is what the adjective *apragmonos* ("did his own work") is intended to suggest. For Platonic justice, as we know, consists in doing one's own work because one's soul is ruled by its rational part (4, 443c9–444a2).

When Cephalus was younger, he was a money-lover, ruled by his appetites for food, drink, and sex (9, 580d10–581a1). That is why, with the waning of those appetites, he is "very glad to have escaped from all that" (1, 329c3–4). As in the case of Odysseus, this escape is clearly represented as moral improvement. What it is an escape *to* is less clear. Socrates says you "do not seem particularly to love money" (1, 330b8–c1), suggesting that Cephalus, whatever he might have been, is no longer an out-and-out money-lover. That he isn't an honor-lover is, if anything, yet plainer. But that leaves just one possibility: Cephalus, too, is in some sense ruled by reason. What choice of lives will his soul make when, having completed its thousand-year journey, it finds itself at the spindle of Necessity? It isn't much of a reach to imagine it following in Odysseus' footsteps—especially if it sees what happened to Cephalus' children after his death.

22. Greek tragedies often had tyrants as characters.

Cephalus, Odysseus, Socrates

Rule by treason is a good thing in Socrates' book. But how good it is depends on the cognitive resources reason has at its disposal. Possession of ethical craft represents the acme here, but no one outside Kallipolis seems to have it, not even Socrates (6, 496a11–497a5). That is why all such a philosopher can accomplish is (1) to "keep quiet and do his own work (*hēsuchian echōn kai ta hautou prattōn*)" and (2) to be "satisfied if he can somehow lead his present life pure of injustice and impious acts, and depart from it with good hope, blameless and content (*meta kalēs elpidos hileōs te kai eumenēs apallaxetai*)" (6, 496d6–e2). What should no longer be entirely surprising is that accomplishment (1) puts Socrates' life-achievement squarely on a par with that of Odysseus (*ta hautou prattōn* is a near synonym of *apragmonos*; *hēsuchian echōn* of *idiōtou*), accomplishment (2) with that of Cephalus (notice *elpis* at 1, 331a2 and *eukolos*—a near synonym of *eumenēs*—at 329d5, 330a6).

Adeimantus is impressed that a philosopher manages to achieve even that much: "Well, that is no small thing for him to have accomplished before departing." Socrates himself is less impressed: "But no very great one either, since he did not chance upon a suitable constitution. In a suitable one, his own growth will be fuller and he will save (*sōsei*) the community, as well as himself" (6, 497a1–5). The keyword here is the verb *sō(i)zein*, which makes a double reappearance in the penultimate sentence of the *Republic*: "And so, Glaucon, his [Er's] story was saved (*esōthē*) and not lost; and it would save (*sōseien*) us, too, if we were persuaded by it" (10, 621b8–c1). With ethical craft to guide his choices, we may infer, the philosopher can get beyond mere *hope* of personal salvation to salvation itself, and beyond personal salvation to political salvation. But that is in part because his craft includes both the theoretical component on which (the elenctic or unreformed) Socrates focused and the experiential one introduced by Plato and represented by Cephalus and Odysseus.

CHAPTER 4

⌇

Glaucon's Thrasymachean Challenge

Plato's brothers, Glaucon and Adeimantus, spend roughly ten Stephanus pages—which, even in a long dialogue like the *Republic*, is a lot—trying to tell Socrates what they want him to do as regards justice. Yet it has proved extremely difficult to say what their message—"Glaucon's challenge" as it is often called—is and what its provenance. The challenge begins with a division of goods into three kinds or classes:

> *Final*: . . . a sort of good we would choose to have not because we desire its consequences, but because we welcome it for its own sake—enjoying, for example, and all the harmless pleasures that have no consequences afterwards beyond enjoying having them. (2, 357b4–8)

> *Instrumental*: . . . a third kind of good, which includes physical training, medical treatment when sick, and both medicine itself and other ways of making money. We would say that these are burdensome but beneficial to us, and we would not choose to have them for their own sake, but for the sake of the wages and other things that are their consequences. (2, 357c6–d2)

> *Compound*: . . . a sort of good we love for its own sake, and also for the sake of its consequences—knowing, for example, and seeing and being healthy. For we welcome such things, I imagine, on both counts. (2, 357c2–4)

The class of final goods includes harmless pleasures that we enjoy while they last. Yet if these must have no further consequences, it is hard to think of clear cases. Even a pleasant sensation or moment of daydreaming or bit of pointless play is likely to have some further desirable effects—for example, it might make us feel more relaxed or give us energy for other projects (see Aristotle, *NE* 10.6, 1176b27–35). It may be that what Glaucon has in mind is goods that need have no further consequences with any substantial effect on their desirability. A passage from the *Laws* speaks of harmless pleasure only as "causing no particular harm or benefit *worth seriously talking about.*" Such pleasure, the Athenian Stranger says, should be called "play" (*Lg.* 2, 667e5–8). Since play is not a sensation, Glaucon's pleasures probably aren't sensations either but activities that are worthy of choice simply because they are enjoyable.

If intrinsic goods are those that would, for example, pass the test of being good even if nothing else existed or no animate beings did, final goods are not intrinsic ones. Instead, they are things we welcome by themselves—things we love or choose not as a means to something else we desire, but in some sense as ends. Hence the goods Glaucon is interested in seem to be those that are good because good for us, or worthy of desire, love, or choice by us. That they are good for us *because of themselves*, however, strongly suggests that their being so is the result of some features or properties that are intrinsic to them. Adeimantus' subsequent talk of things that are "genuine goods by nature" (2, 367c9–d1) is of a piece with this idea.

According to Giovanni Ferrari, the class of instrumental goods "comprises things that, taken in themselves, are painful or tiresome, and ... not just neutral means to desirable consequences." Glaucon's, he claims, is "a cultured aristocrat's classification of goods," since pursuing ends by nonneutral means is "demoted to the rank of a tiresome and laborious category of good."[1] If he is right, the division is not exhaustive, since it omits neutral means to desirable consequences, and it is not general, since it is, so to speak, class specific. Yet Glaucon presents the division not as his own view of goods, but as one that *we*—including the masses—at least implicitly accept in assigning justice to the class of instrumental goods (2, 358a4–6). Moreover, since we have to expend some time and energy and incur some opportunity costs in acquiring or doing supposedly neutral goods, these, too, are surely instrumental in nature.

The existence of compound goods might be taken to suggest, as it has been by Bernard Williams, that the distinction between final and instrumental goods "is not one between different classes of goods; it is a distinction between kinds of goodness or ways in which things can be found good, and not ... a distinction between different things."[2] Nonetheless, the properties (or powers) that make something a final good are of a distinct

1. G. R. F. Ferrari, *City and Soul in Plato's Republic* (Sangt Augustin: Akademia Verlag, 2003), pp. 17–18.
2. B. A. O. Williams, "Plato's Construction of Intrinsic Goodness," in *The Sense of the Past*, ed. Myles Burnyeat (Princeton: Princeton University Press, 2006), p. 123.

sort—a sort that compound goods possess along with some others of a different sort that make them also good for their consequences. This explains—which it is otherwise hard to do—why Socrates thinks that compound goods, not final ones, are "the finest" (2, 358a1): they have the good-making powers of final goods and instrumental goods combined.

Asked to which of these classes justice belongs, Socrates responds that it is a compound good, the sort that anyone "who is going to be blessed with happiness must love both because of itself and because of its consequences" (2, 358a1–3). The various formulations Glaucon and Adeimantus subsequently give of their challenge are their attempts to specify what they think would constitute success in justifying the "because of itself" component of this response. The first is Glaucon's:

> *Formulation 1*: I want to hear what justice and injustice are, and what power each has when it is simply by itself in the soul. I want to leave out of account the wages and the consequences of each of them. (2, 358b4–7)

By focusing on justice as a power in the soul, Glaucon strongly suggests—if he does not simply say—that his interest is not primarily in just actions, but in justice as a psychological state or state of character. More precisely, his interest is in this state, considered not as a dormant capacity but as an active or activated one: it is not health (*hugieia*), he mentions, but being healthy (*to hugiainein*).[3]

Now a state—activated or otherwise—might well be a compound good even though not all the actions it causes or motivates its possessor to do are themselves such goods. Aristotle shows clear awareness of this:

> Happiness is a complete activation or use of virtue, and not a qualified use but an unqualified one. By qualified uses, I mean those that are necessary; by unqualified, I mean those that are fine. For example, in the case of just actions, just retributions and punishments spring from virtue, but are necessary uses of it, and are fine only in a necessary way, since it would be more choiceworthy if no individual or city needed such things. On the other hand, just actions that aim at honors and prosperity are unqualifiedly finest. The former involve choosing something that is somehow bad, whereas the latter are the opposite: they construct and generate goods. To be sure, an excellent man will deal with poverty, disease, and other sorts of bad luck in a fine way. But blessed happiness requires their opposites. (*Pol.* 7.13, 1332a9–21)

---

3. A point noticed by Ferrari, *City and Soul*, p. 18. Compare Aristotle, *NE* 1.8, 1098b30–1099a7.

Socrates, too, seems committed to making the same distinction. "If we had to come to an agreement," he says, "about whether a man similar in nature and training to this city of ours [and hence courageous, temperate, just, and wise] would embezzle gold or silver he had accepted for deposit, who do you think would consider him *more likely to do so* than men of a different sort?" (4, 442e4–443a1). The implication, apparently, is that being just and passing "the everyday tests" for being so (4, 442e1) may be compatible with not always doing (conventionally) just actions.[4] We must be careful, in any case, not to slip unwittingly into considering actions, when traits of character are alone relevant.

Glaucon's next formulation is his most complex and detailed:

> *Formulation 2*: I want to hear justice praised simply by itself, and I think that I am most likely to learn this from you. That is why I am going to speak at length in praise of the unjust life: by doing so, I will be showing you the way I want to hear you denouncing injustice and praising justice. (2, 358d2–7)

Putting this together with Formulation 1, we have the idea of justice as having a power and of the just life as so related to it (or to that power) that praise of the one counts as the desired sort of praise of the other. It is an idea whose foundations lie in the immediately preceding pages. The definitional power of justice, Socrates and Thrasymachus finally agree, is to enable a soul to live well or be happy (1, 351d7–352a10). For the soul's function is to live, and virtues are defined by relation to the functions they perfect (1, 353d3–354a5). Praise of the just life counts as praise of justice itself, we may infer, because the power of justice in which Glaucon is specifically interested is its definitional power.

The remainder of Formulation 2 is an attempt to so isolate justice that this power comes into clear focus.

> As for the decision itself about the life of the two we are discussing, if we contrast the extremes of justice and injustice, we shall be able to make the decision correctly, but if we don't, we won't. What, then, is the contrast I have in mind? It is this. We will subtract nothing from the injustice of the unjust person, and nothing from the justice of the just one. On the contrary, we will take each to be perfect in his own pursuit. First, then, let the unjust person act like a clever craftsman. An eminent ship's captain or doctor, for example,

---

4. A point noticed by David Sedley, "Philosophy, the Forms, and the Art of Ruling," in *The Cambridge Companion to Plato's Republic*, ed. G. R. F. Ferrari (Cambridge: Cambridge University Press, 2007), p. 279.

knows the difference between what his craft can and cannot do. He attempts the first but lets the second go by. And if he happens to slip, he can put things right. In the same way, if he is to be completely unjust, let the unjust person correctly attempt unjust acts and remain undetected. The one who is caught should be thought inept. For the extreme of injustice is to be reputed just without actually being so. And our completely unjust person must be given complete injustice—nothing must be subtracted from it. We must allow that, while doing the greatest injustice, he has nonetheless provided himself with the greatest reputation for justice.... Having hypothesized such a person, let's now put the just man next to him in our argument—someone who is simple and noble and who, as Aeschylus says, does not want to be reputed good, but to be so. We must take away his reputation. For a reputation for justice would bring him honor and rewards, so that it would not be clear whether he is being just for the sake of justice, or for the sake of those honors and rewards. We must strip him of everything except justice, and make his situation the opposite of the unjust person's. Though he does no injustice, he must have the greatest reputation for it, so that he may be tested with regard to justice by seeing whether or not he can withstand a bad reputation and its consequences. Let him stay like that unchanged until he is dead—just, but all his life believed to be unjust. In this way, both will reach the extremes, the one of justice and the other of injustice, and we will be able to judge which of them is happier. (2, 360d8–361d3)

The idea of stripping away from justice whatever is not part of its definitional power is explicated by reference to that of stripping away a reputation for justice and the consequences that flow from it. The motivation is plain enough: it is justice that is to be defended, not reputed justice. The addition to justice of a reputation for positive injustice is more difficult. "It is not clear, in particular," as Williams writes, "whether the genuinely just man 'appears' unjust because he has an unconventional notion of justice, so that the world judges unfavorably the character he really has, or because it misunderstands what his character is."[5] What is clear, though, is that when we turn to the perfectly unjust person it is no accident that he has a reputation for justice, since it is part of his supposedly craftlike injustice to ensure that he has one. That is to say, the power to provide such a reputation for himself is one of the powers injustice by itself is taken to have, more or less by definition. Hence it seems safe to suppose that the reason the just person's reputation can be stripped away is that justice's definitional power—as what enables a soul to live well—does not

5. Williams, "Construction," p. 120 n. 5.

include the power to control the sort of reputation its possessor will have with other people.

A perfectly just person can enjoy a reputation for injustice his entire life either because his justice is hard for people to understand, because he has been the subject of a successful smear campaign, or for some other reason altogether. If he will be happier than the unjust person even in such circumstances, justice will not merely be a compound good, it will be one much more desirable for its own sake than for its good consequences. Adeimantus supposes, indeed, that this is a part of what Socrates is being challenged to prove. Since neither Socrates nor Glaucon objects, he is surely right.

What Glaucon says that what he wants to be shown is that the just person, simply because he is just, is happier than the unjust one. The comparative formulation is important, since one person can be happier than another even if neither is very happy in absolute terms. Hence a just person who is suffering all the terrible things that follow from a bad reputation, including even the rack, does not have to be all that happy. It is enough that he be happier than the unjust one who enjoys a good reputation. That, too, might seem an implausibly high standard for a defense of justice to be required to meet.[6] But is it? We might think here of the somewhat analogous case of health. Someone with bad flu may look and feel much sicker than someone with asymptomatic heart disease, but he is healthier all the same. Yet, it is easy to be distracted by the rack, as by appearances and feelings, into giving too much weight to symptoms and not enough to underlying conditions. Socrates makes this point himself in discussing tyrants. To judge them adequately, he thinks, we need the psychological equivalent of medicine, so that we will not be "dazzled by the façade that tyrants adopt for the outside world" (9, 577a3–5), namely, the "illusionist painting of virtue" (2, 365c4) in which Adeimantus thinks the unjust person wraps himself in order to win a good reputation by hiding the pathology within. The good judge is someone who can see through this—as the doctor can see through apparent health—to the true condition of the soul it cloaks. The good judge of how happy justice makes us had better proceed in the same way—looking to our true state and not simply to how happy we look or feel.

6. David Wiggins, *Ethics: Twelve Lectures on the Philosophy of Morality* (Cambridge, Mass.: Harvard University Press, 2006), p. 18, speaks of "the utterly peculiar and special terms under which the Platonically just man is doomed to live" and concludes that "a sane philosophy of morality" will set Glaucon's thought experiment aside on the grounds that in it the "health of the soul itself, along with all happiness and sanity, will long since have flown out the window."

In his next attempt to say what he wants, Adeimantus seems at first to be speaking of the belief-mediated consequences of justice itself:

Formulation 3: Amazing Socrates, we said, of all of you who claim to praise justice, beginning from the earliest heroes of old whose accounts survive up to the men of the present day, not one has ever blamed injustice or praised justice except by mentioning the reputations, honors, and rewards that are their consequences. No one has ever adequately described what each does itself, through its own power, by its presence in the soul of the person who possesses it, even if it remains hidden from gods and humans. No one, whether in poetry or in private discussions, has adequately argued that injustice is the greatest evil a soul can have in it, and justice the greatest good. (2, 366d7–367a1)

In an earlier passage, though, he moves seamlessly from consequences of that sort to others that are quite different, namely, the consequences of reputed justice or of a just reputation:

When fathers speak to their sons to give them advice, they say that one must be just, as do all those who have others in their charge. But they do not praise justice itself, only the good reputation it brings: the inducement they offer is that if we are reputed to be just, then, as a result of our reputation, we will get political offices, good marriages, and all the things that Glaucon recently said the just man would get as a result of having a good reputation. (2, 362e6–363a5)

A person's reputation, the thought seems to be, is a consequence of what people believe about him, not of the truth, so that a good manipulator of belief—a good simulator or mimic of justice—can acquire the good reputation without being just.

Adeimantus' final formulation adds an important negative qualification.

Formulation 4: Do not merely demonstrate to us by argument that justice is superior to injustice, but tell us what each one itself does, because of itself, to someone who possesses it that makes the one bad and the other good. Follow Glaucon's advice and do not take reputations into account. For if you do not deprive justice and injustice of their true reputations and attach false ones to them, we will say that it is not justice you are praising, but its reputation, or injustice you are condemning, but its reputation, and that you are encouraging us to be unjust but keep it secret.... You agree that justice is one of the greatest goods, the ones that are worth having for the sake of their consequences, but much more so for their own sake—such as seeing, hearing, knowing, being healthy, of course, and all the others that are genuine goods by nature and not simply by repute. This is what I want you to praise about justice. How does it—simply because of itself—benefit its possessor, and how does injustice harm him? Leave wages and reputations for others to praise. (2, 367b3–d3)

What Adeimantus does not want is a proof that justice is superior. He and his brother already believe that (2, 358c6, 368a5–b3). In this regard, he might be seen as reflecting a criticism of Socrates raised in the *Clitophon*:

> I think you are better than anyone else at exhorting people to care about virtue, but one of two things must be true: either that's the only thing you can do and nothing further—as might happen in the case of any other craft, for example, when someone who isn't a ship's captain rehearses a speech in praise of the captain's craft as something of great value to human beings, and likewise for the other crafts. The very same complaint might be made against you concerning justice—that you are no more a knowledgeable expert (*epistēmoni*) about justice simply because you make beautiful speeches in praise of it. Mind you, that's not my view, mine is that one of two things must be true: either you know nothing about justice, or you don't want to share what you know with me. That is why, I suppose, I go to Thrasymachus and anywhere else I can, because I'm puzzled. But if you're finally ready to stop exhorting me with speeches, and just as if it had been about the craft of gymnastics that you were exhorting me, saying that I shouldn't neglect my body, you would have proceeded to give me what comes next after such exhortation and would explain what kind of thing my body is by nature and what kind of treatment it therefore needs—that's the sort of thing you should do now. You can take it that Clitophon agrees that it's absurd to care for other things, but when it comes to the soul, the very thing we go to all the trouble for, to neglect it. (410b4–e1)[7]

What Adeimantus wants, it seems, is something like what Clitophon describes—an account of what justice is that would explain how it can be superior and merit Socrates' praise, given Thrasymachus' argument, by showing what its effects are on the soul. If reputations are included in the requisite explanation, it will fail, since it won't be justice that is shown to merit the praise, but its reputation.

Hence Adeimantus follows Glaucon in thinking that reputations must be reversed: focus on justice in a man who is reputed unjust and you are guaranteed to be focused on the right target for defense, something

---

7. The authenticity of the *Clitophon*, long disputed, is defended by S. R. Slings, *Plato: Clitophon* (Cambridge: Cambridge University Press, 1999), pp. 215–234.

which, if good at all, must be good "by nature and not simply by repute." Though he does not make the attachment of false reputations depend on what powers are definitional of perfect justice and injustice, as Glaucon does, he probably has much the same point in view. If Socrates is to succeed in defending or praising a justice that does not include being able to ensure a good reputation for its possessor among its definitional powers, his defense must succeed when its possessor has a bad one. Otherwise it may still be only reputed justice that is being defended.

When we think about justice, we tend to think either consequentially or deontologically. Talk about leaving wages and consequences out of the defense of justice, as a result, tends to raise deontological thoughts in our minds. Justice must be shown to be choiceworthy for its own sake. The eudaimonistic, and so apparently consequentialist, nature of Glaucon's challenge is thus something we find puzzling—as is Socrates' own apparent readiness to speak of "the good things that come from being just" as what are crucial to a defense of justice as choiceworthy in the requisite way (10, 612d3–10). But the puzzle largely disappears if what Glaucon and Adeimantus mean by consequences is only such consequences as could equally well be consequences of reputed justice—*simulator-accessible* consequences, as we may call them. Since the class of simulator-accessible consequences is much narrower than the class a consequentialist appeals to, excluding them from the defense of justice is compatible with wanting that defense to be a consequentialist one. And that is precisely the sort, as we have seen, that Glaucon and Adeimantus do seem to want.

If defending justice as desirable for its own sake consists in showing it desirable for the sake of those of its consequences that are not simulator accessible, however, the desirability of other compound goods—knowing, seeing, and being healthy—for their consequences should reside in consequences that are simulator accessible. That they may have such consequences is perhaps obvious enough: someone can fake knowledge (think of Sophists as Plato and Aristotle conceive of them), sight, or health and reap the benefits of doing so. It is very hard to believe, nonetheless, that this is how the masses, who are supposed to employ the division of goods in categorizing justice as an instrumental good, are likely to understand the matter. It is not, in fact, how we are likely to understand it ourselves.[8] The solution to this problem lies in the distinction Glaucon draws between the powers that define justice as a virtue and other powers or effects it may have. Though his compound goods are not all virtues, they do seem

---

8. A point made by Julia Annas, *An Introduction to Plato's Republic* (Oxford: Clarendon Press, 1981), pp. 65–70.

to be either virtues, broadly speaking, or the desirable functions they perfect. Hence the consequences for which they are desirable are presumably effects they have other than those definitional of them as the virtues or functions they are. What gives the simulator-accessible ones among them their special pertinence in the case of justice is not that they are its only consequences, but simply that they are the only ones appealed to in the conventional defenses of it.

Inadequate Defenses of Justice

While Glaucon looks at popular views about the origins and nature of justice and injustice that have the effect of praising injustice as "naturally good" (2, 358e4), Adeimantus looks at "the arguments that…praise justice and disparage injustice" (2, 362e3–5). His point is that what people praise is *reputed* justice, what they blame, *reputed* injustice. His argument thus takes the form of a survey of received opinion, especially as expressed in the works of Homer and Hesiod, which were used in traditional ethical education, whereas Glaucon's is more focused on opinion's theoretical underpinnings.[9]

According to Glaucon, the story people accept about the origins and nature of justice is something like this:

> People say, you see, that to do injustice is naturally good, and to suffer injustice bad. But the badness of suffering it far exceeds the goodness of doing it. Hence, those who have done and suffered injustice and who have tasted both—the ones who lack the power to do it and avoid suffering it—decide that it is profitable to come to an agreement with each other neither to do injustice nor to suffer it. As a result, they begin to make laws and covenants, and what the law commands they call lawful and just. That, they say, is the origin and very being of justice. It is in between the best and the worst. The best is to do injustice without paying the penalty; the worst is to suffer it without being able to take revenge. Justice is in the middle between these two extremes. People love it not because it is a good thing, but because they are too weak to do injustice with impunity. (2, 358e4–359b5)

9. It is noteworthy that the basis cited for the "ancient quarrel between poetry and philosophy" mentioned in *Republic* 10, (607b6–7) is precisely their different attitudes to justice: "In the course of our discussion, then, did we respond to the other points, without having to invoke the rewards and reputations of justice, as you all said Homer and Hesiod did? Instead, haven't we found that justice itself is the best thing for the soul itself, and that the soul should do what is just, whether it has the ring of Gyges, or not, or even the cap of Hades as well" (10, 612a8–b4).

Were this a story about the absolute origins of justice, it would be plainly incoherent: if there could be no injustice prior to the making of laws and covenants, no one could possibly be led to make them by doing or suffering injustice. The story's true aim, however, is the more circumscribed one of explaining how *democratic* justice—the sort relevant in Athens and in Piraeus, where the conversation is taking place—arose. (Although it can easily be adapted to apply to other cases in which one political group takes over power from another.) Glaucon refers specifically to "what the masses think" about justice (2, 358a4). He explains what its origins are in a situation in which it is those who are "too weak to do injustice with impunity" (2, 359b2)—presumably the mass of ordinary people, not the privileged and powerful few who make the laws and covenants. Finally, he refers to the effect of the laws as forcing people to "honor equality (*tou isou*)" (2, 359c5–6), which is a distinctively democratic goal: "Democracy comes about, I suppose, when the poor are victorious, kill or expel the others, and give the rest an equal (*isou*) share in the constitution and ruling offices" (8, 557a3–4).

What we are to imagine is a group of such people, already in a non-democratic political community, who have committed injustice (broken its laws), got away with it (perhaps simply by chance or police ineptitude), and seen how naturally good that is. At the same time they have also suffered injustice without being able to take revenge and have seen how naturally worse that is. Since the only explanation on offer for their inability to take revenge is lack of power compared to the perpetrator, it follows that within this community there must have been perpetrators sufficiently powerful to inflict injustice with impunity. To offer protection against such perpetrators, the agreement the masses subsequently make with each other must constitute the masses themselves as a new, yet more powerful, (collective) agent that is able to "kill or expel the others." This is what makes their subsequent legislation an effective replacement for the laws of their previous community.

It is sometimes said that this account of the origins of justice is "the ancestor of honorable contractualist accounts."[10] Once we see that it is not an account of radical origins, such ancestry seems more problematic. Glaucon is not explaining how we got out of a state of nature. Nor is he explaining the legitimacy of laws by appeal to anything like the general will, or what rational agents would all agree to. This is clear from what he immediately goes on to say about someone who is "truly a man." As someone with enough power to be unjust (to break the laws) with impunity, *he* would not make

10. Williams, "Construction," p. 119.

an agreement not to do injustice on the condition of not having to suffer it—"for him that would be insanity" (2, 359b4–5). Power is the only source of legitimacy countenanced. That is why Glaucon ends the story by saying that this "is the nature of justice, according to the argument . . . and those are its natural origins" (2, 359b6–7). The origins are natural—not convention-al—because they have to do entirely with natural differences in power. The justice is natural, not conventional, for parallel reasons: it gains its author-ity not from the fact that it is embodied in conventions, but from the fact that those conventions are an expression of effective natural power.

All the same there is an element not of ethical but of (benign) seman-tic conventionalism in what Glaucon describes. Imagine that there are no laws. Still there are lots of natural harms being inflicted on people, some-times with impunity. Getting killed, sexually assaulted, deprived of shel-ter or food—all these are among the thousand natural shocks that flesh is heir to. When someone or some group emerges that is strong enough to make laws, it is these harms they will want to protect themselves against through legislation and designate as "unjust." Natural harms before, they thereby become injustices.

That a sufficiently powerful agent would not choose justice is presented as evidence that it is not a final or a compound good, but an instrumental second best, lying between the natural good of doing injustice with impu-nity, and the much worse natural evil of suffering it without recourse. The story of the ring of Gyges is intended to reinforce this point by showing that all who practice justice "do so unwillingly, as something compulsory, not as something good" (2, 358c3–4; also 359b7–9, 359c4–6, 360c6–7). What the ring does, as we know, is enable its wearer to practice injustice—break the law—with impunity by making him invisible. What it is taken to imply is a view of human nature and the human good.

A just person—someone who obeys the laws of his community—seems quite different from an unjust one. Give him Gyges' ring, so the story goes, and you will soon see that deep down the two are the same:

> Suppose we grant to the just and the unjust person the freedom to do whatever he likes. We can then follow both of them and see where their appetite would lead. And we will catch the just person red-handed traveling the same road as the unjust one. The reason for this is the desire to do better (*pleonexia*). This is what every nature naturally pursues as good. But by law and force it is made to deviate from this path and honor equality. (2, 359c1–6)

What lies on that road for the just person, according to popular opinion, is stealing what he wants from the marketplace, having sex with anyone he wants, having the power of life and death over people, and doing "all the other things that would make him the equal of a god among humans" (2, 360b4–c3). And why would he do all that? Because on his view, as allegedly on everyone's, the natural good for anything with a nature (whether god or man) consists in letting its appetites "grow as large as possible, without restraint" (which is what *pleonexia* consists in) and, "when these are as large as possible, having the power to serve them" (*Grg.* 491e8–492a1). Hence if someone did not want to do injustice, given the opportunity Gyges' ring affords, he would be thought to be "most wretched and most foolish by those aware of the situation. Though, of course, they would praise him in public, deceiving each other, for fear of suffering injustice" (2, 360d5–7).

Going back for a moment to the account of the origins and nature of justice, let us consider what it implies, in particular, about moral motivation—about where in our motivational set justice gets a grip. The person who is truly a man, who is strong enough that his opportunism faces nothing but opportunity, simply does what nature, when unrestrained by law, urges, and so pursues pleonectic satisfaction without let or hindrance. The perfectly unjust man who lives under law has the same motivational set as the one who is truly a man, but fewer opportunities to act from the relevant part of it without getting caught. The masses, who also live under law, are opportunists too, but since they lack both power and craft, they have little or no opportunity to act as nature urges. What is constant as we move down this list is the natural desire for the natural good of pleonectic satisfaction. All that changes is the degree of constraint law and convention impose on it. People are just, to whatever extent they are, because they are compelled to be.

We have already taken an advance draft on Glaucon's argument that the life of the perfectly unjust person, who necessarily enjoys a reputation for justice, is happier than that of a perfectly just person with an unjust reputation. If the human good really is Calliclean, his argument will be very hard to resist, since the perfectly unjust man does seem to do a much better job of satisfying his enlarged appetites than the perfectly just one— especially when the bad consequences of reputed injustice are factored into the equation. We would expect, therefore, that Socrates' response will need to persuade us that our (and the gods') nature has been misrepresented, and with it our (and their) natural good.

From Adeimantus' archive of the sorts of conventional defenses of justice to which he does not want Socrates to add, we may select just one:

> As for what people say, they say that there is no advantage in my being just if I am not also reputed just; whereas the troubles and penalties of being just are apparent. On the other hand, the unjust person, who has secured for himself a

reputation for justice, lives the life of a god. Since, then, opinion forcibly over-comes truth, and controls happiness, as the wise men say, I must surely turn entirely to it. I should create an illusionist painting of virtue around me to deceive those who come near, but keep behind it the wise Archilochus' greedy and cunning fox. (2, 365b4–c6)

Here the idea of simulation and control of belief or public opinion is explicit. Being just involves troubles and penalties but no advantages unless one is also reputed just. Simulation of justice thus becomes the wise course, since it combines the advantages of a just reputation with the absence of the troubles and penalties of being just. That means that it is not justice but reputed justice that is being defended. The defenses are unsatisfactory, then, because they are all couched exclusively in terms of simulator-accessible consequences.

The Thrasymachean Provenance of the Challenge

When Glaucon says that in the view of the masses justice is an instru-mental good (2, 358a4–6), Socrates responds: "I know that is the gen-eral view. Thrasymachus has been faulting justice and praising injustice on these grounds for some time. But it seems that I am a slow learner" (2, 358a7–9). Glaucon replies that he will help Socrates to understand by developing Thrasymachus' account: "I think Thrasymachus gave up before he had to, as if he were a snake you had charmed.... So, if you agree, I will renew the argument of Thrasymachus" (2, 358b2–c1). A few lines later, he explains that while he himself is not persuaded by that argument, his ears are "deafened listening to Thrasymachus and countless others" propound it (2, 358c7–d1). Later still, Adeimantus says that if Socrates fails to leave reputations out of the defense, he will be agreeing with Thrasymachus "that justice is the good of another, the advantage of the stronger, while injustice is one's own advantage and profit, though not the advantage of the weaker" (2, 367c2–5). Socrates himself subsequently reminds us that it is Thrasymachus' argument to which his own is opposed: "either [we must] be persuaded by Thrasymachus to practice injustice, or, by the argument that is now coming to light, to practice justice" (8, 545b1–2). Finally, at the end of his defense of justice, it is again Thrasymachus' position that he presents as having been turned upside down: "It is not to harm the slave that we say he should be ruled, as Thrasymachus supposed was true of all subjects, but because it is better for everyone to be ruled by a divine and wise ruler" (9, 590d1–4). From early to late, then, the position presented as in need of critical discussion is that of Thrasymachus. Moreover he, too, seems to agree that this position really is his, since to these characterizations—unlike to Socrates' initial ones (1, 338d2–3, 340d2)—he offers no objection or emendation. It is possible, of course, that everyone, including Thrasymachus himself, is getting him wrong anyway, but, given this evidence, it is surely unlikely. When even very perceptive critics tell us that Thrasymachus' and Glaucon's "accounts seem to be opposed to one another," therefore, or that the only Thrasymachean view the brothers really share is "that the life of justice is in some sense a *second best*," we should resist.[11]

Thrasymachus' initial account of justice, which he subsequently emends and fills out in various ways, is this:

> Each type of rule makes laws that are advantageous for itself: democracy makes democratic ones, tyranny tyrannical ones, and so on with the others. And by so legislating, each declares that what is just for its subjects is what is advantageous for itself—the ruler—and it punishes anyone who deviates from this as lawless and unjust. That, Socrates, is what I say justice is, the same in all cities, what is advantageous for the established rule. Since the established rule is surely stronger, anyone who does the rational calculation correctly will conclude that the just is the same everywhere—what is advantageous for the stronger. (1, 338e1–339a4)

In operation in the account are four ideas: first, of power in the service of what is advantageous to its possessors; second, of that power finding expression in political rule of different constitutional sorts, depending on who or what possesses it; third, of a *nominal* definition of justice—an explanation of the meaning of the word "justice" in a particular city—as consisting in obedience to its laws (1, 339c10–11); and, fourth, of a real definition of justice as what is advantageous to the stronger, which is invariant across constitutions ("the same in all cities"). Though, as we shall see, the nominal and real definitions are related, it is important not to conflate them, since it muddies the crucial issue of whether Thrasymachus is a conventionalist about justice or some sort of realist.

The third idea in Thrasymachus' account is a political one. It offers an explanation in terms of power of the variety of constitutional types. It is taken up by Glaucon, as we saw, with particular reference to democratic constitutions, understood as those in which the masses make the laws, and "call lawful and just…what the law commands" (2, 359a3–4). Thus he accepts Thrasymachus' nominal definition of justice as obedience to the law.

11. Williams, "Construction," p. 119.

Thrasymachus' second idea is a broadly psychological one to the effect that people pursue their advantage to the extent that their power allows. If they have the power to make laws, they will make laws advantageous to themselves. The masses are no different. When by banding together they constitute themselves as a new, stronger Thrasymachean ruler, the laws they make will reveal as much. Thus Glaucon also accepts Thrasymachus' real definition of justice as what is advantageous to the stronger.

Thrasymachus' prize example of the truth of his views is the perfectly unjust tyrant, whom he describes as a man of "great power (*ton megala dunamenon*) who does better (*pleonektein*)." As the phraseology indicates, he is clearly the prototype for Glaucon's "man who has the power (*ton dunamenon*)" to do injustice with impunity, the one who is "truly a man" (2, 359b2–4), able to "to do better (*pleonexian*)" (2, 359c4). As an expert at the craft of ruling (1, 340d2–341a4), he is also the prototype for Glaucon's perfectly unjust person, who, because he is like doctors, ship captains, or other "clever craftsmen" (2, 360e6), ensures that he has a reputation for justice.

Glaucon's Thrasymachus is not simply a realist about justice, to be sure, but a realist of a particular sort, namely, a *naturalist*. Though Thrasymachus does not himself mention nature or natures in laying out his views when he is being cross-examined by Socrates, we see how much a part of his way of thinking they are. He readily accepts, for example, that injustice produces in every one of its possessors "the very same effects which it is in its nature to produce" (1, 352a6–7) and shows no discomfort at all in talking about the "natural aim" of a craft (1, 341d8–9) or what a ruler does or does not "naturally seek" (1, 347d5) in practicing one.

The Thrasymachean provenance of the views of Glaucon and Adeimantus seems to be assured. But if their views are Thrasymachean, Plato must think Thrasymachus a worthy opponent. Why have Glaucon and Adeimantus claim to be his heirs otherwise? Why have Socrates identify his opponent as Thrasymachus? Why devote so long a dialogue to his views? None of this means that Thrasymachus *is* a worthy opponent, of course, or that the views Plato ascribes to Glaucon and Adeimantus coincide with—or are even consistent with—those he ascribes to Thrasymachus. Plato could have nodded on both counts. That he nonetheless *intended* a coincidence of views is scarcely to be doubted, given what he writes. That he did not nod is surely likely, but that is just to say that we should favor interpretations that make him consistent.

Thrasymachus' Definition of Justice

Socrates' conversation with Cephalus and Polemarchus is advertised as a search for a definition of justice: "speaking of that thing itself, justice, [what] are we to say it *is*...?" (1, 331c1–2); "the following is not the definition (*horos*) of justice" (1, 331d2). At the end of the conversation with Polemarchus, this point is emphasized again: "Since it has become apparent that neither justice nor the just consists in benefiting friends and harming enemies, what else should one say it *is*?" (1, 336a9–10). Thrasymachus, moreover, is presented as understanding all this perfectly well: "If you really want to know what justice *is*," he says to Socrates, "give us an answer yourself and tell us what *you* say the just *is*" (1, 336c2–6). When Socrates proclaims himself unable to comply (1, 336e9–337a1; compare 2, 354c1) and Thrasymachus is persuaded to answer in his place, what he says is: "justice is no other thing than what is advantageous for the stronger" (1, 338c2–3). Plato seems to be doing everything, therefore, to represent this statement—*advantage stronger*, as we may call it—as being Thrasymachus' definition of justice. Even if, to repeat, we had some reason to think it was an inconsistent definition or one inconsistent with other things Thrasymachus says or one that failed to meet our standards for definition at all, our confidence that it is what the text presents as his definition should not be shaken.

When Socrates responds by asking for a clarification of how the notion of the stronger is to be understood (1, 338c5–d1), Thrasymachus tells the story we looked at earlier. What is stronger in each city is the ruling element—for example, the masses in a democracy. This element makes laws advantageous to itself. It applies the term "just" to those subjects who are obedient to them and "unjust" to those who violate them, rewarding the one and punishing the other. When a subject does what justice (law) requires of him, therefore, he does what is advantageous for the established rule, that is, for the stronger. This claim is *the fact-based account* (since it is often taken to be based on empirical observation of actual people and cities rather than being theoretical or conceptual in nature); the rulers involved are actual rulers; they are actually stronger and make actual laws.

Justice is the advantage of the stronger. It is also what the rulers legislate: "whatever laws the rulers make must be obeyed, and that is what is just" (1, 339c10–11). But rulers are liable to error, so that they make some laws incorrectly—that is to say, not for their own advantage. Hence it is apparently just to do the opposite of what Thrasymachus claimed, since "the weaker are then ordered to do what is disadvantageous for the stronger" (1, 339b9–e8). When Polemarchus enthusiastically seconds this criticism

(1, 340a10–b5), Clitophon, previously silent, steps in on Thrasymachus'
behalf. What Thrasymachus meant by *advantage stronger*, he claims, is this:
"what the stronger *believes* to be advantageous for him. That is what he
maintained the weaker must do, and that is what he maintained is what is
just" (1, 340b6–8). Thrasymachus implicitly rejects this interpretation of
his views, however, opting instead for an entirely different line of defense.
Pointedly ignoring Clitophon and Polemarchus, he addresses himself
directly to Socrates: "Do you think," he asks, "that I would call someone
who is in error stronger at the very moment he errs?" (1, 340c6–7). Socrates
replies, "I did think you meant that, when you agreed that the rulers are
not infallible, but sometimes make errors" (1, 340c8–d1). Thrasymachus
angrily denies that this is what he had in mind:

> I think we express ourselves in words that, taken literally, do say that a doctor
> is in error, or an accountant, or a grammarian. But each of these, to the extent
> that he is what we call him, never makes errors, so that, according to the precise
> account (and you are a stickler for precise accounts), no craftsman ever makes
> errors. It is when his knowledge fails him that he makes an error, and in virtue
> of the fact that he made that error he is no craftsman. No craftsman, wise man,
> or ruler makes an error at the moment when he is ruling, even though everyone
> will say that a physician or a ruler makes errors. It is in this loose way that you
> must also take the answer I gave just now. But the most precise answer is this:
> A ruler, to the extent that he is a ruler, never makes errors, and unerringly
> decrees what is best for himself, and that is what his subject must do. Thus,
> as I said from the first, it is just to do what is advantageous for the stronger.
> (1, 340d6–341a4)

What Thrasymachus refers to here as his most precise answer is *the theory-
based account* (since it is often taken to be theoretical or conceptual rather
than empirical in nature). The rulers in question are ideal rulers, who are
ideally stronger and make ideal laws.

Though few critics think well of the theory-based account or the argument for it, most are agreed that it shows unequivocally that Thrasymachus
is not (or not now) a conventionalist about justice. That something accords
with a conventional law, made by the acknowledged ruler or legislative
body, is not what makes it just for him. To be just it must accord with a *correct* law—one that is advantageous for the stronger ruler. Yet such critics
have had little trouble accepting that the fact-based account does embody
a sort of conventionalism that is inconsistent with the theory-based
account: "It is not until after Socrates has begun to spring his trap that
Thrasymachus moves to reject the conventionalism which has caused the

problems for his opening claim."[12] In constructing this trap, however, Socrates recognizes from the beginning that Thrasymachus has a standard of correctness for actual laws in mind, namely, that they "prescribe what is advantageous for the rulers themselves" (1, 339c7–8). This is an embarrassment for the view that the fact-based account is conventionalist, since if it were, there could be no such standard, and we would have to wonder why Plato sends Socrates off on so wrong a foot. But if the fact-based account isn't conventionalist, it is to that extent at least not in conflict with the theory-based account.

While actual and ideal rulers, laws, and the rest are useful expository devices, it is a mistake to treat actual rulers as the sort we find in cities and make empirical claims about, and ideal rulers as creatures of Thrasymachean theory or fantasy, about whom we make a priori or conceptual claims. For Thrasymachus makes it quite clear that actual rulers are ideal at those times when they are practicing the craft of ruling and therefore not making errors. Hence when actual rulers are ruling correctly, they are ideal rulers, and so—tautologically—*never* make errors. The actual rulers in a city are generally the stronger element there. How else could they rule? But when they make a law not in their own interest, they manifest not strength but weakness in doing so, since they are allowing others to do better than themselves.

Properly understood, then, the fact-based account is a mix of empirical observation (some cities are democracies, some aristocracies, and so on), apparently uncontroversial political interpretation (the stronger element in a city is what rules it), and a controversial normative claim to the effect that when rulers rule correctly they rule in their own interest. Socrates has no trouble in accepting the empirical observation—or the political interpretation, for that matter (1, 338d9–10).[13] In fact, he agrees with Thrasymachus that political strength consists in mastery of the craft of ruling and that masters of a craft never make errors (1, 342a2–b7). What he disagrees about is only the normative claim (1, 339a5–6), and so about how the craft of ruling is to be defined. He thinks it aims not at the advantage of the stronger rulers but at that of the weaker subjects (1, 342e7–11).

Where the fact-based account speaks of "each type of rule" or ruling element making laws that are "advantageous *for itself*" (1, 338e1–2), the

12. S. Everson, "The Incoherence of Thrasymachus," *Oxford Studies in Ancient Philosophy* 16 (1998): 123.

13. "That the stronger rule, while the weaker are ruled" is "a kind of rule that is necessary" and "the one most widely spread among living things, and in accord with nature" (*Lg.* 3, 690b4–8).

theory-based account speaks instead of "a ruler" unerringly decreeing "what is best *for himself*" (2, 341a1–2). Thus the latter seems to character-ize rulers as straightforwardly *self*-interested in a way that the former does not. The interests, for example, of the masses need not coincide with the self-interest of individual democrats. (If any one of them were to become powerful enough to tyrannize the city, Thrasymachus thinks, we would see this plainly.) But this just raises the question of what precisely the fact-based account means by "what is advantageous for X" when X is a rul-ing entity that is not a single person. Indeed, it raises this question even when, as in a kingship, X is a single person, since we can legitimately draw a distinction between what is advantageous for him qua king and what is advantageous for him qua individual. The one unproblematic case, which has the merit of being the clearest proof Thrasymachus thinks he can give of his account is that of the tyrant (1, 344a1–3). For, in his view, there is simply no gap between someone's interests as tyrant and his interests as an individual. With that unproblematic case as our guide, we can be sure of this much: as it is in the tyrant's interest to do what will maintain his rule, so, too, it must be in the interest of the masses, or any other ruling element, to do the same thing. All ruling elements are, in this sense, *self*-interested.

In the *Laws* we find a discussion whose pertinence to Thrasymachus is readily apparent:

> Athenian: You realize that some people maintain that there are as
>   many different kinds of laws as there are of governing
>   elements. . . . These people take the line that legislation
>   should not be directed to waging war or attaining the whole
>   of virtue, but should look to what is advantageous for the
>   established governing element, whatever it is, so that it rules
>   in perpetuity and is never overthrown. They say that the best
>   way to formulate the naturalistic definition (*horon*) of justice
>   is like this.[14]
> Cleinias: How?
> Athenian: That it is what is advantageous for the stronger.
> Cleinias: Could you be a bit clearer.
> Athenian: The point is this: Surely, they say, it is the strong element in a
>   city that at any given moment establishes the laws. Right?
> Cleinias: True enough.
> Athenian: So do you imagine, they say, that when the masses are
>   victorious, or some other governing element, or even a

14. Note *horos* at 1, 331d2.

	tyrant, it will intentionally establish laws aimed primarily at something other than what is advantageous for maintaining its own rule?
Cleinias:	Of course not.
Athenian:	And if someone breaks these established laws, won't their establisher, calling "just things" what is required by them, punish him as a doer of injustice?
Cleinias:	Likely so.
Athenian:	Therefore, these things would always, for this reason and in this way, be what is just.
Cleinias:	According to this argument, at any rate. (*Lg.* 4, 714b3–d10)

Here *advantage stronger* is characterized both as the definition of justice and as naturalistic. It thus provides compelling additional support for the reading of the fact-based account we earlier developed by appeal to the *Republic* alone.

We can reasonably go on now to look at some criticisms of *advantage stronger* considered specifically as a definition, keeping in mind that our response may be to question the notion of definition they use or presuppose. It has been objected, for example, that *advantage stronger* cannot be a definition because it is not analytic.[15] Since *advantage stronger* is a real definition, however, and real definitions need not be analytic (think of "water is H_2O"), this is not a serious problem. Similarly, it has been objected that *advantage stronger* cannot be a correct definition if "we take a definition as specifying some property with which justice is to be identified," since identical properties must have the same extensions, but it is "highly implausible" that every act advantageous to the stronger must be just.[16] We might respond that a good real definition need not be an identity statement of the sort envisaged. When Oscar Wilde tells us that sentimentality is the bank holiday of cynicism, he is indicating the morally or psychologically most significant thing about it. He would hardly feel that his insight was undermined were it pointed out to him that not all instances of cynicism on holiday are instances of sentimentality. Thrasymachus could reasonably make the same sort of response, claiming that the politically or prudentially most significant fact about justice is captured by *advantage stronger*.

That point aside, the criticism is also not conclusive for other reasons. Once Thrasymachus has stated *advantage stronger*, he goes on to present the

15. G. F. Hourani, "Thrasymachus' Definition of Justice in Plato's *Republic*," *Phronesis* 7 (1962): 117–120.
16. Everson, "Incoherence," p. 109.

fact-based account as the clarification of it Socrates requests. Part of what
that account does, therefore, is to explain how the phrase "advantageous
for the stronger" is to be understood. It tells us what the property of being
advantageous for the stronger is identical to. First, the property of being
the stronger is identified with the property of being the ruling element:

Being the stronger = Being the ruling element.

It is political strength, or strength as manifested in political rule, that is
at issue, and not, for example, the physical sort possessed by Polydamas
the pancratist fighter (1, 338c8). So the property of being advantageous
for the stronger is identical to the property of being advantageous for the
ruler:

Being advantageous for the stronger = Being advantageous for the ruler.

Next, the property of being just is identified with the property of being
obedient to laws made correctly by the ruling element, so that

Being just = Being obedient to correct laws

and

Being obedient to correct laws = Being advantageous for the ruling
element.

To have the property of being advantageous for the stronger, therefore, an
act must have the property of being obedient to correct laws. So not simply *any* case of being advantageous to the stronger will be just, any more
than any case of superior strength will result in possessing the property
of being the stronger.

When a strict Thrasymachean ideal ruler sits down to develop a set of
correct laws, he chooses the set obedience to which will maximize his—
the ruler's—advantage. Does this mean that every time a subject obeys
a law in the set, the act he performs will be maximally advantageous
for the advantage of the ruler or will better promote his advantage than
any other act the subject could have done? Surely, there is no reason to
think so. An enemy of the ruler may have acquired a canister of nerve gas.
A friend of the ruler may be able to steal it, which would be to the ruler's
advantage. Yet a law in the set forbids theft, and the friend is just and
law abiding. Nevertheless this is still the set of laws obedience to which is

most advantageous to the ruler. In this regard, the advantageousness of laws is like that of states of character; it mustn't be equated or confused with the advantageousness of actions.

It remains to incorporate Thrasymachus' nominal definition of "justice" as obedience to the law into his account. In a democracy, "justice" will be given its semantic content (its sense or connotation) by the laws that have been enacted there. If those laws are all correct (if they are advantageous for the masses), "justice" will then unambiguously refer to (will have as its referent or denotation) what *is* justice, namely, what is advantageous for the stronger. When some of the laws are incorrect, the situation will be more complex. What we should then say is that the nominal definition is given by the laws but that justice is incorrectly specified by it. When people describe as "just" what is prescribed by an incorrect law, they will be linguistically correct but factually mistaken. When our dictionaries gave "large fish" as (part of) the meaning of "whale," we were in the same situation when we described a whale as a large fish.

Justice as the Good of Another

In a passage immediately preceding his account of the tyrant, Thrasymachus gives a further characterization of justice:

> [1] *Justice is really the good-of-another,* what is advantageous to the stronger and the ruler, and harmful to the one who obeys and serves. [2] Injustice is the opposite, it rules those simpleminded—for that is what they really are— just people, and the ones it rules do what is advantageous for the other who is stronger; and they make the one they serve happy, but they do not make them- selves the least bit happy. (1, 343c3–d1)

(1) seems to be a recapitulation of the fact-based account, suggesting that in the phrase "the good of another," the other referred to is the ruler, that is, the legislating element in the city. (2) seems broader in compass, as the examples Thrasymachus gives in apparent support of it make clear:

> [3] You must consider it as follows, Socrates, or you will be the most naïve of all: A just man must always get less than an unjust one. First, in their contracts with one another, when a just man is partner to an unjust, you will never find, when the partnership ends, that the just one gets more than the unjust, but less. Second, in matters relating to the city, when taxes are to be paid, a just man pays more on an equal amount of property, an unjust one less; but when

the city is giving out refunds, a just man gets nothing, while an unjust one makes a large profit. Finally, when each of them holds political office, a just person—even if he is not penalized in other ways—finds that his private affairs deteriorate more, because he has to neglect them, that he gains no advantage from the public purse because of his justice, and that he is hated by his relatives and acquaintances, because he is unwilling to do them an unjust favor. The opposite is true of an unjust man in every respect. I mean, of course, the person I described before: the man of great power who does better. (1, 343d2–344a2)

While justice is what is advantageous to the legislating element in a city, it is also advantageous to ordinary unjust (or law-breaking) people who are clever enough—stronger enough in that way—not to get caught. When Socrates asks Thrasymachus whether he considers unjust people to be "wise and good," he responds, "Yes, if they commit perfect injustice and can bring cities and whole nations under their power. Perhaps, you thought I meant pickpockets? Not that such crimes aren't also profitable, if they are not found out" (1, 348d5–8). Hence if the evidence Thrasymachus gives in (3) is to be so much as relevant to the case he is making, the "another" referred to in (1) cannot simply be the stronger legislating element in the city.

This fact has important bearing on the apparent inconsistency critics have detected between *good of another* and *advantage stronger*. If the stronger acts justly according to *good of another*, he will, they say, act for the good of another, so that his action will not be advantageous for himself. Hence it will not be advantageous for the stronger either, since in this case the stronger is himself. According to *advantage stronger*, therefore, it will not be just.[17] Though this may seem an inconsistency, in fact it isn't one. The terms "stronger," "another," "ruler," and "subject" are comparative or contrastive. As we saw, they do not always refer to legislating elements or their subjects. Hence it is always important to find the right comparison or contrast class. At the end of the passage of which *good of another* is a part, Thrasymachus says: "As I said from the beginning, justice is what is advantageous for the stronger, while injustice is profitable and advantageous *for oneself*" (1, 344c7–9). So it is from the viewpoint of oneself that *good of another* should also be understood. Hence the relevant "another" in (1) is simply someone *other and stronger than oneself*. If one is an ideal ruler, who unerringly makes correct laws, no one fits this bill. When one obeys these laws oneself, therefore, and acts justly, one's justice is—albeit vacuously—advantageous for everyone other and stronger than oneself,

17. Everson, "Incoherence," p. 116.

since that class is empty. So in that case, too, justice is advantageous for the stronger and the good of another (if there is one).

Though it is perhaps a bit harder to see, something similar holds when we turn to lesser unjust agents. If X can be unjust (can break the relevant correct laws) in his dealings with Y without being caught—that is, caught *by anyone*—then, there is no one other than X that is relevantly stronger than he, not even the generally stronger legislating entity in X's city. When X acts justly toward Y, which is precisely what, as a clever craftsman, he will do when he cannot get away with acting otherwise, his *act*, since it will be in accord with correct laws, will be of a sort that is advantageous to the stronger ruler. His *state of character*, his disposition toward those laws, which is to disobey them when he can get away with it, is a different matter. It is advantageous only to himself—than whom, in this regard, no one is stronger, since no one catches him. But in (3), as in Glaucon's challenge, the focus is states of character, not actions. It is the *unjust man* (the one disposed by his character to break the law when he can get away with it) and the *just man* (the one disposed to abide by it even when he could get away with it breaking it) that are being compared. It is "when the partnership ends" that we should see who has done best, not at each point along the way. Opportunism requires opportunity.

Though (3) shows that (1)–(2) is not about stronger legislating entities alone, its continuation presents that element as a special case of relative power in operation. Whenever X can get away with treating Y unjustly, X is stronger than and rules Y and Y is weaker than, serves, and is subject to X. So when X is the stronger legislating entity, the same holds. Rule and strength are expressions of natural power, not of conventional status. It is this fact, indeed, that explains why the tyrant is an illustration of *advantage stronger* at all, let alone the very clearest illustration. Here is how Thrasymachus introduces him:

[4] The man of great power who does better—he is the one you should consider, if you want to figure out how much more advantageous it is for the individual to be unjust rather than just. [5] You will understand this most easily if you turn your thoughts to injustice of the most perfect sort, the sort that makes those who do injustice happiest, and those who suffer it—those who are unwilling to do injustice—most wretched. The sort I mean is tyranny, because it uses both covert means and force to appropriate the property of others—whether it is sacred or secular, public or private—not little by little, but all at once. If someone commits a part of this sort of injustice and gets caught, he is punished and greatly reproached—temple-robbers, kidnappers, housebreakers, robbers, and thieves are what these partly unjust people are called when they commit

those harms. When someone appropriates the possessions of the citizens, on the other hand, and then kidnaps and enslaves the possessors as well, instead of these shameful names he is called happy and blessed, not only by the citizens themselves, but even by all who learn that he has committed the whole of injustice. For it is not the fear of doing injustice, but of suffering it, that elicits the reproaches of those who revile injustice. So, you see, Socrates, injustice, if it is on a large enough scale, is stronger, freer, and more masterful than justice. And, as I said from the beginning, justice is what is advantageous for the stronger, while injustice is profitable and advantageous for oneself. (1, 344a1–c9)

(4) refers to the masters of the craft of ruling who appear in the theory-based account. These include legislators, but also—as (3) makes clear—any citizen who is able successfully to combine real injustice with reputed justice. (5) presents the tyrant as the perfect embodiment of that sort of injustice, because, unlike such "partly unjust people" as temple robbers, kidnappers, housebreakers, robbers, and thieves, he commits "the whole of injustice," and gets away with it.

Temple robbers and the rest commit injustice in a straightforward manner by breaking the relevant laws of their city. (No natural harm is correctly called an injustice, remember, unless it breaks a law.) The tyrant seems quite different. He does not so much break the laws as overthrow both them and the previously stronger legislating entity that made and enforced them. Is he really unjust, or is he the perpetrator of a successful revolutionary coup? It is by presenting him as simply a more extreme case of straightforwardly unjust people that Thrasymachus allows us to see him in the former light—as straightforwardly but also perfectly unjust.

The tyrant is the ancestor of Glaucon's perfectly unjust man, who combines real injustice with reputed justice. We can now appreciate more fully why that is true. For the stronger, laws function as the ultimate "illusionist painting of virtue" with which to surround himself. So effective is it, in fact, that we can typically see through it only from the outside and by dint of adopting a historical perspective, a diachronic view. It is when the tyrant is represented as using his newfound greater strength to break all the laws of the previous regime that he can be seen as simply a more powerful temple robber or pickpocket. In a moment, though, he will disappear behind his legislation—really unjust but reputed just.

CHAPTER 5

✣

Souls, Soul-Parts, and Persons

Republic 4 argues that a human soul has three parts or elements: appetite (*epithumētikon*), spirit (*thumoeides*), and reason (*logistikon*). Socrates speaks, too, of "others that may be in-between" (4, 443d7–8) the canonical three. While this no doubt allows for some relaxation of strict tripartite-ism, it raises a problem of its own: why would any other elements or parts there might be have to be "in between" the others? But that is just a special case of the more general problem of explaining what these soul-parts are and how they are related to the soul itself and to the person whose soul it is.

Reason

When reason is first introduced, its functions seem to be predominantly practical. It is the element in the soul (1) "with which it calculates" (4, 439d5), the one (2) that is "really wise and exercises foresight on behalf of the whole soul" and so is its proper or appropriate ruler (4, 441e3–5), (3) that "guards the whole soul and the body against external enemies … by deliberating" (4, 442b5–7), and (4) that has "within it the knowledge of what is advantageous both for each part and for the whole, the community composed of all three" (4, 442c5–7). Later, however, reason takes on a more contemplative or theoretical look. It is the element (5) "with which we learn" (9, 580d9), the one (6) that is "always straining to know where the truth lies" (9, 581b6–7), (7) that it is appropriate to call "learning-loving and philosophic" (9, 581b10–11), and (8) that, when it rules in someone's soul, causes him to think that the pleasures of making money and being honored are "far behind" that of "knowing where the truth lies and always enjoying some variety of it while he is learning," and to praise his own life as the most pleasant (9, 581c1–11). When we recall that the philosopher's preferred life is one of contemplating the forms (7, 519b7–521c8), our confidence might grow that if a fracture or fissure were to open within reason, it would occur between (4) and (5).

That none occurs there—or that none is presented as occurring there—is due, in part at least, to a single doctrine or pair of doctrines. First, "the most important thing to learn about" is the form of the good (6, 505a2), since "it is by their relation to it that just things and the others become useful and beneficial" (6, 505a3–4), so that "if we do not know it, . . . even the fullest possible knowledge of other things is of no benefit to us, any more than if we acquire any possession without the good" (6, 505a6–b1). The putatively theoretical knowledge described in (5)–(8) is thus knowledge of something with profound practical import. Second, while justice and beauty are—as we shall put it later on—*ambivalent*, so that "many people would choose things that are reputedly just or beautiful, even if they are not so, and to act, acquire things, and form beliefs accordingly," goodness isn't: "no one is satisfied to acquire things that are reputed good, but, on the contrary, everyone seeks the things that are good" and "disdains mere reputation," so that the good is "what every soul pursues and for its sake does everything" (6, 505d5–e2).

The joint import of these two doctrines is that the good is pursued because every soul wants good things and so wants to know what things are really good, useful, and beneficial—something only knowledge of the form of the good can provide. But what eventually emerges as the most beneficial thing, the one the *Philebus* calls "the [best] good *in a human being*" (64a1), is knowing or contemplating that very form so that the pleasure of "knowing where the truth lies" emerges as the most pleasant pleasure, and the philosophic life around which it is organized, the happiest (9, 576d6–588a10).

What makes it just and appropriate for reason to rule the soul (or the appetitive and spirited elements) is explained in (2)–(4). Reason is wise (it has knowledge of the form of the good) and exercises foresight on behalf of the whole soul by making use of that knowledge. When it rules, it isn't simply its own interests it considers, therefore, but those of the other parts as well: "when the entire soul follows the philosophic element and does not engage in faction, the result is that each element does its own work and is just, and, in particular, each enjoys its own pleasures, the best pleasures and—to the degree possible—the truest" (9, 586e4–587a2). On the other hand, when "one of the other parts gains mastery, the result is that it cannot discover its own pleasure"—since it doesn't have access to the only reliable paradigm for evaluating the goodness of pleasures—and "compels the other parts to pursue an alien, and not a true pleasure" (9, 587a4–6). With each part satisfied by the best and truest pleasures available to it, faction is banished and, from "having been many," the reason-ruled soul becomes "entirely one, temperate and harmonious" (4, 443e1–2). For the form of the good, as we shall see, is an ideal of rational order or rational unity, which as such induces a like order and unity in the soul of the one who loves and contemplates it (6, 500c3–d3).

Though this rational order flows into the reason-ruled soul as a whole, its consequences for reason are different from those for the other soul-parts. The following passage begins to explain why:

> We must not think…that the soul in its truest nature is full of complexity, dis-similarity, and conflict with itself.…It is not easy, you see, for something to be immortal when (*te*) it is composed of many elements and (*kai*) is not composed in the most beautiful way—which is how the soul now seemed to us.…Yet both our recent argument, and others as well, compel us to accept that the soul *is* immortal. But what it is like in truth, seen as it should be, not maimed by its partnership with the body and other bad things, which is how we see it now, what it is like when it has become pure—*that* we can adequately see only by means of rational calculation. And you will find it to be a much more beauti-ful thing than we thought and get a much clearer view of the cases of justice and injustice and of all the other things that we have so far discussed. So far what we have said about the soul is true of it as it appears at present. But the condition we have seen it in is like that of the sea god Glaucus, whose original nature cannot easily be made out by those who catch glimpses of him, because some of the original parts of his body have been broken off, others have been worn away and altogether mutilated by the waves, while other things—shells, seaweeds, and rocks—have been fastened to him, so that he looks more like any wild beast than what he naturally was. Such, too, is the condition of the soul when we see it beset by myriad bad things. But, Glaucon, we should be looking in another direction…toward its love of wisdom. We must keep in mind what it grasps and the kinds of things it longs to associate with, because it is akin to what is divine and immortal and what always exists, and what it would become if it followed this longing with its whole being and if that impulse lifted it out of the sea in which it now is, and struck off the rocks and shells which, because it now feasts on earth, have grown around it in a wild, earthy, and stony profu-sion as a result of those so-called happy feastings. And then you would see its true nature, whether multiform or uniform, or somehow some other way. But we have given a pretty good account now, I think, of what its condition is and what elements it possesses in human life. (10, 611b1–612a6)

The soul is partnered with the body, but also with other bad things, which—as the reference to feasting makes clear—are (or include) appetites. As the shells, seaweed, and rocks that have become fastened to him obscure Glaucus' true nature, so these appetites obscure the true nature of the soul.

An earlier passage completes the explanation by telling us in plainer terms what this true nature is:

> The other so-called virtues of the soul do seem to be closely akin to those of the body: they really are not present in it initially, but are added later by habit and practice. The virtue of wisdom, on the other hand, belongs above all, so it seems, to something more divine, which never loses its power, but is either useful and beneficial or useless and harmful, depending on the way it is led around....If this element of this sort of nature had been hammered at right from childhood, and struck free of the leaden weights, as it were, of kinship with becoming, which have been fastened to it by eating and other such pleasures and indulgences, which turn its soul's vision downward—if, I say, it got rid of these and turned toward truly real things, then the same element of the same people would see them most sharply, just as it now does the things it is now turned toward. (7, 518d9–b5)

What is struck free of the appetites and so on that get fastened to it by eating or feasting is the rational part alone, which is the locus of wisdom (4, 442c4–7). Hence what we would see to be the soul's true nature, were these removed, is reason, which—like the forms to which it is akin—is uniform, not multiform. The virtues other than wisdom are so-called virtues *of the soul*, apparently, because they are virtues not of reason alone, which is the true soul, but of the soul when it is embodied.

One problem for this way of interpreting these texts is raised by the sentence: "it is not easy...for something to be immortal when (*te*) it is composed of many elements and (*kai*) is not composed in the most beautiful way." For it seems to allow that even a complex soul could be immortal if it were beautifully put together. *Te...kai*, though, is "often used to unite complements," where "the second may be stronger than the first."[1] This is how consistency requires it to be taken here. The sense is: "when it is composed of many elements and, moreover, not composed in the most beautiful way." Only one possibility is thus in view—that of a soul that cannot easily be immortal, because it is composed of many elements. To

---

1. H. W. Smyth, *Greek Grammar* (Cambridge, Mass.: Harvard University Press, 1980), p. 667, 2974.

be sure, the complex soul does become *"entirely one"* (4, 443e1–2), when reason rules in it. But the unity it then achieves, since it is "out of many," is not of the natural or metaphysical sort that constitutes an absolute barrier to disintegration and belongs to reason alone.

As naturally uniform and unified, reason is akin to the uniform and unified forms. In flowing into the whole soul, therefore, the rational order of the good meets in reason its psychological analogue or partner. Nonetheless, even reason can be turned away from the forms toward the world of becoming, to which the other elements in the soul are akin. It is in this unnatural state that it appears complex and multiform, just as Glaucus does, even though he, too, is really simple and divine. The tripartite soul is truly complex. What falsely appears complex is reason maimed by its association with the other soul-parts and the body. As Glaucus is a simple divine being, we—to the extent that we are truly human—are our reason:

> Fashion a single species of complex, many-headed beast, with a ring of tame and savage animal heads that it can grow and change at will. . . . Now fashion another single species—of lion—and a single one of human being. But make the first much the largest and the second, second in size. . . . Now join the three in one, so that that they somehow grow together naturally. . . . Then fashion around the outside the image of one of them, that of the human being, so that to anyone who cannot see what is inside, but sees only the outer shell, it will look like a single creature, a human being. (9, 588c7–e2)

If we take this verbal image seriously, reason isn't just something immortal and so capable of autonomous existence when separated from the other (mortal) soul-parts, but is the true human being rather than a mere (or proper) part of one.[2] Appetite and spirit, by contrast, like the shells, seaweed, and rocks attached to Glaucus, are of a different order altogether.

Reason—the more divine element in the soul—always has sharp vision, but it can be controlled by vice, that is, by the rule in the soul of appetite or spirit (4, 443c9–444e1). The effect of such rule is to turn it downward toward the visible world of becoming, rather than allowing it to look upward toward the intelligible world of being and the forms to which it is akin (7, 525b2–c6). But the psychological power concerned with becoming is belief (7, 534a2–3; also 6, 508d3–8). Hence it should be the rational part (turned downward) that is responsible for it.

---

2. Aristotle also claims that we are—or are most of all—our understanding (*nous*), which is the divine element in our souls (*NE* 9.4, 1166a16–17; 10.7, 1178a2–8).

Though philosophically felicitous, this conclusion—like the doctrine of the unity and simplicity of reason—can seem textually problematic:

> Haven't measuring, counting, and weighing proved to be most welcome assistants in these cases [of optical illusion and illusionist painting], ensuring that what appears bigger or smaller or more numerous or heavier does not rule within us, but rather what has calculated or measured or even weighed?...And that is the task of the soul's rational element?...But quite often, when it has measured and indicates that some things are larger or smaller than others, or the same size, the opposite simultaneously appears to it to hold of these same things....And didn't we say that it is impossible for the same thing to believe opposites about the same thing at the same time?...So the element in the soul that believes contrary to the measurements and the one that believes in accord with the measurements could not be the same. But the one that puts its trust in measurement and calculation would be the best element in the soul....So the one that opposes it would be one of the inferior elements in us. That, then, was what I wanted to get agreement about when I said that...imitation really consorts with an element in us that is far from wisdom, and that nothing healthy or true can come from their relationship or friendship. (10, 602d6–603b3)

It is to reason, for example, that stick X appears longer than stick Y. It is reason that does not *believe* in accord with that appearance that X is longer than Y. If these psychological relations—*appears to* and *believes*—are genuine opposites or contraries, one must be possessed by one subpart of reason and the other by a different subpart, since "the same thing cannot do or undergo opposite things, not, at any rate, in the same respect, in relation to the same thing, at the same time" (4, 436b9–c2). Whether they are genuine opposites is another question.[3]

An inferior element in us believes, contrary to measurement, that X is longer than Y. In accord with what are *its* beliefs formed? The only candidate in view is *what appears to reason*. But this appearance cannot be the same as the inferior element's belief, which is only "in accord with" the appearance. Similarly, reason's own belief, as contrary to the appearance, must also be different from it. What appears to reason certainly conflicts in this case with what reason believes. But this conflict is not of the sort that requires psychic division, since perceiving and believing are not the same psychological relation. Hence the passage gives us no grounds for dividing reason into subparts or elements.

---

3. A question answered affirmatively by M. F. Burnyeat, "Culture and Society in Plato's *Republic*," *The Tanner Lectures on Human Values* 20 (1999): 223–227.

The phrase "one of the inferior parts within us" denotes appetite, which is the part that lacks reason (10, 604d8; 4, 439d7). But spirit, too, is probably included in its denotation, since spirit can be bestial (3, 411e1) and become irrationally angry (4, 441c2). In any case, Socrates himself later cites anger as among the things that appearances and their imitation on the tragic or comic stage "nurture and water, when they should be dried up, and establish as rulers in us when—if we are to become better and happier rather than worse and more wretched—they should be ruled" (10, 606d1–7). That is why we get the odd shift from the soul being ruled by what appears bigger or smaller—that is, by something that isn't a soul-part—to its being ruled by something that is such a part, namely, reason. It doesn't matter what part gets nurtured and watered into ruling the soul. As long as appearances are doing the watering and nurturing, the results will be bad.

Though the text we have been considering does not present us with a divided rational part, it does present us with an inferior part, whether appetite or spirit, that has beliefs. And this is no anomaly. For temperance to exist in the soul, reason, appetite, and spirit must "share the belief that reason should rule," and "not engage in faction against it" (4, 442c9–d2). Moreover assent and dissent (4, 437b1) are among the opposites that only a divided soul can have simultaneously toward the same thing. It is probably to this text, indeed, that ours refers, with belief treated as equivalent to assent by a soul or soul-part.

A belief, however, can be either what is believed or assented to—a content of some sort—or the cognitive attitude of assent (or dissent) that is held to it. In a fully virtuous, reason-ruled soul, content and assent are always united, since the soul-parts assent in unison to whatever content reason provides. But in a soul ruled by one of the other soul-parts, the two elements in belief can come apart. In the case of a perceptual belief, for instance, the relevant content, as we saw, is an appearance to reason. On the basis of measurement and calculation, reason dissents from this appearance and so believes contrary to it. But this doesn't mean that the soul's ruling element will follow suit. It may assent to the appearance. Since it rules the soul, its assent will carry the day, affecting subsequent belief, calculation, and action.

When we ask what does the believing in the tripartite soul, then, we have to be clear about which side of belief we have in mind. What makes available a belief's *content* is always the rational part. What determines the *attitude* adopted to that content, whether assent or dissent, is the part that rules in the soul. Since a full belief consists of both a content and an attitude to it, only the rational part forms beliefs autonomously, or without help from the other parts of the soul, because it alone provides access to content. The other parts, by contrast, form beliefs only in cooperation with reason, which provides them with contents to assent to or reject. What these soul-parts have on their own are not beliefs proper, then, but sub-doxastic dispositions to assent to or dissent from contents. The fact that these dispositions are acquired and shaped by habituation, not by education proper (7, 522a4–7), is of a piece with this conclusion.

What is true of beliefs in this regard must also be true of appetites, desires, and any other psychological functions involving content that is broadly cognitive or propositional. The content, whether perceptual or intelligible, involves the rational part, while the attitude to it—the assent or dissent, pursuit or avoidance—is determined by the part that rules the soul, which may be the rational part itself. It follows that nothing in the soul is autonomously capable of any of these psychological functions except the rational one—though it may need to be in a body to perform some of them (such as perceiving). There is a clear sense, therefore, in which the rational element alone is *a* soul.

Appetite

Appetite is the element in the soul (1) "with which it feels passion, hungers, thirsts, and is stirred by other appetites, the irrational and appetitive element," and (2) that is "friend to certain ways of being filled and certain pleasures" (4, 439d6–8). It is the element (3) whose rule in a person's soul leads him to say that compared to the pleasure of making a profit, the pleasures "of being honored or of learning are worthless unless there is something in them that makes money," and to give "the highest praise to his own life" as most pleasant (9, 581c1–d3).

It is with the appetitive element, (1) tells us, that the soul feels appetites, which are desires for "the pleasures of food, sex, and drink and those closely akin to them" (4, 436a10–b2). The fact that hunger and thirst are "the most conspicuous examples" (4, 437d2–3) helps explain why (2) characterizes appetites generally as "friend to certain ways of being filled." For the passive partner, at least, even sexual desire might seem to be like that. A cognate characterization is given later on, when "hunger, thirst, and the like" are described as "emptinesses related to the state of the body" (9, 585a8–b1). Though "closely akin" and "the like" are vague phrases, we get the picture. Appetites are desires that can be credibly or intuitively represented as specifically body related. Thus the needs or desires for shelter and clothing, for example, though not in any obvious way sorts of emptiness, are presumably appetites, all the same (2, 369c9–d4).

Because they are related to the body, appetites can be consistently represented as pulling reason away from the intelligible world of the forms, where it belongs, down toward the visible world of becoming, which is the body's own natural bailiwick. In the *Phaedo* the view is expressed in its starkest terms:

As long as we have a body, and our soul is contaminated by such a bad thing, we shall never adequately attain what we desire—which, we say, is the truth. The body keeps us busy in a thousand ways because of the nourishment it must have—besides, if any illnesses befall it, they impede our hunt for what *is*. It fills us, too, with multifarious passions, appetites, fears and phantoms, and with all sorts of other trash, so that we are really and truly, as the saying goes, never able to think about anything because of it. It is nothing other than the body and bodily appetites, indeed, that cause wars and factions and conflicts. For it is over the acquisition of wealth that all wars take place,[4] and it is because of the body that we are compelled to acquire wealth, since we are enslaved to its service. And so for all these reasons it keeps us too busy to practice philosophy. Worst of all, if we *do* get any leisure from it, and turn to investigate some issue, in the middle of our inquiries there it is again creating uproar, disturbance, and fear all over the place, so that the truth cannot be discerned in a pure way because of it. But, in fact, it has been shown to us that if we are ever going to know anything in a pure way, we must be apart from the body and must look at things by themselves with the soul itself. It is then, it seems, that the thing we desire and whose lovers we claim to be—wisdom—will be ours, and that happens, the argument indicates, when we are dead, not while we are alive. For if we cannot know anything in a pure way when we are together with the body, then one of two things holds: either there is nowhere we can acquire knowledge, or it is when we are dead—since it is then that the soul will be all by itself, separate from the body, and not before. And so, while we are alive, we shall come closest to knowledge, it seems, if we have as little to do with the body as possible and as little association with it, beyond what is absolutely unavoidable, and do not allow ourselves to be infected by its nature, but remain purified of it, until the god himself releases us. (66b5–67a6)

For a true human being—for reason—it is clearly a bad thing to be embodied and attached to appetite. All the same, while it is embodied, reason has no choice but to see to the welfare of the whole soul and body, since its own welfare depends on theirs.[5] On earth, contemplation requires a village, so

---

4. Compare 2, 373d7–e8.
5. Suicide is not an option, except in exceptional circumstances, for reasons canvassed at *Phd.* 61d3–c8.

to speak. We need food and drink, shelter and clothing, protection from violence and predators, and, no doubt, some love and affection, too.

When we meet the democratic man, this way of understanding appetites suffers a setback:

> He lives from day to day, gratifying the appetite of the moment. Sometimes he drinks heavily while listening to the flute, while at others he drinks only water and is on a diet. Sometimes he goes in for physical training, while there are others when he is idle and neglects everything. Sometimes he spends his time engaged in what he takes to be philosophy. Often, though, he takes part in politics, leaping to his feet and saying and doing whatever happens to come into his mind. If he admires some military men, that is the direction he is carried in, if some moneymakers, then in that different one. There is neither order nor necessity in his life, yet he calls it pleasant, free, and blessedly happy, and follows it throughout his entire life. (8, 561c6–d8)

It suffers another setback when we read the following passage about jokes and comic theater:

> What is forcibly kept in check in our personal misfortunes and has an insatiable hunger for weeping and lamenting—since that is what it has a natural appetite for—is the very element that gets satisfaction and enjoyment from the poets.... If there are jokes you would be ashamed to tell yourself, but that you very much enjoy when you hear them in a comedy, or even in private, and that you don't hate as something bad, aren't you doing the same as with the things you pity? For the element in you that wanted to tell the jokes, but which you held back by means of reason, because you were afraid of being reputed a buffoon, you now release, and by making it strong in that way, you are often led unawares into becoming a comedian in your own life. (10, 606a3–c9)

A hungry, thirsty, randy *appetitive* part is all well and good, as perhaps is one that desires physical training, but what makes a desire to do philosophy, or participate in politics, or to lament or tell jokes an *appetite*? Why think that there is one single part with which a soul does or feels all these?

Socrates uses the verb *epithumein* not just to express what appetite alone does or what a soul or person does with it but in an obviously looser and more popular sense.[6] He describes the three soul parts as having "three kinds of... appetites" (9, 580d6–7), Cephalus as having "appetites

---

6. Noticed by Hendrik Lorenz, *The Brute Within* (Oxford: Clarendon Press, 2006), pp. 45–46.

for discussions and their pleasures" (1, 328d4–5), Thrasymachus as "pretending to have an appetite to speak in order to win a good reputation" (1, 338a5–6), honor-lovers as "having an appetite for honor as a whole" (5, 475b1–2), and even a philosopher or wisdom-lover as having "an appetite for wisdom" (5, 475b8–9). In these texts, an appetite seems to be simply a strong desire of whatever sort. Though we should not overlook this fact or causally spurn the assistance it might provide with how to understand the democratic man or the theater enthusiast, we must be careful not to allow it to let us off too many hooks. Even if we set aside the apparently problematic appetites as loosely and popularly so called, we still have to explain what it is about the desires for food, drink, sex, and the rest—which are appetites in the strict sense—that makes them the contents of a single part of the soul.

Socrates shows himself well aware of this problem:

> In just the way a city is divided into three classes, the soul of each person is also divided in three.... It seems to me that the three also have three kinds of pleasure, one peculiar to each, and the same for appetites and kinds of rule.... One element, we say, is that with which a person learns; another, that with which he feels anger. As for the third, because it is multiform, we had no one special name for it, but named it after the biggest and strongest thing it has in it. I mean, we called it the appetitive element, because of the intensity of its appetites for food, drink, sex, and all the things that go along with them. We also called it the money-loving element,[7] because such appetites are most easily satisfied by means of money.... So if we said its pleasure and love are for profit, wouldn't that best bring it together under one heading for the purposes of our argument, and make clear to us what we mean when we speak of this part of the soul? And would we be right in calling it money-loving and profit-loving? (9, 580d2–581a7)

The appetitive part certainly includes unproblematic appetites—sexual desire or passion, hunger, and thirst—as some of its contents, but what makes it a single part of the soul is that its characteristic pleasure and love are for money or profit, since its constituent desires are most easily satisfied by means of it. This does not mean, obviously, that you can drink, eat, or have sex with money. Socrates' point is that money is the best single instrumental means to satisfying these appetites, since you can buy real food, drink, and sex with it. What makes appetite a unified part is that it has or can have a unified goal. Its unity is thus telic or teleological. There is

7. At 8, 553c5; implied at 4, 442a6–7.

one, single thing that it loves, and it is that which confers on it such unity as it has. The philosophy the democratic man dallies with, we might infer, is the sort that money can buy—for example, from a Sophist.

The discussion of appetites, which divides them into necessary and unnecessary ones, reveals the good concealed in this teleological picture of appetite:

> In order not to have a discussion in the dark, would you like us first to define which appetites are necessary and which are not?...Well, then, wouldn't those we cannot deny rightly be called necessary? And also those whose satisfaction benefits us? For we are by nature compelled to try to satisfy them both. Isn't that so?...So we would be right to apply the term necessary to them? What about those someone could get rid of if he started practicing from childhood, those whose presence does no good but may even do the opposite? If we said that all of them were unnecessary, would we be right?...Let's pick an example of each, so that we have a pattern to follow....Wouldn't the desire to eat to the point of health and well-being and the desire for bread and relishes be necessary ones?...The desire for bread is surely necessary on both counts, in that it is beneficial and that unless it is satisfied we die....And so is the one for relishes in so far as it is beneficial and conduces to well-being. What about an appetite that goes beyond these and seeks other sorts of foods, that if it is restrained from childhood and educated, most people can hold in check, and that is harmful to the body or harmful to the soul's capacity for wisdom and temperance? Wouldn't it be correct to call it unnecessary?...Wouldn't we also say that the latter are spendthrift, then, whereas the former are moneymaking because they are useful where work is concerned?...And won't we say the same about sexual appetites and the rest? (8, 558d8–559b6)

Necessary appetites are thus divided into two classes, those (such as the one for bread) whose satisfaction is both beneficial and essential for life and those whose satisfaction is beneficial and conduces to well-being (but is not essential for life). Both are necessary, because we are compelled by nature to satisfy them both.[8] Appetites are unnecessary when we are not compelled by nature to satisfy them, because early education and upbringing can get rid of them (or allow us to keep them under control). They also fall into two classes, those whose presence is harmful to the body and those whose presence is harmful to the soul's capacity for wisdom and temperance. The good or benefit that comes from the satisfaction

---

8. This is relevant to the claim that every "soul pursues" what is really good and "for its sake does everything" (6, 505d7–e2).

of necessary appetites is associated with money (an association fore-shadowed at 4, 442a6–7), as are the harms brought by unnecessary ones (spendthriftness).

Even unnecessary appetites of the worst because lawless sort are "prob-ably present in all of us, but they are held in check by the laws and by our better appetites allied with reason" (9, 571b4–6).[9] It is only in "a few people that they have been got rid of or that only a few weak ones remain, while in others they are stronger or more numerous" (9, 571b6–c1). Thus our better appetites—that is to say, the necessary or moneymaking ones—are assigned a sort of policing role in relation to the unnecessary ones (as they are at 8, 554d9–e2). The fact that they are then allied with reason is further evidence that money is a sort of good, since reason is intrinsically related to an ideal of goodness, rational order, and unity.

Because unity and goodness enter the appetitive part only with the appearance therein of the love of money and the structure that this love imposes on it, we are better able to understand the claim, crucial to the account of incontinence, that thirst is in its nature for drink and not for good drink, and similarly for the other appetites (4, 437d1–438a5). The claim, as we can now see, is that there is nothing intrinsic to hunger—to change to the example Socrates develops in *Republic* 8—that makes it either a necessary appetite (essential for life or promoting of well-being) or an unnecessary one (nonbeneficial or harmful but eliminable or con-trollable). It all depends on how training and upbringing have shaped or qualified it. A hunger satisfied by a healthy amount of bread or some other staple is necessary, as is one for relishes, or healthy garnishes, whereas one that goes "beyond these and seeks other sorts of foods is unneces-sary" (8, 559b8–9). The good drink that thirst is not by nature for is not good-tasting or high-quality drink, in other words, but beneficial drink—drink that is good for the relevant person. The unqualified appetites are, in that sense, good-independent. As a result, there is nothing about them that could serve as a unifier of appetite. They are irreducibly many, because they are by nature for irreducibly distinct things—drink, food, sex, and so on.

It is here, surely, that we find an explanation for the claim that appe-tite's unity is somehow not as tight or natural as that of spirit or reason. It is multiform, as they, evidently, are not. The unforgettable image of appe-tite as "a single species of complex many-headed beast," later identified as being "snakelike" (9, 590b1), that has "a ring of tame and savage animal heads all of which it can grow or change from within" (9, 588c7–10), gives

---

9. Notice that the cognate phrase "the fine and good appetites" (8, 561b9–c1) must refer to strict, not loose and popular, appetites.

vivid expression to this fact. Since lawless and unnecessary appetites, such as cannibalistic or incestuous desires, are described as constituting "the bestial and savage element" (9, 571b3–c5), they are presumably represented by the savage heads, while other appetites—the necessary ones, certainly, but perhaps the lawful but unnecessary ones as well—are represented by the tame heads. A head grows as the appetite it represents empties and craves satisfaction, evidently, only to have another take its place once it is sated or filled, as happens in the appetite-ruled democratic person: "putting all his pleasures on an equal footing, he lives, always surrendering rule over himself to whichever desire comes along, as if it were chosen by lot, until it is satisfied; and after that to another, dishonoring none but satisfying all equally" (8, 561b3–6).

Though the love of money can impose (a degree of) unity on the appetitive element, the discussion of the oligarchic person reveals how circumscribed it is. For the unnecessary appetites perforce still exist in him unmoderated, ready to spring into action when the occasion arises:

> Where someone like that has a good reputation and is thought to be just, something good of his is forcibly holding in check the other bad appetites within, not persuading them that they had better not, nor taming them with arguments, but using compulsion and fear, because he is terrified of losing his other possessions. ... Yes, by Zeus, my friend, you will find most of them, when they have other people's money to spend, have [unnecessary] appetites in them akin to those of the drone. (8, 554c12–d7)

As a result, Socrates says, the oligarchic person is not "one but somehow twofold, although his better [necessary] appetites would generally master his worse [unnecessary] appetites" (8, 554d9–e2).[10] He is twofold, notice, because his ruling appetitive part—the one with which he identifies, as we might put it—is itself divided. The (generally overlooked) fact that this divide occurs within appetite itself is surely important. What is equally important is that it does not split that element into two *parts*, but into a part unified by its love of money on the one hand and a collection of essentially disunited—because unnecessary—appetites on the other.

Socrates' talk of the oligarchic man as not persuading his unnecessary appetites "that they had better not" or "taming them with a word"

---

10. He is probably relying on a claim introduced earlier in connection not with souls but with cities: "in all constitutions, change originates in the ruling element itself when faction breaks out within it; but if this group remains of one mind (*homonoountos*; compare *homonoētikēs* at 8, 554e5), then—however small it is—change is impossible" (8, 545d1–3).

(8, 554d1–2; compare 4, 442a1) naturally reraises the question of appetite's cognitive resources. In this case, as opposed to that of belief attribution, the text is somewhat plainer. The dronish or unnecessary appetites exist in the oligarch, we are told, because of "his lack of education" (8, 554b7–8). Moreover, as we saw, it is the education and restraint of appetite "from childhood" (8, 559b9–10) that leads to the elimination of unnecessary appetites or the restriction of their operation to fantasies and dreams. In *Republic* 4, musical and physical training are identified as what makes the three parts of the soul harmonious and concordant (4, 441e7–442a2), which is exactly what the oligarch's soul fails to be: "the true virtue of a single-minded and harmonious soul would somehow far escape him" (8, 554e4–6). But musical training, as the counterpart of physical training, is what "educated the guardians through habits, conveying by harmony a certain harmoniousness of temper, not knowledge, and by rhythm a certain rhythmical quality," and its constituent accounts or stories "cultivated other habits akin to these" (7, 522a4–7). Glaucon's insistence on habits and his contrast of them with knowledge make it plain that the persuasion of appetite and the taming of it with words or accounts isn't to be conceived on the model of a two-party conversation. Appetite is persuaded and tamed through the process of being habituated. But there is no need, having recognized this fact, to dumb the process of habituation unduly down. Appetites, like other desires, have intentional contents (hunger is for *food*, thirst for *drink*), and to that extent cognitive ones; they are not blind reflexes. It is on these contents, too, that habituation works, shaping thirst, for example, to be discerning, so that only beneficial drink will arouse or satisfy it.

Spirit

Spirit is the part of the soul (1) "with which it gets angry" (4, 439e2–3; also 9, 580d9–10). It is the one (2) that always has as its whole aim "mastery, victory, and high repute," and so is "victory-loving and honor-loving" (9, 581a9–b4), (3) that is "the natural auxiliary of the rationally calculating element, if it has not been corrupted by bad upbringing" (4, 441a2–3), and that is not seen "partnering with the appetites to do what reason has decided should not be done" (4, 440b4–7), but rather "in the faction that takes place in the soul, is far more likely to take arms on the side of reason" (4, 440e3–4). (4) When spirit rules in a person's soul, it makes him say that the pleasure of being honored casts the pleasures of making money or of learning into the shade (9, 581d5–7), so that he praises his own kind of life as most pleasant (9, 581c1–11).

The natural tendency of spirit, we learn when it is first mentioned, is to make "the whole soul fearless and unconquerable in any situation" (2, 375b2–3). In a revealing metaphor, spirit is characterized as "the very sinews" of the soul (3, 411b3), the thing that holds it together in the face of an adversity that might otherwise cause it to melt or collapse: the opposite of spiritedness is gentleness (2, 375c7–8) and softness (3, 410d1). It is the analogue, after all, of the protective military guardians in a city. Though it is present in everyone right from birth (4, 441a7–8), some people are nonetheless naturally spirited, others not (3, 411b6; 5, 456a4–5).

A person's spirit can apparently be engaged or sparked directly by events in the outside world (as in the case of Leontius' spirited disgust or Odysseus' anger), but it can also be engaged by what occurs within: "don't we often notice on other occasions that when appetite forces someone contrary to his rational calculation, he reproaches himself and feels anger at the thing in him doing the forcing, and just as if there were two warring factions, such a person's spirit becomes the ally of his reason?" (4, 440a9–b4). Moreover, spirit is sensitive not just to the rationality or incontinent irrationality of its own behavior but to its justice. Hence the very sort of painful or life-threatening treatment that would normally arouse spirit will not do so when it takes the form of just punishment: "what about when a person thinks he is doing some injustice? Isn't it true that the nobler he is, the less capable he is of feeling angry if he suffers hunger, cold, or the like at the hands of someone whom he believes to be inflicting this on him justly, and won't his spirit, as I say, refuse to be aroused?" (4, 440b9–c4). What is self-reproach when directed toward the incontinent or unjust self, thus becomes something more like righteous indignation when engaged on behalf of the unjustly treated one:

> But what about when a person believes he is being unjustly treated? Doesn't his spirit boil then and grow harsh and fight as an ally of what he holds to be just? And even if it suffers hunger, cold, and every imposition of that sort, doesn't it stand firm and win out over them, not ceasing its noble efforts until either it achieves its purpose, or dies, or, like a dog being called to heel by a shepherd, is called back by the reason alongside it and becomes gentle? (4, 440c6–d3)

In the cases of incontinent and unjust behavior or treatment, spirit seems to have the whole self as either good or bad in its purview. In the cases of Leontius' disgust and Odysseus' anger, it seems more like an ordinary appetite or desire. Socrates himself says of spirit that it initially seemed like "something appetitive." In the end, though, he says, it emerged as something else, somehow more allied with reason (4, 440e1–4). In another phrase, it is "the middle element" (8, 550b6), in between appetite and reason, with the result that rule by it is "somehow in the middle between aristocracy and oligarchy" (8, 547c6).

Leontius' appetite wants to look at the naked corpses, but his spirit is "disgusted (*duscherainoi*)" (4, 439e8) by them and turns him away. The question is, what is it disgusted at? Is it the naked corpses? Or is it Leontius himself (or his appetitive part) for wanting to look at them? When, mastered by his appetite, Leontius succumbs to incontinence, what he says to his appetites is, "Look for yourselves, you evil wretches, take your fill of the beautiful sight" (4, 440a3–4). This strongly suggests that he himself—as possessing and succumbing to those evil appetites—is disgust's target. The verb *duscherainein*, used to characterize his attitude to himself and his appetites, confirms this interpretation. Throughout the *Republic*, it is primarily used to express a distinctive evaluative attitude.[11] Thus Glaucon's perfectly unjust man is not, as he should be, "disgusted by doing injustice" (2, 362b5), while the guardians are, as they should be, "disgusted" by—and so unwilling to imitate—the lamentations of famous men at the loss of family and possessions (3, 388a1). Moreover, as the latter example suggests, it is an evaluative attitude directed not so much at (in this case) actions, but at the agent himself for performing them:

> When a moderate man comes upon the words or actions of a good man in the course of a narration, he will be willing to report them as if he were that man himself, and he won't be ashamed of that sort of imitation. He will be most willing to imitate the good man when he is acting in a faultless and intelligent manner, but less willing and more reluctant to do so, when he is upset by disease, passion, drunkenness, or some other misfortune. When he comes upon a character who is beneath him, however, he will be unwilling to make himself resemble this inferior character in any serious way—except perhaps for a brief period in which he is doing something good. On the contrary, he will be ashamed to do something like that, both because he is unpracticed in the imitation of such people, and also because to shape and mould himself on an inferior pattern disgusts him. In his mind he despises that, except when it is for the sake of amusement. (3, 396c6–e1)

What the moderate man is disgusted by and ashamed of—what he despises—is himself for acting like a bad person.

The evaluative vocabulary that spirit employs—or that a person motivated by it employs on its behalf—is that of justice and injustice, good and

---

11. The one exception is 5, 475b11, where *peri ta mathēmata duscheranionta* means "to be choosy or fastidious about learning things."

bad, shameful (ugly) and beautiful (fine). But its grip on this vocabulary is in an important sense incomplete:

> Then aren't these the reasons, Glaucon, that musical training is most important? First, because rhythm and harmony permeate the innermost element of the soul, affect it more powerfully than anything else, and bring it grace, such education makes one graceful, if one is properly trained, and the opposite, if one is not. Second, because anyone who has been properly trained will quickly notice if something has been omitted from a thing or if it has not been well crafted or well grown. And so, since he feels disgust correctly, he will praise fine things, be pleased by them, take them into his soul, and, though being nourished by them, become fine and good. What is ugly or shameful, on the other hand, he will correctly condemn and hate while he is still young, before he is able to grasp the reason. And, because he has been so trained, he will welcome the reason when it comes, and recognize it easily because of its kinship with himself. (3, 401d4–402a4)

Properly habituated by musical and gymnastic training, the spirited element is in harmony with reason, sticking to its "pronouncements" in the face of adversity (4, 442b10–c2). In this condition, it spontaneously loves and hates in the right way, ensuring that its possessor exhibits "political courage" (4, 429b1–430c4). But to exhibit full-blown courage, more is required: the rational element must be wise, so that its pronouncements, stemming as they then do from knowledge of the good, will be the most genuinely beneficial ones (6, 504c9–505b3).

In his discussion of political courage, Socrates carefully extends the purview of that virtue to include resistance not just to pains and fears, but to pleasures and appetites (4, 429d1, 430b1–2; compare 3, 412d9–414a6). Leontius' incontinent gazing at corpses is thus a failure of courage: his spirit cannot withstand the tempting appetitive pleasures of looking at pale naked bodies.[12] He is defeated—primarily in his own eyes, hence the self-disgust—by those pleasures much as a Homeric hero is by his opponent. And in that defeat the honor that goes to victory is lost.

---

12. If we know anything about the historical Leontius, it is that he was infamous in Athens for his love of boys as pale as corpses, suggesting that his appetite is sexual in nature. But we know this only if the *Leōtrophidēs* of the dramatist Theopompus is indeed our Leontius, who must have been sufficiently infamous for something, in any case, for everyone involved in the conversation to know what Socrates is talking about.

Socrates twice cites the Homeric passage about the triumph of Odysseus' reason over his spirit but never quotes it in full. Like well-brought-up Athenian boys and (perhaps) girls, we are supposed to be familiar with it:

> There devising evils in his spirit for the suitors,
> Odysseus lay awake; and out of the palace issued
> those women who in the past had been going to bed with the
>   suitors,
> full of cheerfulness and greeting each other with laughter.
> But the spirit deep in the breast of Odysseus was stirred by this,
> And much he pondered in the division of mind and spirit,
> whether to spring on them and kill each one, or rather
> to let them lie this one more time with the insolent (*huperphialoisi*)
>   suitors,
> for the last and latest time; but the heart was growling within him.
> And as a bitch, facing an unknown man, stands over
> her callow puppies, and growls and rages to fight, so Odysseus'
> heart was growling inside him as he looked on these wicked actions.
> He struck himself on the chest and spoke to his heart and
>   scolded it:
> Bear up, my heart. You have had worse to endure before this
> on that day when the irresistible Cyclops ate up
> my strong companions, but you endured it until intelligence
> got you out of the cave, though you expected to perish.
>
> (*Od.* 20.5–21)[13]

Odysseus is devising evil in his spirit for the suitors because they are *huperphialos*, which is usually, but not always, something pejorative. When, still in disguise as a beggar, he wants to try to draw the great bow that is, in fact, his own, Antinoös responds:

> Ah, wretched stranger, you have no mindfulness, not even a little.
> It is not enough that you dine in peace, among us, who are men of
>   quality (*huperphialoisi*),[14]
> and are deprived of no fair portion, but listen

---

13. Richmond Lattimore, *The Odyssey of Homer* (New York: Harper and Row, 1975).

14. See Joseph Russo, Manuel Fernández-Gailano, and Alfred Heubeck, *A Commentary on Homer's Odyssey*, vol. 3 (Oxford: Clarendon Press, 1992), p. 179.

to our conversation and what we say? But there is no other
vagabond and newcomer who is allowed to hear us
talk.

(Od. 21.287–292)

Whether being *huperphialos* is a bad thing, thus seems to depend on relative status, relative honor. Diomedes, a mere mortal, is *huperphialos* for attacking the immortal gods (*Il.* 5.881). The Cylopes, on the other hand, are *huperphialos* because they are puissant enough to "build a most beautiful wall for the famous city" (Bacchylides 11.78).[15] If Odysseus were truly a wretched beggar, the suitors would not be insolent in treating him and his household in the way they do, since a fair portion is one proportional to honor and status. Because he is far from wretched, their treatment amounts to an assault on his honor. It is as such that it galvanizes his spirited anger.

The anger ignited by the serving maids is partly derivative from the already smoldering one Odysseus feels at the insolent suitors: they are going off to sleep with men who are dishonoring him. At the same time—as the simile of the bitch with her puppies reveals—they are his property: it is their master they are dishonoring and betraying.[16] Unlike intelligence (*mētis*) or mind (*phrenes*), this anger is instantaneous, unreflective, and uncalculating. It motivates Odysseus quickly to reestablish mastery, achieve victory, and thereby regain honor and high repute.

In the case of both Leontius and Odysseus, then, spirit's characteristic love of honor is—albeit implicitly—in play. In the former, that love is defeated by appetite (Leontius is incontinent, weak-willed); in the latter, it is defeated by reason (Odysseus is continent, self-controlled). In both men, there is psychological conflict, which the basic characterization of spirit lays at the feet of bad upbringing. For spirit, in contrast to appetite, is the natural auxiliary of reason, both allied with it and subordinate to it, unless corrupted. What we want to understand now is why that is so.

Appetite naturally contains unnecessary, because harmful or nonbeneficial, appetites—appetites that cannot be brought into harmony or unity of purpose. That is why it is not naturally on the side of reason. It takes musical and gymnastic training to purge or repress unnecessary appetites,

15. David A. Campbell, *Greek Lyric*, vol. 4 (Cambridge Mass.: Harvard University Press, 1992), p. 183.

16. "Odysseus' rage at the maidservants reveals the possessiveness of the master beneath the beggar's disguise, and may also hint at sexual jealousy, since it was not uncommon for powerful nobles to have sexual relations with their female servants (1, 429–433). In this sense (even though Odysseus did not intend sexual relations with the maids), they 'belonged' to him, which makes his extreme anger here more understandable" (Russo et al., *Commentary on Homer's Odyssey*, pp. 108–109).

so that only the necessary, beneficial, and reason-allied ones remain as motivators of action. Appetite's unity and harmony with reason is thus an essentially cultural or political achievement.

The basis of appetite's unity is its characteristic love for a single, unified goal (money), which is the best means of satisfying its essentially diverse contents. On systematic grounds alone, then, spirit's unity and natural alliance with reason should have a cognate explanation. We noticed earlier that spirit is what holds the person together and preserves his unity and coherence in the face of threats to it. That is why its virtue, courage, is "a sort of preservation" (4, 429a5). As a natural conatus for unity, spirit is allied with reason as itself the paramount unifying force. Because it wants to be successful, however, to triumph over what threatens it with dissolution, spirit requires not just conatus but to get things right. It is reason, with its cognitive and ratiocinative capacities, that is best suited to that task. Consequently, spirit, given its nature, will not just be allied with reason, but subservient to it, so that what it will first and foremost preserve is "the *correct and law-inculcated belief* about what should inspire terror and what should not" (4, 430b3–5)—a belief that has its source in reason's knowledge of the form of the good (4, 442b10–c7).

What becomes of spirit during its subsequent education through music and gymnastic training is what brings honor into the picture. The object of honor, like that of the sort of disgust we looked at, is the whole person. At first, this (proto-) person is, as it were, a natural being or product—a human animal. The effect of socialization is to give it a second nature. Now it is a (full-blown) person with a social position and status. As a natural being, its preservation was one thing. As a social being, it is much richer and more complex. A sufficiently serious social slight can result in suicidal shame, as it does in Sophocles' *Ajax*. Honor—being accorded a respect appropriate to one's status—can become more important than animal life itself.

Nonetheless, just as in the case of appetite, the unity that the love of honor brings to the spirited part is imperfectly transmissible to the whole soul. Here the timocratic man is the pertinent example. His spirit-ruled soul is the result of bad education, in which "the true Muse, the companion of discussion and philosophy," is neglected and physical training is honored more than its musical correlate (8, 548b7–c2). Consequently, an appetite for money remains unmoderated in his soul, just as it does in that of the oligarch. On the other hand, the timocrat's adoration of gold and silver is not out in the open, like the oligarch's, but secret, indulged only in private (8, 548a5–b2).[17] Its scope in his life, like that of lawless unnecessary

---

17. Honor, as something conferred by others on the basis of what they see, has trouble providing the motivation needed to rule out private appetitive indulgence.

appetites in most of ours, is thus more circumscribed. Nothing is explicitly said about the enslavement of the timocrat's rational element to the pursuit of honor rather than truth. But the effect of the lopsided education he receives is to make him an "unmusical hater of argument" (3, 411d7), who does not use "argument to persuade, but force and savagery" (3, 411d7–8), making him the very opposite of the argument-loving philosopher (*La.* 188c4–189b7; *Phd.* 89d1–91b7). Reason, we may infer, is as coerced in him as spirit in the oligarch (8, 555a1–6).

People who conceive the good as honor, Aristotle claims, fail to do justice to its somewhat ambiguous nature. For honor "seems to depend more on those who honor than on the one honored" and so is too superficial to be the human good, which is "something of our own and hard to take from us." Here the honor at issue is *donor honor*. And about it, Aristotle is surely correct. For if the donors are foolish or imperceptive or vicious, nothing a person does, no matter how meritorious, will be any guarantee of getting it. As Aristotle continues his investigation, *recipient honor* comes into play. Cultivated people, he says, "seek to be honored by practically wise people, among people who know them, and for their virtue" (*NE* 1.5, 1095b21–30). This is the honor we possess when we have the virtue that rightly attracts donor honor from right-thinking and right-perceiving donors. It is the honor philosopher-kings possess. In between these two, Socrates discerns a third sort, which is the honor we possess when the virtue we exhibit is itself dependent on those who do genuinely possess recipient honor. This is the sort the honor-loving guardians go for. They reliably do what the truly virtuous do, since they genuinely possess virtue's *manifest* properties—the very ones right-thinking and right-perceiving people look to in correctly bestowing honor.[18] Nonetheless, on the inside, there is something they lack—something that comes not from others, but from themselves. While not as deep as recipient honor, this in-between kind does seem sufficiently more substantive than donor honor to count as a genuine sort of human good.

Ruling the Soul

A canonical soul-part description specifies: first, an instrumental role, or what the soul does by means of the part, whether rational calculation or

18. It is this fact that explains spirit's particular attachment to what is *kalon* (fine, noble, or beautiful) as something *incandescent*—an idea we shall soon explore. Compare Gabriel Richardson Lear, "Plato on Learning to Love Beauty," in *The Blackwell Guide to Plato's Republic*, ed. Gerasimos Santas (Oxford: Blackwell, 2006), pp. 104–124.

feeling anger or thirst; second, a characteristic love (truth, honor, money); third, a characteristic pleasure associated with that love; fourth, a characteristic type of rule (aristocratic, timocratic, oligarchic). The second, as we have seen, is the key to understanding what makes a soul-part a unified element in the soul. But it is the fourth that most illuminates what a soul-part is—namely, a unit that can rule the soul by bending the other parts to its will, to its own characteristic love. What most illuminates the different parts, therefore, are the objects of these loves: money, honor, the (form of the) good.

What distinguishes one such object from another is the distinctive sort or degree of unity that a ruling love for it can impose on the soul. How much intrasoul coercion as opposed to persuasion does love for it involve? How much potential for conflict does love for it leave open and in what areas? How much starving or dissatisfaction of the elements being ruled and of itself does it involve? These are the considerations that provide a basis for the claim that, for example, spirit is (as a unifier) in between appetite and reason. Provided we accept that money is a minimal unifier and the good a maximal one, it also provides a basis for believing that if there were other such unifiers, with corresponding loves, they would be in between the three canonical ones.

Because soul-parts are like this, the sort of conflict that reveals their existence is conflict over rule of the soul—conflict whose resolution identifies the soul involved as, for example, incontinent (Leontius) or continent (Odysseus). For in the harmonious, reason-ruled soul, no such conflict occurs—at least, not in the ideal case. In the ideal case, indeed, soul-*parts* are almost invisible. But rule is a notion at once normative (rule by any part aims at the real good, even if, as in case of appetite and spirit, it also involves a misconception of that good) and, in a way to be explained, *higher order*. Take the love or desire for money. From the logical point of view, it is a first-order desire, as is the desire for honor or the good. But its existence, like theirs, presupposes that of other desires to whose satisfaction it has (derivatively) an attitude, so to speak. If it rules in a soul, all the soul's other desires and resources will be employed to best achieve its goal, even if, as in the case of money, its goal is a means to satisfying some of them. The sort of conflict that reveals the existence of soul-parts, therefore, always involves something that is *in this sense* higher order.

We are naturally inclined to think of soul-parts in the context of an overall psychology, and to ask which part performs which psychological function or houses which psychological state or attitude. Which part perceives, imagines, or remembers? Which feels grief, jealousy, shame, or pride? Faced with interaction between soul-parts, we are beset with worries about vicious regresses—does spirit need a rational element of its own in order to listen to reason?—and unexplanatory homuncularism.[19] The fact that the rational part, alone of the parts, is *a* soul should help allay these worries. But it does so by radically reconceiving the very idea of a soul-part. The rational part is alone *a* soul. Appetite and spirit are nonsouls, parasites on the rational part that can alter its functioning and change its goals. But that is to speak of soul-parts from the eternal point of view. From the temporal point of view, appetite and spirit are, when properly ruled, reason's providers and defenders—the analogues of the producers and guardians in Kallipolis, as reason is itself the analogue of the philosopher-kings.

Souls and Persons

The idea that the rational element in the soul—or *rational soul* as we may now more usefully call it—is alone, properly speaking, *a* soul is confirmed by accounts we find elsewhere in Plato's dialogues. Here is a fairly early example from the *Phaedo*:

> Soul is most similar to that which is divine, immortal, intelligible, uniform, and unsusceptible to disintegration, and always remains in the same state and condition as itself. Body, on the other hand, is most similar to what is merely human, mortal, unintelligible, multiform, susceptible to disintegration, and never in the same state as itself. (80b1–5)

The reason for the difference is that soul is incomposite, body composite: "what has been put together and is naturally composite is the sort of thing that is susceptible of being divided in the respect in which it was put together; whereas if something is really incomposite, then it alone is really incomposite if indeed anything is" (78c1–4). As a result, psychological capacities attributed to parts of the incarnate soul in the *Republic* are attributed not to soul but to body (66b5–d3). At the same time, souls that have lost the bodies they have on earth—although not perhaps those they have in Hades—can have the sorts of appetites (81e1), fears (81c11), and types of character (81e2–3) that could hardly be possessed by rational soul alone. Rather than see this as an out-and-out contradiction, we should perhaps see it as prefiguring, if not presupposing, a view like the *Republic*'s. Rational soul is alone a soul—simple, indissoluble, eternal. But,

19. See Bernard Williams, "The Analogy of City and Soul in Plato's *Republic*," in *The Sense of the Past: Essays in the History of Philosophy,* ed. Myles Burnyeat (Princeton: Princeton University Press, 2006), pp. 108–117.

when embodied, it acquires characteristics that disguise its true nature. Thus when a complex embodied soul is divided "in the respect in which it was put together" with the body, what we get is rational soul, on the one hand, and some other elements that are not themselves souls but accretions to them, on the other.

A later portrait from the *Phaedrus*, which is one of the best known of all, represents reason, spirit, and appetite as a charioteer and a pair of horses:

> To say what sort of thing soul is would require a long exposition, and one calling for utterly divine powers; to say what it resembles requires a shorter one, and one within merely human capacities. So let us speak in the latter way. Let it then resemble the combined power of a winged team of horses and their charioteer. Now in the case of gods, horses and charioteers are all both good and of good stock; whereas in the case of the rest there is a mixture. In the first place, the ruler in our case has charge of a pair; secondly, one of them he finds noble and good, and of similar stock, while the other is of the opposite stock, and opposite in its nature; so that the driving in our case is necessarily difficult and troublesome. How then it is that some living creatures are called mortal and some immortal, we must now try to say. All soul has the supervision of all that is soulless, and ranges about the whole universe, coming to be now in one form, now in another. Now when it is perfectly winged, it travels through air and governs the whole cosmos; but the one that has lost its wings is swept along until it lays hold of something solid, where it settles down, taking on an earthly body, which seems to move itself because of the power of soul, and the whole is called a living creature, soul and body fixed together, and acquires the name "mortal"; immortal it is not, as any reason that has been calculated out shows, but because we have not seen a god or adequately grasped one with our understanding, we imagine a kind of immortal living creature that has both a soul and a body, combined for all time. (246a3–d2)

The perfectly winged soul that travels through air or space is entirely nonsolid and bodiless. When it loses its wings, it takes on an earthly body, and the resulting psychophysical compound is called a living creature. But loss of wing power is a matter of degree. The gods that end up on the stars and the planets are also immortal souls that have lost something of that power, but because their horses and charioteer are better than ours, they never sink down to earth but stay up in the heavens.

Though Plato sometimes allows the stars and planets themselves to be called "gods" (*Ti.* 40a2–d5), he is also explicit, as he is the *Republic* and here in the *Phaedrus*, that this is like calling the snake-lion-human complex a "human being." It's harmless enough as long as you don't take it literally. For the stars and planets are psychophysical compounds, and just as rational soul alone is the true human being, so it is the souls of the stars and planets that are alone gods:

> Consider the stars and the moon, the years, months, and all the seasons: what other account can we give except this same one? Since a soul or souls are evidently the causes of all these things, and good souls possessed of every virtue, we shall declare these souls to be gods. (*Lg.* 10, 899b3–7)

So it isn't the celestial bodies that are truly immortal, but the souls that have laid hold of them. If we imagine otherwise, it can only be because we don't understand what a god is.

Because the stars and planets are not immortal, they can in some sense be divided into body and soul. Yet they will never, in fact, come apart into these two components. When the Demiurge addresses them, he explains why this is so:

> Gods, works divine whose maker and father I am, whatever has come to be by my hands cannot be dissolved without my consent. Now while it is true that everything that is put together can be dissolved, still only someone evil would consent to the dissolution of what has been beautifully fitted together and is in good condition. That is why you, as creatures that have come to be, are neither completely immortal nor completely exempt from dissolution. Still, you will not be dissolved nor will death be your lot, since you have received the guarantee of my will. (*Ti.* 41a7–b5)

These manufactured gods are thus a nice intermediate case. They do not have the absolutely indissoluble unity possessed by rational soul, but they do have a type of unity that mortal creatures, whose souls and terrestrial bodies can come apart, lack. Metaphysical unity is all or nothing; psychophysical unity, a matter of degree. Since acquiring a body involves acquiring accretions to rational soul (the pair of horses), the same holds for the unity of a complex soul. Its unity isn't absolute and metaphysical, but mediated by Demiurgic will.

We are used to thinking of souls as immortal, less used to thinking of them as transmigrating. Yet that, too, is something Plato made a part of his portrait of them. At the spindle of Necessity, for example, where souls choose their next incarnations, Er saw the soul that once belonged to Orpheus choosing a swan's life, and a swan "changing to the choice of a human life" (*R.* 10, 620a3–8). In the *Timaeus*, too, reincarnation retains its prominence:

> Once souls were of necessity implanted in bodies, and these bodies had things coming to them and leaving them, the first innate capacity they would of

necessity come to have would be sense perception, which arises out of compelled disturbances. This they would all have. The second would be erotic desire,
mingled with pleasure and pain. And they would come to have fear and spirit
as well, plus whatever goes along with these, as well as all their natural opposites. And if they could master these, their lives would be just, whereas if they
were mastered by them, they would be unjust. And if someone lived a good life
throughout his proper span of time, he would at the end return to his dwelling
place in his companion star, to live a life of happiness that agreed with his character, but if he failed in this, he would be born a second time, now as a woman.
And if even then he still could not refrain from evil, he would be changed once
again, this time into some wild animal that resembled the wicked character he
had acquired. And he would have no rest from these toilsome transformations
until he had dragged that massive accretion of fire-water-air-earth into conformity with the revolution of the Same and uniform within him, and so subor-
dinated that turbulent, irrational mass by means of reason. This would return
him to his original condition of excellence. (42a3–d2)

Choice is not mentioned here, which may be a significant difference—
although the mechanisms that determine how a soul will be incarnated
seem compatible with it. Nonetheless, the picture still presents us with
the need to make sense of a single soul that acquires erotic desire and
spirit only when it acquires a body, and that can subsequently be placed
in very different sorts of animal bodies, with different consequences for
it. It doesn't take much to see that rational soul is alone well suited to
play both these roles. For the complex tripartite soul already has erotic
desire and spirit and so cannot acquire them, and if a soul is to learn
from an incarnation or to make a choice of another one or to subordinate anything at all to reason, it must have a rational cognitive capacity
of some sort.

The mention of a soul's "companion star" refers us to the *Phaedrus*, where
souls are portrayed as followers of different gods—or, in the language of
the *Timaeus*, as associated with or located on different stars or planets. At
a point in their revolutions, these gods "travel to the summit of the arch
of the heavens" (247a8–b2). From there, they can view "the region above
the heavens," and the forms that dwell in it (247c3–e2). But in order to do
this their souls must enter that upper region:

When those souls that are called immortal have reached the top, they travel
outside and take their stand upon the outer part of the heavens, and positioned
like this they are carried round by its revolution, and gaze on the things outside
the heavens. (247b6–c2)

At other points in its revolution, such a soul is inside the heavens, and so is both embodied and tripartite—although its body isn't of the earthly sort that a human soul takes on when it is incarnated terrestrially: in the *Timaeus* the bodies of the gods are "mostly fire" (40a2–3). When it travels outside, though, it apparently leaves even these astral bodies (or whatever we are to call them) in some sense behind. It is this sort of soul that is "called immortal." That it is rational soul is clear:

> This region [outside the heavens] is occupied by being that really *is*, that is without color or shape, intangible, and that only the captain of the soul—the understanding—can contemplate, and that is the kind of thing with which true knowledge is concerned. Thus because a god's thought is nourished by under-standing and knowledge that is pure, and so too every soul that is concerned to receive what is appropriate to it, it is glad at last to see what *is* and is nourished and made happy by contemplating what is true, until the revolution brings it around in a circle to the same point. (*Phdr.* 247c6–d5)

Rational soul does not lose contact with its astral body altogether. It con-tinues to be carried around by its revolution. But because of the paths these astral bodies reliably travel, rational soul is able regularly to escape from the realm of body while yet remaining attached to it.

A human soul that is the follower of a particular god also travels to the heavens' summit, provided it has trained its appetitive horse well (247b3–5; compare *Phd.* 66d3–7)—something not all such souls succeed in doing. But its charioteer or captain—rational soul—can keep itself in the realm of the forms only intermittently, subject as it is to "disturbance by its horses" (248a4). As a result, it "scarcely catches sight of the things that *are*, while another captain now rises, now sinks, and because of the compulsion exerted by its horses sees some things but not others" (248a4–6). It is how much of the forms its captain does manage to see—and how often—that determines what happens to it. It may remain on its star or planet, follow-ing in the orbit of its god, but whenever "through inability to follow it fails to see, and through some mischance is weighed down with forgetfulness and deficiency, and because of the weight loses its wings, it falls to earth" (248c5–8).

If a soul is good enough never to be sent to earth at all, we should pre-sumably imagine its life on the model of that of its god: sometimes, but less reliably, less frequently, and less continuously than he or she, its rational part gets to travel outside the heavens while yet remaining attached to its astral body and so to the spirited and appetitive elements that the horses represent. But even if a soul isn't good enough for that, its fall to earth is, so to speak, graduated. In its first incarnation, no soul, however minimal its wing power, is "planted in any wild beast" (248d1). That fate can come only in much later incarnations and only to those whose wings resolutely refuse to grow (249b3–5). Instead, souls are initially planted in terrestrial human beings—snake-lion-human complexes—with different types of characters. Thus "the one that saw most shall be planted in a seed from which will grow a man who will become a philosopher or a lover of beauty or one devoted to the Muses or prone to love; the second in the seed of a law-abiding king, or someone fit for generalship and ruling," until, in the eighth place, we reach the seed from which a Sophist or demagogue will grow, and, in the ninth, a tyrant (248d1–e3). And so it continues through thousand-year cycles of reincarnation and choices of lives, until, after ten thousand years, "each soul returns to the place from which it has come" (248e5–6).

A god's rational soul, while it is initially separate from every sort of body, then, is never subsequently in that condition. Once it is joined to an astral body by the Demiurge, it cannot be separated from it. That is why gods cannot suffer the equivalent of death by having their rational soul come apart from the only body they have. We can suffer death. That is one thing that distinguishes us from them. But we do not do so by having our rational soul come apart from our astral body—none of the portraits of soul envisages that. If they did, our souls would be better off than those of the gods, not worse. Instead, we die by having our complex soul come apart from our earthly body: we die on earth, not on our home star or planet. Whether we say that it is our complex soul or our rational soul that gets incarnated matters, when what is alone absolutely immortal and simple in us takes on the sort of astral body it has on its home star or planet. Thereafter, our souls, like those of the gods, are always complex, always tripartite, always embodied. Yet to the degree that we can make sense of that beginning as an event in our lives or the life of our soul, it is our rational soul alone that we must take to be ourselves. That is why, as "an immortal thing," we should be seriously concerned with what happens to us throughout "the whole of time" rather than in the relatively short period "from childhood to old age" (*R.* 10, 608c6–d11; also 6, 498d1–7).

In the *Republic*, Socrates identifies rational soul with the human element in the snake-lion-human complex that is a terrestrial human being. In the *Phaedrus*, he is apparently more circumspect:

> I am not yet capable, in accordance with the Delphic inscription, of "knowing myself."...So I inquire...into myself, to see whether I am actually a beast

more complex and appetite-consumed (*epitethumenon*) than Typhon,[20] or both a tamer and a simpler creature, sharing some divine and un-Typhonic portion by nature. (229e5–230a6)

The question he raises is one we would think better posed by leaving human beings out of the picture. For while we might concede that rationality is something that human beings have a portion of by nature, and might even concede that there is something divine about it, we would surely hesitate to concede that that is all there really is to being human. Appetite and spirit—to stick to things already in play—seem equally important.

"Person," of course, is something of a term of art, but if we agree that a person is "an intelligent being, that has reason and reflection, and can consider itself as itself, the same thinking thing in different times and places,"[21] then there is much to be said for thinking that only rational soul—only the soul's rational part—is a person. For as portrayed, in any case, rational soul must in some way remember what happens to it in its many different incarnations, whether in animal or human bodies, and especially in those glimpses it catches of the forms when it is, as it were, as out of body as it is possible for it to be:

> For a soul that has never seen the truth will not take human shape. For a human being must comprehend what is said in accord with a form, arising from many perceptions and being collected together into one through calculation; and this is a recollection of those things that our [rational] soul once saw when it travelled in company with a god and treated with contempt the things we now say are, and rose up into what really *is*. (*Phdr.* 249b5–c4)

The answer to Socrates' question, then, is that he is a person, a rational soul. This person is by nature simple or incomposite, but by Demiurgic fiat it is part of the sort of appetite-spirit-reason complex that is a human soul and is so moreover, even when the terrestrial body it inhabits is that of another species of animal.

In some of the dialogues in which we meet the apparently unreformed Socrates, we encounter a resolutely intellectualist psychology, according to which virtue is wisdom or craft knowledge of virtue and incontinence

---

20. Typhon (or Typhoeus) was a dragon with a hundred snake-heads, whose voice was at times like that of a lion. He was the last obstacle between Zeus and the kingship of the gods (Hesiod, *Th.* 820–868). The adjective *atuphou* ("un-Typhonic") may mean "lacking in pride."

21. John Locke, *An Essay Concerning Human Understanding* (Oxford: Clarendon Press, 1979), p. 335.

impossible. It is often claimed that in the *Republic* and the other dialogues we have just been looking at, this psychology is abandoned in favor of a nonintellectualist one in which virtue involves conative as well as cognitive conditions, and in which weakness of will is possible. Though this claim is surely true, we might equally well say that Socratic psychology is the psychology of rational soul and that nothing said about complex tripartite soul presupposes that—considered as such—there is anything wrong with it.

CHAPTER 6

✧

From Beauty to Goodness

Beauty (*to kalon*)[1] possesses a feature that serves at once to distinguish it from goodness and to group it together with certain other Platonic forms:

> Isn't it also clear that many people would choose things that are reputed to be just or beautiful, even if they are not, and to act, acquire things, and form beliefs accordingly? Yet no one is satisfied to acquire things that are reputed to be good. On the contrary, everyone seeks the things that *are* good. In this area, everyone disdains mere reputation. . . . That, then, is what every soul pursues, and for its sake does everything. (*R*. 6, 505d5–e2)

People know that they want what is genuinely good, not what is merely believed or reputed to be good. Yet they cannot readily distinguish the advantages of being beautiful from those of seeming beautiful, those of being just from those of having a just reputation. (That, indeed, is the nub of the challenge Glaucon and Adeimantus pose in *Republic* 2, when they ask how being just can produce greater eudaimonistic benefits—greater happiness—than having a reputation for justice while being unjust.) Beauty and justice are thus *ambivalent* in a way that goodness—and it alone, it seems—is not.

In Diotima's elenchus-like examination of Socrates in the *Symposium*, a moment arrives at which he cannot say what the person who possesses beautiful things gets by possessing them but can say what the person who possesses good things will get: "That, I said, I'm better placed to answer: he'll be happy. Yes, she said, because those who are happy are happy

---

1. What is *kalon* is what is beautiful or sexually attractive ("hot" as we might say), as opposed to ugly, but also what is fine or noble, as opposed to shameful.

through possessing good things, and one no longer needs to go on to ask, And what reason does the person who wishes to be happy have for wishing it? Your answer seems final. True, I said" (204d4–205a3). It is because beauty is ambivalent while goodness isn't that Socrates is in this better position. Good things bring us happiness, but do beautiful ones? Maybe it's the apparently beautiful ones that do that.

The specification of a desire is incomplete when all we know is its object *x*. We also need to know what it motivates us to do to *x*. We desire not food but to eat food, not a book but to read a book. Though they don't single out this feature of desire for explicit mention, Socrates and Diotima are sensitive to it. What we desire, they agree, is *to possess* good things. The question immediately arises of why that is what we desire to do to them. Once we are reminded that possessing them will allow us to use them to make ourselves happy, we have much of what we need—a final explanation that puts a stop to why-questions.

Conceptual relationships—especially when they are obvious to those with even a minimal grasp of the concepts involved—make for easy agreement; but that agreement can also conceal deep disagreement: "Almost everyone is agreed about what to call [the topmost of all achievable goods]: both ordinary people and people of quality say happiness, and suppose that living well and doing well are the same thing as being happy. But they are in dispute about what happiness *is*" (Aristotle, *NE* 1.4, 1095a17–21). Socrates makes essentially the same point. "Whatever name a city applies to the good, that surely is what it aims at when it legislates" (*Tht.* 177e4–6). That the good is what is aimed at is a simple conceptual truth. That *this* (for instance, what is advantageous to the stronger) is the good is not a conceptual truth and may not even be a truth of any kind. In fact, as Socrates tells Adeimantus, our grip on the good is notably insecure: "The soul has a hunch that the good is something, but is puzzled and cannot adequately grasp just what it is or acquire the sort of stable belief about it that it has about the other things (*ta alla*), and so it misses the benefit, if any, that even those other things may give" (*R.* 6, 505e1–5).

The source and nature of the soul's puzzlement is revealed by a point made elsewhere about stable beliefs:

> True beliefs are a very fine thing as long as they stay in their place … so that they are not worth very much, until someone ties them down by rationally calculating the explanation. This, my friend Meno, is recollection, as we have agreed in what we said before. When they are tied down, they first of all become pieces of knowledge, and then stable. (*Men.* 97e5–98a7; compare *Smp.* 202a5–9)

Our grasp of the substantive good is unstable, we may infer, because of the difficulty involved in giving an explanatory account of it or calculating its explanation. That is what Socrates has just been saying to Adeimantus. The masses believe that pleasure is the good, he says, but admit that there are bad pleasures. The more refined believe the good is wisdom or knowledge but identify the wisdom in question as knowledge of the good. With one explanation ending in contradiction, the other in circularity, puzzlement reigns and security eludes us (*R.* 6, 505b5–d3). Thus goodness has a characteristic feature of its own: it is *elusive.* Moreover, we know why it has this feature. It is a first principle—indeed *the* ultimate first principle of everything (7, 532a5–533d1). Hence the question of its explanation— which is an intensified version of a puzzle infecting all first principles—is bound to be particularly vexed.

The things contrasted with the good, as ones we do have secure beliefs about, are referred to as *ta alla*—"the other things" (6, 505e4). The immediate reference is to justice and beauty, which were under discussion a few lines before. Socrates seems to imply that we do have secure beliefs about these. Yet secure beliefs—beliefs tied down—are items of knowledge, and he is explicit that we cannot have knowledge about justice or beauty until we first have it about the good itself: "I imagine that just and beautiful things won't have acquired much of a guardian in someone who does not even know why they are good. And I have a hunch that no one will have adequate knowledge of them until he knows this" (6, 505a4–7; also 7, 534b8–c6). Hence his original thought must be something closer to this: There is no problem about *how* to tie down our beliefs about beauty, justice, and other such subordinate good things. All we have to do is relate them appropriately to the good. There is such a problem about how to do the same for the elusive good itself.

Though beauty shares with other Platonic forms the feature of being ambivalent, it has a special place among them and among the images of them in the world around us that our senses reveal:

> In the earthly likenesses of justice and moderation and other things that are valuable to souls, there is no light, but through dulled organs just a few approach their images and with difficulty observe the nature of what is imaged in them. Beauty, however, could be seen blazing out at that time when our souls, along with a happy company, saw a blessed sight before them.... And now that we have come to earth we have, through the clearest of our senses, found it gleaming most clearly. For of all the sense perceptions coming to us through the body, sight is the sharpest. We do not see wisdom. The feelings of love it would cause in us would be terrible, if it allowed some clear image

of it itself to reach our sight, and so too with the other lovable things. As it is, though, beauty alone has acquired this privilege, of being most clearly visible and most lovable. (*Phdr.* 250b1–e1)

The class of things valuable to souls, which includes the forms of justice, moderation, wisdom, and beauty, is the same as the class of lovable or desirable things generally. The "earthly likenesses" of some of these—justice and moderation—contain no light, and so the organs that perceive them are dulled.[2] At first, wisdom seems to differ from these in having no earthly likenesses, so that our eyes are literally blind to it ("we do not see wisdom"). But the next sentence suggests that its problem is no different from that of the others: it lacks the inner light that would allow "some *clear* image of it itself to reach our sight." It is this that beauty alone has the privilege of allowing. Since the form of beauty has this feature at least in part, it seems, because it itself can be seen blazing out in a way that other forms do not, we may say that beauty's preeminent visibility is due to its *incandescence.*

Love as Begetting in Beauty

That the class of things valuable to souls is being treated as identical to that of lovable or desirable ones generally is established by the fact that Diotima relies on their identity to solve a problem. If—as Socrates has agreed—the wish or love of good things is common to all human beings, why don't we say that everyone is in love, but rather "that some people are in love, others not" (*Smp.* 205a5–b2)? The answer she proposes is that just as poetry has usurped the name *poiēsis*, which applies to the "productive activities that belong to all the different kinds of crafts" (205b8–c9), so a part of love has usurped a name that properly belongs to the whole:

> The whole of desire for good things and for happiness is "the supreme and treacherous love" that is found in everyone; but those who direct themselves to it in all sorts of other ways, in making money, or in their love of physical training, or in philosophy, are neither said to be "in love" nor to be "lovers,"

2. R. Hackforth, *Plato's Phaedrus* (Cambridge: Cambridge University Press, 1952), p. 94, claims that the dulled organs are "the inadequate reasoning powers of man." But the fact that they are dulled by the absence of light implies that they are the eyes, which are "dimmed and seem nearly blind" when "the light of day" gives way to the dimmer "lights of night," namely, the stars (*R.* 6, 508c4–7). Notice the generalizing claim made at *Phdr.* 250d5–6: "if it [wisdom] allowed some clear image of itself to reach *our sight,* and so too with *the other lovable objects.*"

while those who proceed by giving themselves to just one kind of love have the name of the whole, "love"—and they're the ones who are "in love" and "lovers." (205d1–7)

Properly or nonfiguratively speaking, love is the desire for *all the good things in the possession of which happiness consists*. So they are the ones valuable to a soul. Narrow interpersonal erotic love may be the sort that is said to makes us *lovers*, or that we are said to be *in*, but it is the broader sort that is the true natural kind.

It is with love of this broader sort that Diotima's account is intended to deal:

> There is nothing else that people are in love with except what is good. Or do you think there is? By Zeus, I certainly don't, I replied. Is it true then to say, without qualification, that people love what is good? Yes, I said. But, she said, oughtn't we to add that what they love includes their *possessing* what is good? We ought. And then, she said, not only possessing it, but *always* possessing it? We must add that too. In that case, she said, we can sum up by saying that love is of permanent possession of what is good. What you say is very true. Given, then, that love is always of this, she said, in what way and through what activity would eagerness and effort in those pursuing it be called love? What really is this work (*ergon*)? Can you say? If I could, Diotima, I said, I certainly wouldn't be admiring you for your wisdom, and visiting you to learn just these very things. In that case, she said, I'll tell you. It is begetting in beauty (*tokos en kalō(i)*), in respect both to body and to soul. (205e6–206b8)

The object of love is the permanent possession of good things. But what is it that would constitute such possession? What does love motivate us to do? The answer specifies what Diotima calls the *ergon* of love—its work, function, or job in the soul (*R.* 1, 352e3–4, 353a10–11). That work, she claims, is to (motivate us to) beget in beauty either through our bodies or though our souls. *It* is what the permanent possession of good things consists in. That is why she feels entitled to infer that love is "not ... of beauty," but "of procreation and begetting in beauty" (206e3–5).

That love is for the permanent possession of good things, we may accept. Nonetheless, that the permanent possession of good things should consist in begetting specifically in beauty is difficult to understand. The difficulty is deepened by a passage in the *Republic* discussing the love of learning:

> A real lover of learning strives by nature for what *is*.... He does not linger over each of the many things that are reputed to be, but keeps on going, without

dulling his love or desisting from it, until he grasps what is the nature of each thing itself with the part of his soul that is fitted to grasp a thing of that sort because of its kinship with it. Once he is drawn near to it, has intercourse with what *is* really, and has begotten understanding and truth, he knows, truly lives, is nourished, and—at that point, but not before—is relieved from his labor pains. (6, 490a9–b7)

Knowledge is achieved when the form of the good—"the most important object of learning"—is finally grasped (6, 505a2). So the love of it, too, consists in a begetting that should, if the *Symposium* is right, be a begetting in beauty. But why should the love of learning consist in that? Why doesn't it consist in giving birth in goodness? One important feature of what we uncovered earlier is that it seems designed to answer this question. Some good things—namely, beautiful ones—are incandescent; we can just see that they are good or valuable. So they can provide a reliable starting point in valuing—a path to the elusive good itself.

For beautiful things to motivate us to do anything to get them, once we do see their goodness, however, their incandescence is not enough. We must also lack them (*Smp.* 200a9–b2). Since desires are painful states of emptiness or inanition either of the body or of the soul, the appropriate filling up of which is pleasure (*R.* 9, 585a8–b4, 585d11), the question naturally arises of what the painful lack is that makes us love or desire beauty. In the next part of her account, Diotima provides a complex answer:

All human beings (*anthrōpoi*), Socrates, are pregnant both in respect to body and to soul, and when we reach the right age, we naturally desire to beget. We cannot do it in ugliness, but in beauty we can. [1] The intercourse of man and woman is in fact a begetting. And this affair is something divine: living creatures, despite their mortality, contain this immortal thing, pregnancy and procreation. But it is impossible for this to take place in what is discordant. Ugliness, however, is in discord with everything divine, while beauty is concordant. Thus beauty is both Moira and Eileithyia[3] for birth. [2] For these reasons, if ever what is pregnant approaches beauty, it becomes gracious, melts with joy, and begets and procreates; but when it approaches ugliness, it contracts, frowning with pain, turns away, curls up, and fails to procreate, retaining what it has conceived, and suffering because of it. That is why what is pregnant and already full to bursting feels the great excitement it does about beauty, because it frees it from great pain. For Socrates, she said, love is not, as you think, of beauty, ... [but] of procreating and begetting in beauty. (206c1–e5)

---

3. Moira is Fate and Eileithyia the goddess of childbirth.

Initially, Diotima seems to be attributing both sorts of pregnancy she recognizes to everyone. But in developing her views, she attributes pregnancy in soul exclusively to males. What she probably means by *anthrōpoi*, therefore, is not human beings generally but human *males—anthrōpoi* can mean either. That is why her description of pregnancy and its effects sounds so much like a description of male sexual response.

A human male, painfully pregnant with embryophoric semen, seeks a female in whom to discharge it. Why must he seek a beautiful one for this purpose? Why won't an ugly one do? Diotima's explanation seems to have two quite different strands. (1) is a metaphysical or metabiological theory specifying the condition in the world—harmony between beauty and the divine—that enables begetting to take place. When Diotima extends her account to all animals (207c9–d2), it becomes reasonably certain that what she has in mind is the reproductive cycle. As regulated by the seasons, this is controlled ultimately by the sun, which "not only gives visible things the power to be seen but also provides for their coming-into-being, growth, and nourishment" (*R.* 6, 509b1–3; also 8, 546a3–c8). A female must be ovulating, as we would put it, or a male pregnant, as Diotima would, if conception is to be possible. When a pregnant male responds with desire to a beautiful female, however, what he is responding to directly cannot be this underlying harmony, since it is inaccessible to him. This is where (2) comes in. It is a psychological or epistemological theory specifying the condition in a female—clearly visible, because incandescent, beauty—that draws a pregnant male to her. In our own evolutionary theory of animal reproduction, a bridge between these two sorts of theory is provided by the reliable correlation of (visible) symmetry of face and body with (invisible) reproductive fitness. In Diotima's theory, such a bridge seems unnecessary.

This is how her story might go. At the appropriate age, as regulated by the sun and the seasons, a male becomes pregnant with semen. The resulting discomfort makes him desire a female in whom to discharge it. If the female is ugly, he won't love or desire her: love is of good things and he can just see that she is not something (in the relevant way) good. Failing to desire her, he also fails to get an erection: "it [what is pregnant with semen] contracts, frowning with pain, turns away, curls up, and fails to procreate." A somewhat more inflammatory translation might be: "it goes limp, wrinkles up as if in pain, pulls back, and shrivels." Without an erection, the male can't ejaculate, and so "retaining what it has conceived, and suffering because of it," fails to beget or procreate. When a pregnant male finds a beautiful woman, on the other hand, he desires her as something incandescently good, so that what is pregnant, as Diotima puts it, "rises up in exultation and melts with joy." In other words, ejaculation and begetting occur.

Love, Immortality, and Persistence through Becoming

It might seem that with the account of love as being of the permanent possession of good things, and so of begetting in beauty, we have reached explanatory bedrock, since happiness, which stops all "why" questions, simply consists in such possession. Diotima argues that we must go yet further:

> What do you think, Socrates, is the cause of this love, and this desire? Don't you see how terribly all animals are affected whenever they feel the desire to procreate, whether they go on foot or have wings—all of them stricken with the effects of love, first for intercourse with one another, and then also for nurturing their offspring, so that the weakest are prepared to do battle with the strongest on their offspring's behalf and even to die for them, torturing themselves with hunger so as to rear them, and doing everything else necessary. Human beings, she said, one might suppose, do this as a result of rational calculation; but what cause makes animals be so powerfully affected by love? (207a5–c1)

Though she doesn't explicitly mention it, we see the problem that lies behind her question. Love motivates animals—including human ones—to do things that seem positively inconsistent with their own happiness and wellbeing: the *Republic* refers to "the frustrations and sufferings involved in bringing up children" (5, 465c3). But how can love do that if it is related to happiness in the way Diotima claims?

In our theory of reproduction, this problem is addressed, at least in the case of other animals, by appeal to genes and their so-called interests: they motivate us to do what will get copies of themselves into the next generation, even if we must sacrifice our own interests in the process. In Diotima's theory it is answered by a surprisingly innovative appeal to the desire that, in her account, is most basic of all—that for the permanent possession of good things:

> Love is…of procreation and begetting in beauty….Why, then, is it of procreation? Because procreation is something everlasting and immortal, as far as anything can be for what is mortal; and it is immortality, together with what is good, that must necessarily be desired, according to what has been

agreed before—if indeed love is of permanent possession of what is good. (206e2–207a2)

This is her ground for claiming that begetting is "something divine" (206c6), in that it partakes to a degree in the immortality (206c7) that is the mark of divinity. But it isn't just human begetting that partakes in it: "The same account applies to animals as to human beings" (207c9–d1). So animals, too, love or desire—at least in the sense of having a conatus toward—permanent possession of good things.

Thus far we are squarely in the realm of what is recognizably sexual reproduction, in which two members of a species unite to produce off-spring they then rear. Had Diotima known about the phenomenon of asexual reproduction, which requires only one progenitor, she could have stayed in that realm to produce an intermediate case. Instead, she is forced to leave it altogether—or, better, to expand it out of all recognition:

> Mortal nature seeks so far as it can to exist forever and to be immortal. And it can achieve it only in this way, through the process of coming-into-being, so that it always leaves behind something else that is new in place of the old, since even during the time in which each living creature is said to be alive and to be the same individual—as for example someone is said to be the same person from when he is a child until he comes to be an old man, and yet, if he's called the same, that is despite the fact that he's never made up of the same things, but is always being renewed and losing what he had before, whether it's hair, or flesh, or bones, or blood, in fact the whole body. And don't suppose that this is just true in the case of the body; in the case of the soul, too, its traits, habits, opinions, desires, pleasures, pains, fears—none of these is ever the same in any individual, but some are coming into existence, others passing away. (207d1–e5)

Moreover, this isn't the only sort of change to which our traits, habits, opinions, and so on are subject:

> It's much stranger even than this with the pieces of knowledge we have: not only are some of them coming into existence and others passing away, so that we are never the same even in respect to pieces of knowledge, but in fact each single one of the pieces of knowledge is subject to the same process. For what we call going over things exists because knowledge goes out of us; forgetting is the departure of knowledge, and going over something creates in us again a new memory in place of the one that is leaving us, and so preserves our knowledge in such a way as to make it seem the same. (207e6–208a6)

Thus even an apparently persistent particular piece of knowledge is actually a series of different particular pieces of the same sort. Moreover, there is nothing peculiar to knowledge in this:

> In this way *everything mortal* is preserved, not by always being absolutely the same, as the divine is, but by virtue of the fact that what is departing and decaying with age leaves behind in us something else new, of the same sort that it was. It is by this means, Socrates, she said, that the mortal partakes of immortality, both body and everything else; and what is immortal partakes of it in a different way. (208a6–b4)

The account of animal reproduction has now been absorbed into a vastly more general theory, which we might call *persistence-through-becoming*. It is by appeal to it that Diotima draws her conclusion: "So don't be surprised that everything by nature values what springs from itself; this eagerness, this love, that attends on every creature is for the sake of immortality" (208b4–6).

Suppose that at time t_1 Agathon possesses a particular piece of knowledge k_1 of sort Kappa. If k_1 is beautiful, Agathon can just see it to be good. So he will want to possess it at t_2 as well. To do so he must—perhaps by means of going over it—beget another particular piece k_2 that is also of sort Kappa. What goes for k_1 goes for Agathon as well. If he is to survive from t_1 to t_2, a t_1 time-slice of the sort of being (namely, a human) he is must beget a t_2 time-slice of a being of the same sort. So self-love turns out to be itself a sort of begetting in beauty. (No real surprise there. Just look at the definition of love.) But if Agathon's self-love really is just love for (unconventional) offspring, for offspring of the same sort as Agathon himself, then Agathon's love for his (conventional) offspring is much more like his love for himself than we thought, and the value he places on their survival is much more like the value he places on his own. Diotima's conclusion is now imaginatively, at least, within reach.

In her own elaborating of her theory, however, Diotima takes a puzzlingly different approach to the one we have just sketched:

> If you look at human beings and their love of honor, you'd also be surprised at their irrationality in relation to what I've talked about, unless you keep in mind how terribly they are affected by love of acquiring a name for themselves, and of "laying up immortal glory for all time to come," and how for the sake of that they're ready to run all risks, even more than they are for their children—they'll spend money, undergo any suffering you like, die for it. Do you think, she said, that Alcestis would have died for Admetus, that Achilles would have added his death to Patroclus's, or that your Codrus would have died before his time for

the sake of his children's succession to the kingship, unless they thought at the time that there would be an immortal memory of their own courage, the one we now have of them? Far from it, she said; I imagine it's for the sake of immortal virtue and this sort of glorious reputation that everyone does everything, the more so the better people they are, because they are in love with immortality. Those, then, she said, who are pregnant in their bodies turn their attention more towards women, and their love is directed in this way, securing immortality, a memory of themselves, and happiness, as they suppose, for themselves for all time to come through having children. (208c2–209a1)

What is puzzling is that this elaboration seems to make no use of persistence-through-becoming at all. Perhaps that is why Socrates introduces it with a nicely ambiguous editorial comment. Diotima produced it, he says, in the manner of "an accomplished Sophist" (208c1). What he has in mind is not so much that her response is sophistical, but that it is clever. Instead of using persistence-through-becoming explicitly, it embodies a set of puzzles that the theory helps resolve. In that respect, it is like Socrates' own clever conversations, which Diotima is clearly imitating.

Human beings who love honor, Diotima claims, beget conventional offspring because they want to possess good things permanently. But how could being posthumously remembered for possessing such things count as success in that endeavor? That's the first puzzle. The second is that Diotima's argument applies only to those particularly good human beings who love immortal virtue and honor. What explains the behavior of the less good ones who, like other animals, also beget offspring and sacrifice for them? Nonoffspring can preserve one's memory, as we preserve that of Alcestis and Achilles. Offspring who do not share one's values will hardly continue to honor an ancestor they no longer think worth remembering. How, then, can begetting offspring be either necessary or sufficient for being remembered?

Now let's factor persistence-through-becoming into Diotima's argument. Great courage of the sort Achilles possessed is something *kalon*—something beautiful in the sense of fine or noble. The battlefield (the field of honor) is the canonical location for its exhibition. There it shines forth incandescently. Anyone present who values it will preserve a memory of it. As something produced by Achilles, such a memory (together with the causal trace that sustains it) is one of his (unconventional) offspring. As he lives on in what we ordinarily call his life, by begetting similar offspring, so he lives on in the memory of the (conventional) offspring in whom the memory exists, possessed of courage still. But just as his (conventional) offspring are forward continuers of him, he is a backward continuer of them, so that the good things he possessed, they possess, too. Hence they have a special reason, provided by their desire for their own happiness, to keep the memory of their ancestor's courage alive. Putting it the other way around, he has reason of the same sort to produce them. By comparison with the way a god possesses good things, Achilles' way of permanently possessing them is but a pale imitation. Diotima is quite open about that. Her point is that before what we conventionally call death it is no less so.

The mention of honor, and those who love it, is bound to remind us of the *Republic*'s triadic division of human beings into wisdom-loving or philosophical, honor-loving, and appetitive (or money-loving). Though this division is not explicitly mentioned in the *Symposium*, it seems foreshadowed or presupposed in Diotima's triadic division of begetters in beauty into those pregnant in soul, who love wisdom, those pregnant in body (and also in soul), who love honor, and those pregnant in body, who love something else. The last are the subject of the second of the problems we raised for the part of the account currently under review. Suppose, as the *Republic* would lead us to think, that a person of this sort is an appetitive person. He loves food, drink, and sex, and thinks that happiness consists in their permanent possession. To want to possess them permanently—if persistence-through-becoming is true—is to want a continuer of himself to possess them. At this point, the third puzzle already encountered in the case of honor-lovers, resurfaces. For what, as an appetitive person, he wants a continuer of himself to do is continue himself *as such a person*. But for success in that project it isn't enough to beget (conventional) offspring; he must also ensure somehow that they share his values.

This problem about the sharing of values between ancestors and descendants dramatizes an aspect of begetting in beauty that is easily overlooked: it requires the successful transmission of values—that is, of a tradition of valuing—both intrapersonally and across generations. If Diotima has omitted any explicit reference to this fact so far, it isn't because she is unaware of it. In her long account of that other sort of begetting—the one engaged in by those who are predominantly pregnant in their souls—it will be a prominent exhibit.

Two Types of Blindness to Beauty

A connection between the account of bodily pregnancy we have been exploring and pregnancy in soul is provided by Socrates' account in the *Phaedrus* of how to reconcile beauty's incandescence with its ambivalence. The account begins with a description of the reactions of two different sorts of men to beauty's earthly likenesses:

> Beauty alone has acquired this privilege, of being most clearly visible and most
> lovable. All the same, the man [the nonphilosopher] whose initiation [into the
> most blessed of mysteries that culminate in seeing the forms (250b8–c1)] was
> not recent or who has been corrupted does not move sharply (*oxeōs*) from here
> to there, to beauty itself when he observes its namesake here, hence he does not
> revere it when he looks at it, but surrendering himself to pleasure does his best
> to mount like an animal and sow offspring, and keeping close company with
> excess has no fear or shame in pursuing pleasure contrary to nature. Whereas
> the man [the philosopher] who observed much of what was visible to him before
> [the forms], on seeing a godlike face or some bodily shape that imitates beauty
> well, first shudders and experiences something of the fears he had before, and
> then reveres it as a god as he looks at it, and if he were not afraid of appearing
> thoroughly mad would sacrifice to his beloved as if to a statue (*agalma*) of a god.
> (250d6–251a7)

The nonphilosopher doesn't move sharply from earthly beauty to beauty
itself, because his initiation was not recent or because he has been corrupted. A little later the intent of the first condition is clarified: "each man
lives after the pattern of the god in whose chorus he was, honoring him
by imitating him as far as he can, so long as he is uncorrupted and living
out the first of the lives which he enters here" (252d1–3). Thus one of the
causes of the nonphilosopher's problem is the passing of time as measured
not by years but by number of reincarnations. The second cause—corrup-
tion—is more difficult.

We learn in the *Republic* that the "badness natural to each thing—the
deficiency peculiar to each—is what destroys it, but if that does not destroy
it, there is nothing else left to corrupt it" (10, 609a8–b1). Thus ophthal-
mia, which is naturally bad for the eyes, corrupts them (10, 608e7–609a1).
Here we are talking about literal eye disease. But that can't be the nonphilosopher's problem, since he sees the incandescent beauty of a potential
sex partner all too clearly. When the philosopher descends from the bright
sunlight into the cave, he also has eye problems:

> If he had to compete once again with the perpetual prisoners in recognizing
> the shadows, while his sight was still dim and before his eyes had recovered,
> and if the time for readjustment was not short, wouldn't he provoke ridicule?
> Wouldn't it be said of him that he had returned from his upward journey with
> his eyes corrupted? (7, 516e7–517a4)

The philosopher's difficulty lies in finding the likeness or shadow that
matches the form of beauty he firmly grasps. The easy transference of

the epithet "sharp" (*oxus*) from sight—"of all the sensations coming to us through the body, sight is the sharpest" (*Phdr.* 250d3)—to a mental movement (250e2) instigated by seeing a beautiful person suggests that the nonphilosopher's problem is the reverse, namely, that of finding the form that matches the likeness he sees quite clearly. Because he doesn't have a vivid recollection of beauty itself, the beauty he sees (however sharply) fails to remind him of it sharply enough and so he fails to involve the right feature in his perception. Hence he stops with the earthly likeness, remaining focused on it, when he should move up to its intelligible or heavenly original.

The defect in the nonphilosopher's vision is diagnosed this way:

> Haven't you ever noticed in people who are said to be bad, but clever, how sharp the vision of their little soul is and how sharply it distinguishes the things it is turned towards? This shows that its sight is not inferior, but is forced to serve vice, so that the sharper it sees, the more evils it accomplishes. However, if this element of this sort of nature had been hammered at right from childhood, and struck free of the leaden weights, as it were, of kinship with becoming, which have been fastened to it by eating and other such pleasures and indulgences, which pull its soul's vision downward—if, I say, it got rid of these and turned towards truly real things, then the same element of the same people would see them most sharply, just as it now does the things it is now turned towards. (*R.* 7, 519a1–b5)

The reason the nonphilosopher is *upwardly blind* is that his appetitive desires—which include his sexual ones—pull his soul's vision downward. The philosopher, by contrast, is *downwardly blind*, because his rational desires, his self-defining love for the truth, has pulled his soul's vision up toward the forms (7, 519a7–521b10). The blindness of the nonphilosopher and that of the philosopher thus have cognate causes—causes that are not ophthalmic but appetitive.

The characterization of the nonphilosopher's eye problems or the behavior they cause as *para phusin* or "contrary to nature" (*Phdr.* 251a1) suggests that the desires that lead to them are paiderastic:

> [Whether among human beings or beasts] when what is by nature female enters into partnership with what are by nature males in procreation, you must bear in mind that the pleasure involved seems in accord with nature, but when males do so with males, or females with females, it seems contrary to nature, and the recklessness of those who first engaged in it seems to have been caused by a lack of self-control where pleasure is concerned. (*Lg.* 1, 636c2–7)

Yet the fact that they cause the nonphilosopher to "sow offspring (*paidosporein*)" (*Phdr.* 250e5) suggests that his desires are heterosexual appetites. Of course, the offspring he tries to sow might simply be his (embryophoric) semen, and this he could try to sow as readily in a male as in a female: *Laws* 8 speaks of "sowing (*speirein*) . . . sterile seed in males contrary to nature" (841d4–5). But the rare verb *paidosporein*, which occurs nowhere else in Plato, does seem a peculiarly inept choice to describe such an act, since *paido-* inevitably brings actual children (*paides*), not seed or embryos to mind. One might well think, indeed, that it was selected, perhaps even coined, precisely to rule out the exclusively paiderastic interpretation of what the nonphilosopher attempts.

When Plato says that something is contrary to (or in accord with) nature, the nature in question is always the nature of something. Consequently, it is always appropriate to ask which nature is the relevant one. Usually this is answered by specifying the type of thing the nature belongs to, but in the case of human beings we need more than that, since we might be referring either to the complex human being or to the simpler inner one, which is identical to the soul's rational part (*R.* 9, 588c7–e2). When we speak of a human being's nature, in other words, we may be speaking either of his true nature or his embodied nature. The latter includes appetitive desires; the former doesn't (10, 611b1–612a6).

In the *Laws* passage we looked at, the human nature under discussion must be embodied nature, for heterosexual intercourse cannot be in accord with the nature of something unless it includes appetitive desires. In the *Phaedrus*, the philosopher and the nonphilosopher are introduced following a description of the human soul's reincarnations—reincarnations in which it may pass "into the life of a wild animal" (249b3–4). Thus the nature that the nonphilosopher acts contrary to in doing his best to sow offspring must be his true human nature. Hence he will be acting contrary to it even if the intercourse he attempts is heterosexual. The nonphilosopher is thus an exemplar of the class of men Diotima characterizes as pregnant in body, so the explanation of his behavior applies to them. Such men see sharply the beauty of bodies, but their sexual appetites, which cause upward blindness, prevent them from moving on from there to any other beauty.

Begetting in Beauty

The beauty that attracts a male pregnant in body is that of a female. This suggests that the dative construction in the definition of love as *tokos en kalō(i)* is to be understood as locative. Begetting in beauty is begetting inside a beautiful female—inside a beautiful vessel or container. But once we see that the role of her beauty involves exciting or producing an erection, this interpretation is more difficult to sustain. It is just an accident, if you like, from the point of view of her beauty, that ejaculation takes place inside her. When we extend the formula to the begetting of unconventional offspring, the difficulties multiply. Consider Achilles. What excites him, as an honor-lover, is the beauty of his own acts of courage—good things he would like to possess permanently. The human containers in which he deposits the memories of these actions are his conventional offspring. The trouble is that *their* beauty seems to play no role at all in the account.

In the context of persistence-through-becoming, beautiful acts of courage get analyzed as an ancestral-descendant causal chain of beautiful act tokens of the same courageous type. In such a chain, each ancestral token plays two roles. First, it incites Achilles' love or desire and so causes him to beget a descendant token. Second, it provides a blueprint—a paradigm—for that descendant. It is by looking to it and copying what he sees that he must do his begetting if the beauty of the ancestor is to be inherited by the descendant offspring. Reflecting on the place of beauty in this story suggests that the dative construction *en kalō(i)* actually is one of manner or conformity.[4] To beget in beauty is to beget in conformity to beauty—that is, in conformity to a token of beauty that serves for the male progenitor as a paradigm for his offspring. (We might think of all those interlocutors who respond to Socrates' characteristic question—what *is* F?—by giving examples.)

What makes a token serve that role is not just its beauty but the type of love characteristic of the male progenitor. If, like Achilles, he is an honor-lover, for whom happiness consists primarily in virtuous, honor-attracting states of character and actions, it is tokens of these that will arouse his desire to beget. But he cannot succeed in begetting unconventional offspring of this sort in the long run unless he also begets conventional ones who preserve them in memory. And even that isn't enough. To ensure that they will preserve his memory, he must also transmit his values to them. He must ensure that they will be beautiful—and beautiful in the way that he himself is beautiful. We have only to look at the eugenics program of the *Republic* to imagine how the consequent love he will have for them might manifest itself.

Turning back to someone who, though pregnant in body, is not an honor-lover but an appetitive man, we can see that a similar account

4. See Smyth, *Greek Grammar*, p. 377, 1687 c.

applies to him. What attracts him is the beauty of his own appetitive unconventional offspring. It is in conformity with this beauty that he wants to beget. The (bodily) beauty of a female is essential to this enterprise because it is the sort that he both recognizes and is attracted to—it is the sort that can excite his body to respond appropriately. In a sense, therefore, her beauty is of the sort that he wants to beget in. That such begetting occurs inside her body is irrelevant.

As a woman must be beautiful to produce an erection and subsequent ejaculation in a male pregnant in body, so a boy must be beautiful in body and soul to produce their equivalents in a male pregnant in soul (209a1–c2). For such a male, the equivalent of getting an erection is being "immediately resourceful (*euthus euporei*)," while the equivalent of ejaculating is "producing accounts concerned with virtue" (209b8). As embryophoric semen once deposited in the body of a suitable female begins to grow, so these accounts, once deposited in the soul of a suitable boy, begin to shape it toward virtue, since the purpose of telling them is to educate him in it (209c2; compare *Phdr.* 276c3–277a4). That is why accounts concerned with virtue can constitute "procreated virtue of all sorts" (209e2–3)— the very thing with which a man pregnant in soul is filled. Some of these accounts are poems, like those of Homer and Hesiod, which are used in ethical education; others are the sorts of laws and political constitutions that Lycurgus and Solon are "honored for having procreated" (209d7–9).[5] What is particularly important about them for our purposes, especially those of the legislative and constitutional variety, is that they transmit what their progenitor loves, values, and is pregnant with to the next generation in part by creating (or helping create) a political community that inculcates and transmits them.

The Correct Kind of Boy-Love

The aspects of "the art of love" Diotima has discussed to this point are advertised as ones into which Socrates himself could be initiated (209e5–210a1). He can understand appetitive love (the desire for food, drink, sex, and the like), the love of honor, and the love of virtue for the sake of honor. But will he be able to take the next step? Diotima is not sure: "As for those

---

5. "We ourselves are poets who have to the best of our ability created a tragedy that is the finest and the best; at any rate, our entire constitution is constructed as an imitation of the finest and best way of life—the very thing which we claim is the truest tragedy" (*Lg.* 7, 817b1–5).

aspects relating to the final revelation, the ones for the sake of which I have taught you the rest, if one approaches them correctly—I don't know whether you would be capable of initiation into *them*" (210a1–2). Her uncertainty parallels an accusation made by Adeimantus, and almost certainly stems from the same source:

> Amazing Socrates, of all of you who claim to praise justice, beginning from the earliest heroes of old whose accounts survive up to the men of the present day, not one has ever blamed injustice or praised justice except by mentioning the reputations, honors, and rewards that are their consequences. . . . No one, whether in poetry or *in private discussions*, has adequately argued that injustice is the greatest evil a soul can have in it, and justice the greatest good. (R. 2, 366d7–367a1)

As justice remains ambivalent even after the heroes of old (Achilles), the poets (Homer, Hesiod), and those who deal with it in private discussions (Socrates) have done their best to defend it, so beauty, too, remains that way, given what has so far been said. As a result, love, too, remains in shadow.

In the account that follows of "the correct kind of boy-loving" (211b6), the importance of correctness is emphasized (210a2, 4, 6, 8). Couched in the language of initiation into the cult of a mystery religion, it involves Initiate, a man who is still young (210a5), and—in the early stages, at least—the boy or boys who, one way or another, are the objects of his love. At first it also seems to involve the one who is leading Initiate (210a6). As the equivalent of the *mystagōgos*, who was already initiated into religious mysteries and so could lead others through them, he is a "teacher (*paidagōgos*) of the art of love" (210e2–3), and so must already know it, and (presumably) its goal. Were he essential to the story, the transmission rather than the acquisition of knowledge would apparently have to be its topic; but, in fact, he seems inessential: "This is what it is to approach the art of love," Diotima says, "*or* be led by someone else in it, in the correct way" (211b8–c1). It is nonetheless true that, just as her earlier story appeals to divine inspiration to explain the wisdom possessed by craftsmen, poets, and politicians, so this second part partakes not just in the language of mystery cults but in some of their mystery as well.

Pregnant in soul and body, though less so in the latter, desiring to possess permanently the good things in which happiness consists, and attracted by incandescent bodily beauty, Initiate must first "love a single body and there beget beautiful accounts" (210a7–8). Then, as the result of a cognitive process that is not described but is presumed to be correct or reliable, he must "realize for himself that the beauty that there is in any body whatever is the twin of that in any other, and that if one is to pursue beauty of outward form, it's entirely unreasonable not to regard the beauty in all bodies as one and the same" (210b3–4). Moreover, that cognitive change must be accompanied by a conative one: "having realized that, he must become a lover of all beautiful bodies, and slacken this intense love for one body, disdaining it (*kataphronēsanta*)[6] and considering it a small matter" (210b4–6). Nothing is said about how that conative change is to be brought about. The assumption is that Initiate's sexual desires are weak enough that they do not pose an obstacle—do not render him upwardly blind.

Though the process that results in cognitive change is left largely in the dark, something of its nature may be inferred from its results. The beautiful accounts Initiate produces, for example, are probably attempts to specify what *is* beauty that cite his beloved's body as a paradigm case. Once Initiate realizes—or is made to realize—that other bodies besides that of his beloved are also beautiful, he will need to beget a new account that captures this larger class. Doing so should have the effect of posing him a puzzle: "Why, given that love is for begetting in beauty, should I love only this body and not the larger class?" If his love is compliant, if it is not "entirely unreasonable" but susceptible to reason's intrinsic generality (or universalizability), he will love his beloved's beautiful body less obsessively, because he now also loves all other beautiful bodies, too.

Next, and again as the result of an undescribed but supposedly reliable cognitive process, Initiate must consider "beauty in souls more valuable than beauty in the body" (210b6–7). Again, this cognitive achievement must be coupled by conative change: "so that if someone who is decent in his soul has even a slight physical bloom, even then it's enough for him" (210b6–c2). Loving and caring for his beloved, he "begets and seeks the sorts of accounts that will make young men into better men" (210c2–3). He does this, we are told, so that he "may be compelled in turn to contemplate beauty as it exists in practices and laws, and to observe that all of this is mutually so that he should think beauty of body a small matter" (210c4–6).

---

6. See A. W. Price, *Plato and Aristotle on Love and Friendship* (Oxford: Clarendon Press, 1989), p. 44: "taking *no* interest in physical beauty (216d8) and thinking it of *no* account (e3) go with 'disdaining' it 'to an almost incredible degree' (d8–e1); an unintensified 'disdaining' (more literally, 'looking down upon') need amount to no more than…putting in its place."

As in the earlier stage, then, the undescribed process seems to be one of seeking an account of beauty that will apply to all beautiful bodies and to beautiful souls, practices, and laws as well. These are "mutually related," because beauty in souls—virtue—is a consequence of the sort of education mandated by beautiful laws and social practices. Compared to that beauty, the beauty of bodies no doubt *should* seem a relatively "small thing." On the other hand, the presupposition that laws and social practice will be available to Initiate and that he will have the cognitive resources necessary to study them is surely contentious. So much so, indeed, that we can readily appreciate the attraction of having a knowledgeable teacher lurk ambiguously in the narratival background. At the next stage, Diotima herself refers to him.

"After activities," Diotima says, "he [the teacher or guide] must lead him [Initiate] to the different kinds of knowledge, so that he may in turn see the beauty that belongs to kinds of knowledge" (210c7–8). In *Republic* 7, we are given a (partial) list of these, comprising arithmetic, plane and solid geometry, astronomy, and harmonics, where it is recognized that their existence cannot simply be assumed, since their development is a social or political undertaking that remains incomplete (528b5–c7). In what city or social community are we to imagine Initiate finding these kinds of knowledge—these crafts or sciences—ready to hand, or himself sufficiently educated in them to be able to access and appreciate their beauty? He would need not just a teacher, we see, but one equipped with the sort of supernatural powers to which someone already initiated into a mystery cult might lay claim. Indeed, he would need to share in such powers himself.

The mysterious cognitive process of coming to grasp the beauty belonging to kinds of knowledge has, like its predecessors, a conjoint conative purpose. The guide leads Initiate to it,

> so that...looking now towards a beauty that is vast, and no longer slavishly attached to the beauty belonging to a single thing—a young boy, some individual human being, or one kind of practice—he may cease to be worthless and small minded, as his servitude made him, but instead, turned toward the great sea of beauty and contemplating *that*, may beget many beautiful, even magnificent, accounts and thoughts in a love of wisdom (*philosophia[i]*) that grudges nothing. (210c8–d6)

In this fecund state of philosophical begetting Initiate remains "until having grown and been strengthened there, he may catch sight of a certain single kind of knowledge, which has as its object a beauty of a sort I shall describe to you" (210d6–7).

This beauty, which is "what itself *is* beauty (*ho esti kalon*)" (211d1), is the form of beauty of which, now properly trained in the art of love, Initiate will all of a sudden catch sight (210e4). When he has seen and come to know it, Diotima says, he will "*practically* have the final goal within his reach" (211b7–8). For although it is easy to forget while reading her rapturous description of beauty itself and the joys of contemplating it, beauty—however perfect—is never as such the end of the journey. Instead, as before, when Initiate reaches it, he has some begetting to do:

> Do you think it's a worthless life, she said, if a person turns his gaze in that direction and contemplates that beauty with that by which one must contemplate it [the rational element in the soul] and is able to have intercourse with it? Or are you not convinced, she said, that it is under these conditions alone, as he sees beauty with what has the power to see it, that he will succeed in begetting, not phantom images of virtue, because he is not grasping a phantom image, but true virtue, because he is grasping the truth; and that when he has begotten and nurtured true virtue, it belongs to him to be loved by the gods, and to him, if to any human being, to be immortal? (212a1–7)

At this point, Diotima stops, but in what sense has she come to the end? Has happiness, the permanent possession of good things, been achieved? We are left to solve the mystery for ourselves.

Part of the solution, though, has already been scripted. Initiate, we may suppose, is newly wise and virtuous at time t_1. What he will first have to beget is a t_2-time-slice of his wise and virtuous self: persistence-through-becoming assures us of that much. For such begetting to continue past his so-called death, he must also beget similar time-slices of a younger male, who will outlive him. Hence he must find a boy with a beautiful soul and enough of a physical bloom and educate him, so that he becomes of the same wise and virtuous sort as Initiate himself. Again, the foundations for this have been laid. The love he feels for what we call his own future possession of good things—his own happiness—will then bind him in the same way to the boy.

> He is in love, but with what he does not know; and he neither knows what has happened to him, nor can he even say what it is, but like a man who has caught an eye-disease from someone he can give no account of it, and is unaware that he is seeing himself in his lover as if in a mirror. (*Phdr.* 255d3–6)

Initiate's arrival at the end of his initiation is for that reason also a return to the beginning of his journey. Beautiful boys remain as important to his enterprise as his own later stages.[7]

Socrates' Art of Love and Its Limits

At the beginning of his initiation, Initiate is already pregnant in soul with wisdom and the rest of virtue. What Diotima purports to be describing, therefore, is a lengthy process of giving birth, even if—as in the case of Socrates' examination of the slave-boy in the *Meno*—it may look more like one of embryo implantation. What justifies her description, if anything does, is the etiology proposed in *Republic* 7 for upward blindness combined with the *Phaedrus*'s account of beauty's incandescence. There in Initiate's soul is divine reason; there in the body of a particular boy is incandescent beauty. Start with Initiate's attachment to that. Then show him the right things in the right order (or ask him the right questions) and, on the assumption that the appetites that tie him to the boy's beauty are weak enough, he will simply *see* what he is supposed to see. The mystery of divine inspiration has thus been replaced by the near mystery of an intellect or reason that is guaranteed to work correctly—perhaps because it is itself divine (*Ti.* 90a2–b1).

When Socrates has finished the long report we have been exploring of what Diotima told him about love, he adds an editorial comment about himself:

> That's what Diotima said, and I am persuaded by her; since I am persuaded, I try to persuade everyone else too that for acquiring this possession [namely, true virtue] one couldn't easily get a better coworker with human nature than Love is. That's why I declare that everyone must honor Love, and I myself honor what belongs to him and practice it more than anyone, and call on everyone else to do so, and both now and always I eulogize the power and courage of love to the best of my ability. (212b1–8)

It is a comment that recalls another: "The only thing I say I know is the art of love (*ta erōtika*)" (177d8–9). Since *ta erōtika* is the art of asking elenctic questions, love stands revealed as an elenctic passion—one that

---

7. This challenges the well-known critique of Platonic love developed in Gregory Vlastos, "The Individual as Object of Love in Plato," in his *Platonic Studies* (Princeton: Princeton University Press, 1973), pp. 3–42.

correctly proceeds by elenctic examination. Though canonically undertaken with the help of Socrates, it can also take the form of self-examination (*Chrm.* 166c7–d2; *Hp. Ma.* 298a9–c2). We can see in this a basis for Diotima's apparent uncertainty about Initiate's need for a guide. When elenctic examination proceeds correctly, or in the proper order, it always begins by trying to provide an account of what *is* F before turning to other questions about F (*Smp.* 199c5–8; *R.* 1, 354a13–c3). Herein might lie the basis for Diotima's claim that what Initiate produces at each stage are accounts of love.

When Diotima says that she doesn't know whether Socrates would be capable of initiation into the mysteries of loving boys correctly (*Smp.* 210a1–2), the grounds for her reservations might be found, we thought, in this question: Can Socrates show that beauty (or its contemplation) is related in the right way to virtue and happiness? We noted that Diotima stopped her account of these mysteries before explicitly reengaging with it. She does indeed refer to the fact that Initiate has begotten *true* virtue, but the only connection between it and permanent happiness she so much as intimates requires that the gods notice his virtue and, approving of it, reward him for it. But this is just the sort of connection on which a defense of a virtue as something intrinsically good cannot rely (*R.* 2, 366e6). Diotima's reservations are thus reechoed by her silence, bringing her account full circle.

Erotic Love Reconceived

Reservations, though negative, also have a positive side: "I don't know whether you could, but maybe you could." In the present instance, the basis for the positive side lies mostly in the nonimpossible. In the *Republic* this is what is appealed to whenever the issue arises of whether the ideal city Kallipolis could ever be established in practice (6, 499b1–d6, 502a4–c7). The thought, in its relevant form, is that it is not impossible that Initiate, pregnant in soul and with suitably compliant appetites, should find himself in a world where laws, constitutions, and kinds of knowledge are available for him to study, and in which he either finds a Socrates to help him study them in the right order and way or is correctly guided in this by his own love of beauty. It is not impossible that a love that begins with an incandescently beautiful body should lead (or be led) through Socratic or elenctic questioning to beauty itself and to the begetting of genuine virtue.

Suppose this does happen, so that Initiate, in the manner required by persistence-through-becoming, begets wise and virtuous later stages of himself and others. Are the things he has begotten genuinely good ones in whose permanent possession his true happiness consists? This is not a question to be settled by a supposed fact of daimonic inspiration or divine approval or insight. What is wanted is some sort of justification. The mere assertion that the beautiful itself is true beauty does not provide it. And we know why: beauty is ambivalent. To show that true beauty is genuinely good, we need to relate it appropriately to the one thing that is not ambivalent—the good itself. That we will then come face-to-face with the good's elusiveness is, to be sure, a major problem, but a different one.

In the case of an appetitive male pregnant in body, his genital is what produces embryophoric semen, namely, his testes. His erect penis is simply a delivery system for this—an erotogenic zone, a seat of sexual excitation. An honor-loving pregnant male has two genitals. The first produces embryophoric semen and so conventional offspring. The second produces unconventional offspring—things like honor-attracting courageous actions and memory-traces of them in other people. Inspired by the knowledge that in the *Republic* honor-lovers have a soul ruled by its spirited element or *thumos*, let us call this a *thumigenital*, which is simply *thumos* in its capacity as generator of unconventional offspring. Similarly, a philosopher has three genitals, the two he shares with the honor-lover, and a third unique to him, which, since his soul is ruled by its rational element or *logistikon*, we may call a *logigenital*, which is simply *logos* in its capacity as generator of such unconventional offspring as accounts that can make young men better.

Because there are these three kinds of genitals, we can ask what sort of genital sex is literally or really sex? Most people would say that it is the kind that involves the penis—the *epithumigenital*—since it is what begets conventional offspring, little animals of the sort that we really are. But suppose that what we really are is the rational element in our souls. Then real sex would involve not the testes, but the *logigenital*—reason—and it would be the philosopher talking about virtue to a beautiful boy who would be having real sex, not the man who "does his best to go on four feet like an animal and father offspring" (*Phdr.* 250e4–5). It is conventionally thought—indeed it is in dictionaries—that Platonic sex is aim-inhibited or nongenital. That's not entirely false, obviously, but there is a deeper truth that it conceals.

Implicit in this way of thinking about sex is something that destabilizes or threatens the obviously problematic assumption—common to both *Symposium* and *Phaedrus*—that philosophy, beauty, and the repression of the epitumigenital somehow go together to ensure that a Platonic philosopher must be a beauty-focused, aim-inhibited paiderast. For if the true genital is reason, not the testes, and upward blindness has merely adventitious, non-gender-specific appetitive causes, why should women not be as capable of philosophically begetting in beauty as men? It is a question that intersects with the unsolved mysteries in Diotima's account of loving boys correctly. Laws and social practices, kinds of knowledge, the educational institutions needed to make their study possible—all these must be available if the perception of bodily beauty is to lead to a rational grasp of beauty itself. Imagine a city in which all of them are available and where reason—by dint of knowing not just beauty but the good—has adopted the truly best laws and practices as its own. Imagine it possessed a eugenics program that breeds people whose weak or pliant appetites make them as naturally resistant to upward blindness as possible, and an educational program accessible to all of them, regardless of their sex. Imagine that its social roles are open to all capable of filling them, again regardless of sex. In that city, if the *Republic* is to be our guide, we will find philosophers—including female philosophers—for whom the good, not the beautiful, is the greatest object of study, having all sorts of non-aim-inhibited sex, including the sort that we used to think alone deserved the name. Plato makes the almost certainly fictional Diotima a woman, we might conjecture, in part to signal by the anomalousness of her own status (a female practitioner of a supposedly paiderastic discipline) that philosophy cannot be exactly as she describes.[8]

8. Contrast David M. Halperin, "Why Is Diotima a Woman?" in his *One Hundred Years of Homosexuality* (London: Routledge, 1990), pp. 113–151.

CHAPTER 7

⟨∿⟩

Education and the Acquisition of Knowledge

Some people "boastfully profess," the *Republic* tells us, that education can "pretty much put knowledge (*epistēmē*) into souls that lack it, like putting sight into blind eyes" (7, 518b8–c2). The truth, Socrates claims, is more modest. Education "takes for granted that sight is there, though not turned in the right way or looking where it should look, and contrives to redirect it appropriately" (7, 518d5–7). What possesses sight of the relevant sort is "the instrument in the soul with which each of us learns"— namely, reason (7, 518c5–6; 9, 580d8). That is why education, properly speaking, is the craft of reorienting it alone (7, 518d3–5, 529b5–c1). But because the embodied soul also includes appetitive and spirited elements, education cannot accomplish its task without reorienting them as well, "just as eyes cannot be turned around from darkness to light except by turning the whole body" (7, 518c6–8). A matter of habituation rather than of the acquisition of knowledge (7, 522a3–6), this part of education will remain offstage until the discussion of education proper has been completed and we understand the puzzling contrast Socrates draws between the modest and boastful conceptions of its task.

Knowledge and Belief

The knowledge Socrates thinks cannot be put into the soul, like the sight blind eyes lack, is a *dunamis*—a power or capacity (5, 477d8–e1). Thus conceived, two different factors determine its identity: what it deals with (*epi*) and what it does. Powers that share both are identical; powers that share neither are different (5, 477c6–d5). In the case of knowledge the two factors are these: "knowledge deals with what *is*, to know what *is* as it *is*" (5, 478a7). Later, we learn that understanding, which is identical to knowledge (7, 533e3–4), is "concerned with (*peri*) being" or the intelligible realm, while belief is "concerned with becoming" or the perceptible one (7, 534a2–3). The substitution of *peri* for *epi* suggests that one is simply a stylistic variant of the other. What knowledge (or any other power) deals with is what it is concerned with or what its field of operation is.[1]

Our grip on the other factor, which specifies what knowledge does, is tightened by Socrates' brief characterization of learning's culmination:

> A real lover of learning strives by nature for what *is*.... Once he is drawn near to it, has intercourse with what really *is*, and has begotten understanding and truth, he knows, truly lives, is nourished, and—at that point, but not before—is relieved from his labor pains. (6, 490a9–b7)

What learning grasps at that point is a form, such as that of beauty, whose mode of introduction is explained as follows:

> We say that there are many beauties (*polla kala*), many goods (*polla agatha*), and so on for each such thing, thereby distinguishing them in an account.... We also say there is a beauty itself and a good itself, and so on for all the things that we then posited as many. Now we reverse ourselves and posit a single form of each, since we suppose there is a single one, and call it what *is* each.... And we say that the former are visible but not intelligible, while the forms are intelligible but not visible. (6, 507b1–9)

Putting these texts together, we see that what a learner begets, having grasped beauty itself, is an understanding of it that can be embodied in a true account or definition of its nature. Hence this must be what constitutes knowing *what is* (beauty)—or what *is* (beauty) *as it is*.

Belief, a different power from knowledge, deals not with the form of beauty, but with the other things just referred to—*ta polla kala* (5, 476b4–d8, 478e1–479d8). Since, as far as grammar goes, these could be either beautiful particulars or kinds or types of beauty, "the many beauties," which is similarly ambiguous, recommends itself as an

---

1. Crafts or science are powers (1, 346a2–3), each of which "does its own work and benefits that with which it deals" (1, 346d5–6). But what medicine deals with is the body (1, 342c1–2), which is the very thing medical knowledge seems to be about.

appropriate—if occasionally unnatural—translation. What is characteristic of such items is that there isn't one that won't also "clearly be an ugly"
(5, 479a6), so that they are all "somehow clearly both beauties and uglies"
(5, 479a8–b1), and none is "any more what one says it is than it is not what
one says it is" (5, 479b7–8). They are, as Glaucon puts it, summing up, like
those "double games people play at parties, or the children's riddle about
the eunuch who threw something at a bat—the one about what he threw
at it and what it was in. For these things, too, play a double game and
one cannot understand them as fixedly being or fixedly not being or as
both or as neither" (5, 479a8–c5).[2] The conclusion Socrates draws is that
the masses' "many norms (*nomima*) of beauty and the rest are somehow
rolling around between what is not [beauty] and what purely *is* [beauty]"
(5, 479d2–4). A few pages later, he shows us why he does so:

> Do you think there is any difference, then, between the blind and those who are
> really deprived of the knowledge of each thing that *is*, and have no clear para-
> digm of it in their souls—those who cannot look away, like painters, to what is
> most true, and cannot, by making constant reference to it, and by studying it
> as exactly as possible, establish here on earth norms about beauties, justices, or
> goods, when they need to be established, or guard and preserve those that have
> been established? (6, 484c5–d2)

Since the form, which is what knowledge deals with, is a clear paradigm,
the corresponding many dealt with by belief must be an unclear one.

The reference to paradigms and the contrast between manys and
unique forms recalls a well-known passage from the *Euthyphro* in which
Socrates explains that he is seeking not "one or two of the many pieties,"
but rather "the form itself, by virtue of which all the pieties are pieties,"
so that "by concentrating on it and using it as a paradigm" he may call
"a piety any action of yours or anyone else's that is such as it, and may
deny to be a piety whatever isn't such as it" (6d9–e6). What he wants is
a paradigm that has two features. First, it enables its possessor to judge
particular cases correctly. Second, it is reality's own norm—the one *by*

---

2. The riddle seems to have been this. A man who is not a man saw and did not see
a bird that was not a bird in a tree (*xulon*) that was not a tree; he hit (*ballein*) and did
not hit it with a stone that was not a stone. The answer is that a eunuch with bad eye-
sight saw a bat on a rafter, threw a pumice stone at it and missed. For "he saw a bird"
is ambiguous between "he saw what was actually a bird" and "he saw what he took to
be a bird," *xulon* means both "tree" and "rafter," and *ballein* means both "throw" and
"hit." The rest is obvious.

virtue of which the particular cases are, in fact, of the relevant sort—and so is both justificatory and explanatory (compare *Men.* 97e5–98a7).

When someone possesses a paradigm of beauty of this sort, he understands what *is* beauty and can produce a true account or definition of it. One of the masses, by contrast, who possesses instead the unclear paradigm *ta polla kala*, produces an account that shares in the defects of that paradigm and is the best guide to them. Euthyphro's first account of piety is a case in point: "I say that what *is* piety is precisely what I am doing now: prosecuting those who commit an injustice.... Not prosecuting them, on the other hand, is what is an impiety" (*Euthphr.* 5d8–e2). Socrates responds, "But surely, Euthyphro, there are also other manys that you call pieties" (6d6–7). His point isn't that Euthyphro has cited a particular instance, when what was wanted was a type or kind, but that Euthyphro has picked out the wrong type or kind, since the particular instance he cites as a paradigm that identifies it is unreliable. For some of the actions it will count as pieties are impieties, and vice versa. The paradigm plays a double game, therefore, and cannot be understood as fixedly being piety or fixedly not being piety or as being both or neither.

It is this fact that makes *ta polla kala* the right sort of thing for belief to deal with. When Euthyphro uses his paradigm to make judgments about cases, even when he makes no mistakes in applying it, he will sometimes make true judgments, sometimes false ones. His power or capacity to make judgments about piety is therefore fallible. But fallibility is what distinguishes belief from knowledge: what is believed is sometimes true, sometimes false, whereas what is known is always true (5, 477e7–8). Knowledge is a reliable judgment-making power, belief an unreliable one.

The Scope of Knowledge

A major aim of the *Republic* is to show that a city cannot be maximally just or happy unless philosophers rule it, since they alone have knowledge of forms and the good (5, 473c11–e4; 6, 506a9–b1). To serve that purpose, the knowledge in question must apparently extend beyond what *is* to the perceptible world around us—the world that only becomes. When Socrates imagines himself explaining to the philosophers of Kallipolis why they must rule, he seems to acknowledge as much:

> Each of you in turn must go down to live in the common dwelling place of the
> other citizens and grow accustomed to seeing in the dark. For, when you are used
> to it, you will see infinitely better than the people there and know precisely what

each image is and also what it is an image of, because you have seen the truth about beauties, justices, and goods. (7, 520c1–5; also 3, 402b5–7; 6, 506a4–7)

Other texts, too, seem to countenance the extension of knowledge (*epistēmē*) to the visible or perceptible realm. For example, knowledge (*gnōsis*) of forms and of their visible images is said to belong to "the same craft and discipline" (3, 402b9–c8). Since the most common object of the verb *epistasthai* in Plato is *technē*, which is often a synonym of *epistēmē*, the implication seems to be that we can have *epistēmē* of both.[3] The implication is apparently embraced as explicit doctrine when Socrates asserts that "the knowledge (*epistēmēs*) that alone among all the other sorts of knowledge (*epistēmōn*)" should be called "wisdom" is the knowledge that deliberates "about the city as a whole, and about how its internal relations and its relations with other cities will be the best possible" (4, 428c11–429a3), and that "as regards the same manufactured item, its maker . . . has correct belief about its good and bad qualities, while its user has knowledge (*epistēmēn*)" (10, 601e7–602a1).[4]

Yet there are also passages that seem to deny that *epistēmē* of the perceptible world is possible: "If anyone tries to learn something about perceptibles . . . I would say that he never really learns—since there is no knowledge whatever (*epistēmēn ouden*) to be had of such things" (7, 529b5–c1; also 6, 508d3–8). When cognitive powers are canonically relabeled in *Republic* 7, *epistēmē* is identified with *noēsis*, a power that is exclusively "concerned with being" (7, 533e3–534a3) and with the intelligible realm of forms (6, 511b2–c2).

From the interpretative point of view, then, the *Republic* can itself seem to be playing something of a double game, like those riddles Glaucon talks about. But this is in part because we have left out a crucial element—namely, the interplay of knowledge with perception-based belief that is required if a reliable paradigm is to be applied correctly in particular cases. Speaking in the voice of the Muses, Socrates attributes the ultimate decline in Kallipolis to the need the philosophers have to employ just such a combination of powers in making judgments: "Even though they are wise, the people you have educated to be leaders in your city, will, by using rational calculation combined with sense-perception, nonetheless fail to ascertain the period of good fertility and of infertility for your species" (8, 546b1–3). That is why "it is natural for practice to have less of a grasp

---

3. See J. Lyons, *Structural Semantics: An Analysis of Part of the Vocabulary of Plato* (Oxford: Blackwell, 1963), pp. 139–228.
    4. Compare *Men.* 97a9–b7; *Tht.* 201a4–c2.

of truth than theory does" (5, 473a1–3). Applied is never so rigorous as pure.

All the same, there are procedures that can increase practice's rigor or decrease its margin of error. High on Socrates' list are the ones that involve those other denizens of the intelligible realm—numbers:

> The same object, viewed from nearby, does not appear the same size, I presume, as when viewed from a distance.... And the same things appear bent and straight when seen in water or out of it, or concave and convex because sight is misled by colors, and every other similar sort of confusion is clearly present in our soul.... And haven't measuring, counting, and weighing proved to be most welcome assistants in these cases, ensuring that what appears bigger or smaller or more numerous or heavier does not rule within us, but rather what has calculated or measured or even weighed?... And that is the task of the soul's rational element?... [And it] believes in accord with the measurements. (10, 602d6–603e2)

As counting, measuring, and weighing can correct unaided perception, so knowledge of forms can correct unaided perception of their images, enabling the philosopher to see them "infinitely better" than people without such knowledge. Once this mixed cognition is recognized as more reliable, little of philosophical significance hangs on whether we call it *epistēmē* or not. Plato himself, as we saw, may not be altogether consistent on the topic. What matters for the *Republic*'s overall argument is simply that, whatever we call it, it should be both entirely reliable and unavailable to anyone lacking knowledge of forms.

Resemblance and Reliability

When Socrates attempts to get across the difference in reliability between powers, it is invariably to the difference between a thing and its likeness or image that he appeals. Someone who merely believes is like a dreamer who thinks that a likeness "is not a likeness, but rather the thing itself that it is like" (5, 476c4–5). Someone who grasps the beautiful itself, on the other hand, and "is able to observe both it and the things that participate in it, and does not think that the participants are it, or that it is the participants" (5, 476c7–d3), lives in knowledge of the real waking world. In the allegory of the cave, which illustrates "the effect of education and the lack of it on our nature" (7, 514a1–2), the progress toward knowledge is represented as a four-stage journey upward in which crude likenesses (shadows of puppets of human beings and other things) are replaced by less crude ones (the puppets that cast the shadows) and finally by the things themselves (real human beings and other things).

One obvious advantage of this appeal is that it allows the abstract notion of cognitive reliability to be understood in terms of the familiar idea of degrees of resemblance or accuracy of representation. A disadvantage is that it can mislead if taken literally—if we forget that cognitive reliability of paradigms is the crucial or target notion, while talk of likenesses and originals is a way of explaining it. The following confident claim is an infamous case in point:

> We are adequately assured of this, then, and would remain so, no matter how many ways we examined it: what *is* completely (*pantelōs*) is completely an object of knowledge (*gnōston*), and what *is* in no way at all (*mēdamē[i]*) is an object of complete ignorance (*pantē[i] agnōston*)? (5, 477a2–4)

This does indeed sound like arcane metaphysics. Problematic doctrines about degrees of existence, reality, and truth have all been detected in it. Yet Socrates presents it as something obvious and irresistible even to the mass of people who aren't metaphysicians and know nothing about intelligible forms (5, 476d4–e8). We should expect, therefore, that its literal meaning is somehow leading us astray.

What is *gnōston* (negative: *agnōston*) is what knowledge deals with or is concerned with. Hence, as knowledge of beauty deals with what *is* beauty, so knowledge simpliciter deals with what *is* simpliciter (compare 4, 438c6–e10). The adverb *pantelōs* (negative: *mēdamōs*) belongs not to the language of cognitive reliability, however, but to that of likenesses and originals, in terms of which the former is explained or communicated. The thought is that because an incomplete or imperfect likeness is an unreliable paradigm, a reliable one would have to be a perfect or complete likeness. *Pantelōs* thus adds nothing to the claim that knowledge deals with what *is* except a sort of placeholder for the incomplete likenesses that will have real work to do once belief—which is a power lying in between knowledge and complete ignorance (*agnoia*) in cognitive reliability—enters the picture. Knowledge deals with what completely *is*, ignorance with what *is* not, and belief with "what partakes in both being and not being, and cannot correctly be called purely one or the other" (5, 478e1–3).

Though we now understand how to read such claims, it still comes as a bit of a surprise to learn that what *is* not is "most correctly characterized as not some one thing, but as nothing" (5, 478b11–c1). But once we recall that Socrates is speaking in the language of likenesses, we can see our way forward. Ignorance is a cognitive power that is as opaque as knowledge is clear (5, 478c9–d4). Knowledge is infallible; it always makes true judgments. Ignorance is not (like belief) simply fallible, but erroneous: it always makes false judgments. What would it have to deal with—what sort of paradigm would it have employ—in order to do that? Well, ignorance of beauty would have to deal with what *is* not beauty so that whatever was not a beauty would be judged a beauty by it and vice versa. Hence ignorance simpliciter would have to deal with what *is* not simpliciter. Encode that in the language of likenesses and what we get is the clause we left unexamined: "what *is* in no way at all is an object of complete ignorance."

As persistent as the explanation of cognitively reliable paradigms in terms of likenesses and originals is the association of cognitively unreliable ones, first, with the visible realm and, second, with nonuniqueness or plurality. In the following text both associations are present:

> The same account applies to just and unjust, good and bad, and all the forms: each of them is itself one thing, but because they appear all over the place in partnership with actions and bodies, and with one another, each of them appears to be many things. (5, 476a5–8; also 3, 402b5–c8)

To treat one of these perceptible beauties as if it were beauty itself, therefore, is to make the mistake the masses make of taking an image for an original. To be sure, the masses themselves cannot characterize their mistake in that way, since they have no access at all to the originals in question (5, 476c1–2). But they can be brought to acknowledge that the paradigm they use to make judgments about beauty does not provide them with knowledge of it (5, 476d7–e2).

We have already poached extensively on the argument Socrates develops for this purpose. Central to it, as we noticed, is the acknowledgment by Glaucon, on behalf of the masses (5, 476e7–8), that none of the many beauties is any more a beauty than it is not a beauty (5, 479a8–b1). We might wonder how he can be sure that the masses will acknowledge this. In the manner of contemporary experimental philosophers has he taken a poll? The answer is that if he hasn't, Socrates has. When Euthyphro is asked what piety is, he cites an example from the perceptible world as a paradigm. His paradigm is then shown by Socrates to play a double game. As a result, Euthyphro acknowledges that his answer does not manifest the knowledge of piety to which he laid claim. Since every other person Socrates has examined is like him in this regard, Glaucon's confidence seems well founded. At the same time, Euthyphro is also like Socrates' other interlocutors in that he cannot be led by Socratic questioning to a cognitively reliable account of piety. Presumably, this is the basis for Socrates' own otherwise opaque claim that the masses not only do not believe in the form of beauty, but also "would not be able to follow anyone who tried to lead them to knowledge of it" (5, 476c1–2; compare *Smp.* 210a6). The Socratic dialogues invariably end in *aporia*.

The Role of Political Experience

Though the mathematical sciences—comprising arithmetic, plain and solid geometry, astronomy, and harmony (7, 525b9–531b7)—constitute an important step on the way to knowledge, they also have cognitive deficiencies that prevent them from reaching that goal unaided. *Dialectic* remedies these deficiencies. It seeks to grasp "what each thing itself *is*" (7, 533b1). That is to say, it seeks the form that is a reliable paradigm for judging particular cases and explains why they are such cases. Just how it does all this is something we will need to take up later on. For now it is enough to notice that even when, at the age of thirty-five, the trainee philosophers have completed their five years of dialectical training, they have not completed their education. Instead, they must spend another fifteen years engaged in practical politics, taking command "in matters of war and the other offices suitable for young people, so that they won't be inferior to others in experience" (7, 539e4–6).

If this were simply the occasion on which theory meets practice, we might be inclined to downplay its importance for understanding education and the acquisition of knowledge as such, but that is not Socrates' own picture of the situation:

> In these offices, too, they [the dialectically trained philosophers] must be tested to see whether they will remain steadfast when they are pulled in different directions or give way.... Then, at the age of fifty, those who have survived the tests and are entirely best in every practical task and every branch of knowledge (*epistēmais*) must be led at last to the final goal and compelled to lift up the radiant eye-beams of their souls, and to look towards what itself provides light for everything. And once they have seen the good itself, they must use it as their paradigm and put the city, its citizens, and themselves in order throughout the remainder of their lives, each in turn. (7, 539e6–540b1)

Dialectic's upward path so crucially involves political practice, therefore, that the good cannot be reached without it. That means that knowledge—knowledge of anything—cannot be reached without it either.

The reason for this seems to lie in a doctrine we have already noticed in another context: only the user of a kind of thing (whether it is manufactured or living) has knowledge "about what the good and bad points are in the actual use of the thing he uses," because he "has the most experience of it" (10, 601d8–10). For the kind of thing a philosopher-king alone has this sort of knowledge of is a city—a community consisting of human beings, other living things, various natural and manufactured items, a geographical location, and so on. That explains why he can use the good itself as a paradigm to put his city and himself in order (4, 428c11–429a3; 6, 500b8–501b7).

Cities might seem too modest for something as exalted and superior as the good itself to be the good of. But this is not so. The most important constituents of the philosophers' city, after all, are its human citizens. In part, they are products of nature—they have first natures; in part, they are cultural products, shaped by years of education and training—they have second natures. But even their first natures (their genetic makeup, as we would say) are not entirely nature's unaided work, since they are in part the products of a complex eugenics program, designed to ensure an adequate stock of excellent future philosophers and guardians. Because the "periods of good fertility and infertility" for humans are governed by esoteric facts about the sun, the seasons, and the structure of the cosmos, this program is one place where the good of a city emerges as involving something rather grand (8, 546a1–547a6; compare 6, 488d4–7).

Another—yet more significant—such place lies in human first nature itself. Unlike appetite and spirit, reason is "akin to what is divine and immortal and always exists" and so is itself simple, immortal (10, 611b5–612a6), and "more divine" than they (7, 518d11–e1). Its good, therefore, which is part of the good of the city, is scarcely going to be something narrowly political or worldly. As the good of an immortal, it must be the sort of good that can be available not just for "the entire period from childhood to old age," but for "the whole of time" (6, 486a9–10; 10, 608c6–d3). As the good of a *rational* immortal, it must also be a source of "the pleasure of knowing where the truth lies," in which such a being's peculiar happiness consists (9, 581d10). Thus, however exalted the good itself may be, the good of a city must keep pace with it.

Holism and the Division of Epistemic Labor

With the grasp of the good, the goal of Platonic education has been finally reached. For education, as we recall, is the craft concerned with turning reason around from the visible to the intelligible realm, not of "putting sight into it." The final clause, much insisted on by Socrates, remains none-theless puzzling. Once appropriately reoriented, he seems to think, reason will simply see whatever it's looking at. It is to seeing, indeed, that its oper-ation is invariably likened. Since seeing can be very theory-laden, we might be tempted to think of Platonic education as providing the theory with which its intellectual equivalent must be equipped. Mathematics, dialectic, practical politics would then take on the appearance of a vast theory that reveals or makes visible the good, while the good itself would emerge as the entire structure of forms that is the theory's ontological correlate. Since this theory would alone provide the unhypothetical cognition required for knowledge, some sort of epistemological holism would result, at least where forms were concerned—although cognition of the visible world of becoming might still be plausibly represented as reliabalist in nature.[5] We know about visible things because, with the holistic theory of *something else*—forms—to hand, we can make reliably true judgments about them.

It is an attractive picture. But, for all that, it seems to miss the main point or hit just beside it. When the philosophers finally see the good itself, they have the infallible, unhypothetical cognitive grasp of it that is a paradigm of knowledge. But they have no knowledge of anything else until they take the road back down from it, gaining additional infallible, unhypothetical cognition in the process:

> When the eye of the soul [reason] is really buried in a sort of barbaric bog, dia-lectic gently pulls it out and leads it upwards, using the crafts we described to help it and cooperate with it in turning the soul around. From force of habit, we have often called these branches of knowledge. But they need another name, since they are clearer than belief and darker than knowledge. (7, 534d1–6)

Hence it is only when philosophers descend from the good, making "no use of anything visible at all," that they have knowledge of any other forms (6, 511c1–2). Since they can apparently have knowledge of one form reached in this way, without yet having knowledge of others, holism seems ruled out. There is ample motivation, therefore, to consider an alternative to the attractive picture.

Imagine an eye that has the power to see, but isn't turned in the right direction. Imagine, too, that it has in it many layers of differently distort-ing lenses. Now imagine a craft or science that can, first, turn it around

5. Compare Gail Fine, "Knowledge and Belief in Republic 5–7," in her *Plato I: Metaphysics and Epistemology* (Oxford: Oxford University Press, 1999), pp. 228–229.

until it is facing where it should. This is what training in the mathematical sciences does: it leads reason to look away from the visible world up toward the intelligible one (7, 526e7–8). When reason is looking in the right direction, dialectic enters the picture. What it does is to remove the distorting lenses by systematically solving all the puzzles and problems that cloud reason's vision. At that point, practical political training takes over the unified vision that results and imbues it with rich content. What reason will then be able to see isn't a vast structure—a vast rational order—of forms, but the principle of that order, the good that determines it. That is what makes the Sun analogy appropriate rather than misleading or inept. For the sun obviously isn't a complex whole constituted by visible things, it is visibility's very source. Once the philosophers have that principle in their intellectual grasp, knowledge of other forms becomes possible, but may be piecemeal rather than holistic.

Users of flutes, who know the good and bad points of flutes, tell the flute-makers what sort of flutes to make. But they themselves do not know— and need not know—how to make flutes. The good and bad points of flutes are relative to—or partly determined by—the music that a good city ought to allow and provide training in. And no user of flutes need know what such music is, nor need its makers or composers. For the "harmony and rhythm" of music must be appropriate to the poems they accompany, and the poems must be appropriate in content to the larger social role of the singers in whose education and later civilized life they figure (3, 398d8–9). We can already see where this line of thought leads. Eventually, we will reach the designer of the good city's constitution—the philosopher-kings—whom Socrates, Glaucon, and Adeimantus are impersonating.

How they will stand to the poems we have been discussing is something about which Socrates is quite explicit: "You and I are not poets at present, Adeimantus. But we are founding a city. And it is appropriate for the founders to know (*eidenai*) the patterns on which the poets must base their accounts, and from which they must not deviate. But they should not themselves make up any poems" (2, 378e7–379a4). The philosophers know the patterns the poets must follow. But these patterns, as the discussion makes clear, are neither poems nor detailed blueprints for them. Thus the poets, though they may not have knowledge, or even reliable cognition, of the subject matter—ethical and otherwise—of their poems, have something significant to contribute to the poems the city needs for the education and entertainment of its citizens, all the same. If this contribution requires the philosophers' pattern in order for good poems—that is poems that contribute to the good of the city and its citizens—to result, it is also true that the pattern requires the contribution. We might think, in fact, that the philosopher could not arrive at his pattern—could not know what the pattern of a good poem could possibly be—unless he had learned a lot about poetry from its actual practitioners (see 3, 398e1–400c6). What Plato calls knowledge may require the hypothesis-destroying effects of the good, but what thereby gets transformed is still—like the untransformed mathematical sciences—a huge cognitive achievement on the part of people who may not be philosophers themselves.

Blindness and Reorientation

The self-styled educators, who claim to be able to put knowledge into souls like sight into blind eyes stand revealed now as people who think that the soul does not need an eye (7, 533d2), a divine or godlike element (10, 611b5–612a6), in order to acquire knowledge. If the soul were blind, so that it couldn't see the good itself were the two face-to-face, it could still, by learning everything else the philosopher learns, acquire knowledge. But countenancing the good is a precondition of countenancing forms. Hence, by rejecting it, these educators reject forms too. In the case of beauty, justice, and goodness, they—like the masses—must think that the corresponding manys provide reliable paradigms, adequate for knowledge. It is this that establishes their identity:

> None of those private wage-earners—the ones these people call sophists and consider to be their rivals in craft—teaches anything other than the convictions the masses hold when they are assembled together, and this he calls wisdom....Knowing nothing in reality about which of these convictions or appetites is beautiful or shameful, good or bad, just or unjust, he uses all these terms in conformity with the great beast's [i.e., the masses'] beliefs—calling the things it enjoys good and the things that anger it bad....Don't you think, by Zeus, that someone like that would make a strange educator?...But that such things are truly good and beautiful—have you ever heard anyone presenting an argument for that conclusion which was not absolutely ridiculous?...So then, bearing all that in mind, recall our earlier question: Can the masses in any way tolerate or accept that the beautiful itself (as opposed to the many beauties), or each thing itself (as opposed to the corresponding many) exists?...It is impossible, then, for the masses to be philosophic. (6, 493a6–494a3)

We might have guessed that any educators in Plato who "boastfully declare" that they can teach something important about human values and how to live would turn out to be Sophists!

As we noted at the beginning, reason cannot be turned toward the good and the intelligible world of forms unless the complex soul of which it is a part is turned with it. Much of Platonic education, as a result, is directed at the reorientation of appetite and spirit. The problem with the appetite is that, based in the body (9, 585a8–b1) and focused squarely on the perceptible world where bodily hunger, thirst, and sexual desire find their satisfactions, it can keep reason focused there too, forcing it to serve as its instrument and slave (7, 519a1–b5; also 8, 553b7–d7). Through proper habituation, therefore, it must be pruned of its unnecessary or nonbeneficial members, while its necessary or beneficial ones are moderated and made harmonious with reason's aims and dictates (8, 558d8–559b6). This habituation is provided to future guardians or philosophers primarily by the Platonic version of *mousikē* and *gumnastikē*—the traditional ancient Greek education in poetry, song, music, and dance (2, 376e1–3).[6] Allowed to grow luxurious under the influence of unnecessary appetites (2, 373a4–7, d9–e1), Kallipolis is thereby purified (3, 399e4–5).

By nature multifarious, disunited, body centered, and downward focused, appetite must be hammered at if it is to become reason's ally. The case of spirit is somewhat different, as we saw. Because its love of honor (9, 581a9–b4) naturally orients it toward *to kalon*, which both attracts honor and is allied with the good, it is "the natural auxiliary of the rational element, provided it has not been corrupted by bad upbringing" (4, 441a2–3). The aim of Platonic education is thus to solidify and develop what is already a natural orientation to something itself naturally incandescent and attractive. While it does this primarily by shaping desires and emotions, making them harmonious "through habits" rather than by imparting knowledge (7, 522a4–7), such shaping still has a cognitive as well as a conative aspect. Someone properly trained in *mousikē* and *gumnastikē*, Socrates says, will feel disgust correctly and, because he does,

> will praise beautiful things, be pleased by them, take them into his soul, and, though being nourished by them, become beautiful and good. What is ugly or shameful, on the other hand, he will correctly condemn and hate while he is still young, before he is able to grasp the reason. And, because he has been so trained, he will welcome the reason when it comes, and recognize it easily because of its kinship with himself. (3, 401e4–402a4)

---

6. It may be provided to workers and producers by training in a craft. See my *Philosopher-Kings: The Argument of Plato's Republic* (Princeton: Princeton University Press, 1988; reissued, Indianapolis: Hackett, 2006), pp. 176–178, 186–191.

To hate or be disgusted by the wrong things, therefore, isn't simply to be wrongly motivated, it is to misperceive the world and pass on perceptual misinformation to reason. It is through *mousikē* and *gumnastikē* that reason largely acquires the good-adapted eye it needs to deal reliably with the visible world.

When the vast Platonic educational machine consisting of *mousikē*, *gumnastikē*, the mathematical sciences, dialectic, and practical politics is fully successful, the result is someone possessed of each of the four virtues or excellences Socrates considers: wisdom, courage, temperance, and justice. His reason desires the good. His appetite and spirit see and desire in harmony with reason. The ideal of rational order represented by the good he comes as close to embodying as a human being can (6, 500b1–d2). But Platonic education is fully successful only in a relatively small number of cases (4, 428e9–429a1): people with the natural capacities required of philosopher-kings are rare (5, 476b9–10; 6, 503d10). In most people, the obstacles nature poses are too great for even the most resourceful education to overcome. The results are the guardians (ruled by their spirit) and the producers (ruled by their appetite), which Kallipolis also—fortuitously— needs. But though guardians and producers cannot achieve either virtue or the happiness that it alone ensures, with education's help, they can come as close to the two as their natures allow (9, 580b1–c5). Education is "the one great thing" (4, 423e2), therefore, and *mousikē* and *gumnastikē*, which are its foundation, comprise the guardians' own guardhouse (4, 424c8–d1)— the one that, when breached, heralds political decline (8, 546d4–547a6).

The Epistemic Status of the *Republic* Itself

Any account of the acquisition of knowledge through education is bound itself to be subject to epistemological scrutiny. Plato's account in the *Republic* is no exception. It is noteworthy, in fact, for offering such scrutiny so large a target. How, we wonder, does Plato know all that about the soul and the good and the best way for the one to reach the other? In a particularly candid passage, he has Socrates answer this question. "Only the god," he says, knows whether what the allegory of the cave encodes about education, forms, and the good is true (7, 517b6–7). It is a bold summing up—reminiscent of the conclusion he reaches on his own behalf about the meaning of the Delphic oracle's pronouncement about him (*Ap.* 23a5– b4)—of a larger theme, in which a contrast is drawn between a "longer and more time-consuming road" and the implicitly shorter one taken in the *Republic* (4, 435c9–d4; also 6, 504b1–505b3; 7, 531d2–533a5). That the longer road is the upward and downward path of dialectic seems certain. As for the shorter one, it is surely the one Simmias describes:

> To know the plain truth about such matters is either impossible or extremely difficult in this present life, but to fail to examine what is said about them in every possible way, or to give up before one has investigated them exhaustively from every angle, shows utter softness in a man. You see, where these matters are concerned, it seems to me that one must certainly achieve one of two things: either learn or discover how they stand; or, if that is impossible, then at least adopt the best of the things people say, and the one that stands up best to examination, and, carried on it as on a sort of raft, face the dangers of life's voyage—provided one cannot travel more safely and with less risk on the more secure vessel of some divine saying. (*Phd.* 85c1–d4)

Though there is a hint that Socrates may have sailed on the more secure vessel (6, 496a11–e3), the *Republic* itself can only be the less secure one—a companion for the short road, not the long one.

CHAPTER 8

༄

Craft, Dialectic, and the Form of the Good

A rehearsal, first, of some things that we have noticed or taken for granted in our earlier discussions. As a crucial part of his defense against the writ of impiety brought by Meletus, Socrates distinguishes his own "human wisdom" from a greater or more impressive wisdom that he does not possess (*Ap.* 20d6–e3). It is the Athenians' failure to notice this distinction that has led to his prejudicial reputation as a Sophist (19d8–24b2) and an atheist (18c1–3). Although, toward the end of the chapter human wisdom will make a significant reappearance, the primary focus now will be the wisdom Socrates disavows.

Three facts about this wisdom are immediately apparent. First, it concerns human virtue and how to teach it (20b4–5). Second, it constitutes a sort of epistemic ideal in this area: "I, at any rate, would pride myself and give myself airs," Socrates says, " if I had knowledge of those things. But, in fact, men of Athens, I don't know them" (20c1–3). Third, it is sufficiently familiar that it will be readily intelligible to the jurors on the basis of a brief story. If Callias' sons were colts or calves, Socrates tells them, we "could engage and pay a knowledgeable supervisor—one of those expert horse-breeders or farmers—who could turn them into fine and good examples of their proper virtue or excellence." But who can turn them into examples of "the virtue of human beings and citizens"? Callias replies that Evenus of Paros will do the job for five minas of silver. Socrates' reaction is revelatory: "I thought Evenus blessedly happy if he truly did possess that craft and taught it for so modest a fee" (20a5–c1). Hence the wisdom in question seems to be a knowledge of virtue that is relevantly similar to a craft. We can see, then, why Socrates thinks that the jurors will understand what he was talking about. For craft was sufficiently well understood that others, too, resorted to it in popular appeals. The Hippocratic treatise *On Craft (Peri Technēs)*, for example, undertakes to defend medicine as the authoritative body of knowledge bearing on health precisely by showing that it is a genuine craft. The question is: what did Socrates and his fellow Greeks take crafts to be?

Crafts and Their Defining Features

The Hippocratic writers (*Tech.* 11.20–22 and *VM* 23[1]) are explicit that a doctor must know the explanation (*aitia*) of a disease if he is to give the patient "correct care." In the *Gorgias*, an experienced-based knack (*tribē, empeiria*) is distinguished from a craft, because a knack "has no account…and so does not have the explanation of each thing," and nothing can be a craft if it "lacks an account" (465a2–6).[2] In Aristotle, those who "rely on experience" are described as knowing "the fact that but not the reason why, while those with the craft know the reason why, that is, the explanation" (*Met.* 1.1, 981a28–30). *Explanatoriness* is thus one defining feature of a craft.

The Hippocratic writers (*VM* 20–24) also tell us that part of the knowledge of what *is* man or what man *is* (*ti estin anthrōpos, anthrōpos ti estin*) that a perfected medicine will provide is knowledge of the powers (*dunameis*) of various diets and regimens and their effects on people whose bodies have themselves different structures (*schēmata*) and powers. Since both powers and structures are classed as forms,[3] medical knowledge of what man *is* involves knowing the form of man and the forms of the various things that affect his health. In Plato's dialogues, this connection is yet more explicit. In the *Cratylus*, the form (*eidos*) of F is identified with what itself *is* F (*auto ho estin* F) (389a6–b6). In the *Phaedo* the latter is identified with the being or essence (*ousia*) of F (65d13–e1), and is characterized as a crucial factor in the explanation of a particular thing's being F (100a3). Essentially the same identifications are found in Aristotle. In a craft, the form or essence is

---

1. These treatises are translated as "The Science of Medicine" and "Tradition in Medicine" in G. E. R. Lloyd, *Hippocratic Writings* (Harmondsworth: Penguin, 1978). Mark J. Schiefsky, *Hippocrates: On Ancient Medicine* (Leiden: Brill, 2005), is an edition of the Greek text with translation and extensive commentary.

2. Also *Grg.* 463a7–8, 500e3–c6; *R.* 6, 493b6.

3. There is no such thing as a "hot itself or cold itself (*auto thermon ē psuchron*)" that participates in "no other form (*eidei*)" than the hot or cold (*VM* 15.1); "there are many forms of structures (*eidea schēmatōn*) both inside and outside the body" (*VM* 23.1). See H. C. Baldry, "Plato's 'Technical Terms,'" *Classical Quarterly* 31 (1937): 141–150.

in the soul of the craftsman (*Met.* 7.7, 1032a32–b10) and flows from there into the matter by dint of controlling the movements of his hands and body (*GA* 1.22, 730b8–23). Hence *form-relatedness* also seems to be a defining feature of craft. We should not infer, though, that any particular ontology of forms is being presupposed in all these cases: the Hippocratic writers were physicians, not metaphysicians; Plato adopted an *ante rem* theory of forms, in which forms existed independently of perceptible particulars; Aristotle adopted an *in re* theory, in which the existence of the relevant sort of forms depended on that of particulars.

Socrates often speaks of examining people or their lives (*Ap.* 21c3, 28e4–6, 39c6–8), making it clear that the examined life is one in which elenctic discussion of virtue has a central place: "It is the greatest good for a human being to discuss virtue every day and the other things about which you hear me conversing and examining both myself and others, for the unexamined life is not worth living for a man" (38a2–6). Accounts of the virtues are thus the chief focus of an elenchus: "What I chiefly examine is the account, but the consequence may be that I the questioner and you the answerer may also be examined" (*Prt.* 333c7–9). The primary demand Socrates imposes on ethical wisdom, indeed, is that it must enable its possessor to produce accounts of the virtues that are resistant to elenctic refutation, since only then will they specify forms that can serve both as reliable epistemological paradigms and as explanatory ontological factors (*Euthphr.* 6d9–e6). He claims, too, that if one cannot provide such an account and so does not know what *is* justice or piety or some other virtue, one cannot have any ethical wisdom whatsoever: "The result of the discussion, so far as I am concerned, is that I know nothing. For when I do not know what *is* justice, I will hardly know whether it is a kind of virtue or not, or whether a person who has it is happy or unhappy" (*R.* 1, 354c1–3).[4]

Consider now what Peter Geach has labeled "the Socratic fallacy."[5] This is the view, loosely expressed, that if one doesn't know what *is* F, one cannot know anything else about Fs. If it is intended to apply to knowledge generally, the view is clearly false—hence the "fallacy" in Geach's label. But if is a principle about craft alone, it is both nonfallacious and intelligible. For the idea of explanation is tied to the idea of explanatory structure: if there is to be explanation, there must (minimally) be an explanandum, an explanans, and some sort of connection, causal or inferential, between them. It isn't much of

---

4. Also *Hp. Ma.* 286c8–d2; *La.* 190b7–c5; *Ly.* 212a4–7, 223b4–8; *Prt.* 361c2–6.
5. P. T. Geach,"Plato's *Euthyphro*: An Analysis and Commentary" in his *Logic Matters* (Oxford: Blackwell, 1972), pp. 31–44.

a step from there to the idea of explanatory first principles. If Aristotle is to be our guide, it is a step that Socrates (at least implicitly) took:

> Socrates occupied himself with the virtues of character, and in connection with them became the first to raise the problem of universal definitions. ... It was reasonable that Socrates should seek the essence. For he was seeking to deduce, and essences are the starting-points of deductions. ... For there are two things that may be fairly ascribed to Socrates—inductive arguments and universal definition, both of which are concerned with a first principle of scientific knowledge. (*Met.*13.4, 1078b17–30; also 1.6, 987a29–b8)

To be sure, Aristotle's characterization presupposes his own theory of scientific knowledge (*epistēmē*) and is couched in its idiom, but that should not blind us to the nugget of truth it contains. For failure to know the first principles of a craft or science does prevent someone from having craft knowledge of what follows from them, since explanatoriness is one of craft's defining features.

Perception-Based Crafts

Having examined the politicians and poets and found them altogether lacking in ethical wisdom, it was to the practitioners of the handicrafts that Socrates turned. And what he discovered is that they did have genuine wisdom of a sort:

> Finally, I approached the handicraftsmen. You see, I was conscious of knowing practically nothing myself, but I knew I'd discover that they, at least, would know many fine things. And I wasn't wrong about this. On the contrary, they did know things that I didn't know, and in that respect they were wiser than I. (*Ap.* 22c9–d4)

Did that mean that they were able to give correct elenchus-resistant accounts of the forms or paradigms they looked toward in making their products? Socrates' own answer is apparently no. For the way to find out who is "the most craftsmanlike" practitioner of a given craft, he claims, is to determine "who has studied and practiced it and who has had good teachers in that particular one" (*La.* 185b1–4). Being teachable (learnable), indeed, is another part of what a craft involves: "The power [to determine the causes of diseases] is possessed by anyone whose education is not unorthodox and whose nature is not miserable" (*Tech.* 9, 16–18). Craft is a form of knowledge, and all and only knowledge is teachable (*Prt.* 356e2–361b7).

"Craftsmen can teach, those who rely on experience cannot" (Aristotle, *Met.* 1.1, 981b8–10). People might still be good craftsmen, however, even if they fail this first test, by having "some well-executed product of their craft to show you—and not just one but more than one" (*La.* 185e9–186a1). Though not always sufficient by itself, since poets who compose excellent poems do so by divine inspiration, not craft knowledge (*Ion* 533e5–b6), this test seems to be the crucial one in the case of the handicrafts, enabling both teachers and their students to be identified in an independent way.

The reason the handicraftsmen counted as wise to Socrates, then, is that they were able to show him their well-executed products. According to Aristotle, this is one of two ways that first principles are standardly presented:

> Every science that is based in understanding or that shares in understanding to some extent deals with explanations and first principles, whether in a very rigorous manner or a more simplified one. But all these sciences mark off some being—that is, a genus—and investigate it, but not as a being in the unquali-fied sense or qua being, and for the what *is* it (*to ti estin*) [that is, the first princi-ple] they give no account whatsoever, instead, starting from it—some making it clear to the senses, others assuming the what *is* it as a hypothesis—they then demonstrate the intrinsic attributes of the genus, either in a more strictly nec-essary way or in less strict one. (Aristotle, *Met.* 6.1, 1025b5–13)

Let us say that crafts are *perception-based*, when, like the handicrafts, they do not need to provide elenchus-resistant accounts of their first princi-ples, because these can be presented as perceptible paradigms. Crafts are *hypothesis-based*, on the other hand, when they are forced to treat their first principles as hypotheses, because they aren't the sorts of things that perception can grasp.[6]

---

6. The Hippocratic writers implicitly employ this Aristotelian distinction, sug-gesting that is was a commonly drawn one. Medicine, they claim, has "no need of a newfangled hypothesis, as do obscure and dubious matters" (*VM* 1.3; also 15.1). For medicine's subject matter "is simply and solely the sufferings of ordinary people when they are sick or in pain" (*VM* 2.3); what it employs as treatment are "the same foods and the same drinks as we all use" (*VM* 15.2); and the only "measure by reference to which [its] knowledge can be made exact is bodily feeling" (*VM* 9.3). Hence it does not need hypotheses, since it can make its first principles clear to the senses. That would explain why Socrates thinks that doctors "would become cleverest, if, besides learning the craft of medicine, they associated with the greatest possible number of the most diseased bodies right from childhood, had themselves experienced every illness, and were not by nature very healthy" (*R.* 3, 408d10–e1). For those who have experienced an illness themselves have, as it were, an inner measure or paradigm to use in evaluating patients that the congenitally healthy lack.

This way of looking at the matter is confirmed when we turn to what Socrates says to Glaucon in order to explain what a philosopher is. The person "naturally fitted to engage in philosophy" (*R.* 5, 474b7–c1), he says, is the one who "has a desire for wisdom—not for this part of wisdom rather than that, but all of it" (5, 475b8–9). The trouble, as Glaucon quickly points out, is that lovers of sights, sounds, and—most pertinently—crafts will all then count as philosophers (5, 475d1–e1). Socrates characterizes these as students of "petty crafts (*technudriōn*)" (5, 475e1) and "craftlovers (*philotēchnous*)" (5, 476a10), using coined terms that are clearly related in connotation and rhetorical force to those used to describe a group of craftsmen who appear subsequently. These are the "petty men (*anthrōpiskoi*)—the ones who are most sophisticated at their own petty craft (*technion*)" who "leap readily from their crafts to philosophy" (6, 495c8–d4).[7]

What emerges as definitive of Glaucon's craftlovers is that they believe in *polla kala* (5, 479a3. In the *Apology*, the same defining formula is used to describe the handicraftsmen (22d2). Yet in part because of their genuine knowledge of their craft, these handicraftsmen also had a significant cognitive and ethical defect: "because he performed his own craft well, each of them also thought himself wisest in the other most important things; and this error of theirs seemed to overshadow their wisdom" (*Ap.* 22d5–e1). Since the most important things are the virtues (29e3–30a2; *Alc.* 118a7–12), it seems that what the handicraftsmen did was take their craft knowledge as enabling them to answer Socrates' question about virtue. The leap taken by the petty craftsmen is presumably of the same sort. They leap from knowing what a shoe or a shuttle is to thinking they know what virtue is or how to live. Thus when asked what justice or some other first principle of ethical wisdom *is*, they respond, as they would to a similar request posed about a first principle of their own perception-based crafts, by presenting a perceptible paradigm. We have seen why Socrates thinks this will not work: any one of the *polla kala* that is presented as a supposed paradigm will be no more *kalon* than it is not *kalon* and so will not constitute the sort of reliable paradigm needed for knowledge (5, 478e7–479b2).

In *Republic* 7, things accessible to sense perception are divided into two classes:

> Some sense-perceptions do not summon the understanding to look into them, because the judgment of sense-perception is itself adequate, whereas others encourage it in every way to look into them, because sense-perception does not

---

7. *Anthrōpiskoi* is used just once more, and with the same connotation, at *Phdr.* 243a1, the other terms appear only here.

produce a sound result.... The ones that do not summon the understanding are all those that do not at the same time result in an opposite sense-perception. But the ones that do I call *summoners*. This is when sense-perception does not make one thing any more clear than its opposite, regardless of whether what strikes the senses is close by or far away. What I mean will be clearer if you look at it this way: These, we say, are three fingers—the smallest, the second, and the middle finger.... Assume that I am talking about them as being seen from close by. Now consider this about them with me.... It is obvious, surely, that each of them is equally a finger, and it makes no difference whether it is seen to be in the middle or at either end, whether it is dark or pale, thick or thin, or anything else of that sort. You see, in all these cases, the soul of most people is not compelled to ask the understanding what a finger *is*, since sight does not at any point suggest to it that a finger is at the same time the opposite of a finger. (7, 523a10–d6)

Thus any craft whose first principle is a nonsummoner could presumably answer Socrates' request for an account of what it is by presenting one to the senses. The cardinal feature of summoners, by contrast, is that only the understanding can present them to us in cognitively reliable ways:

Now what about the fingers' bigness and smallness? Does sight perceive them adequately? Does it make no difference to it whether one of them is in the middle or at the end? And is it the same with the sense of touch as regards thickness and thinness, hardness and softness? What about the other senses, then, do they make such things sufficiently clear? Or doesn't each of them work as follows: In the first place, the sense that deals with hardness must also deal with softness; and it reports to the soul that it perceives the same thing to be both hard and soft?... In cases of this sort, then, isn't the soul inevitably puzzled about what this sense-perception means by hardness, if it says that the same thing is also soft, and in the case of the sense-perception of lightness and heaviness, what it means lightness and heaviness are, if what *is* heavy is light or what *is* light heavy?... It is likely, then, that it is in cases of this sort that the soul, summoning calculation and understanding, first tries to determine whether each of the things reported to it is one or two.... If there are obviously two, won't each of them be obviously one and distinct?... If each of them is one, then, and both together are two, the soul will understand that the two are separate. I mean, it would not understand inseparable things as two but as one.... But sight, we say, saw bigness and smallness, not as separate, but as mixed up together.... And to get clear about this, understanding was compelled to see bigness and small-ness, too, not mixed up together, but distinguished—the opposite way from sight.... Isn't it in cases like this that it first occurs to us to ask what bigness is, and smallness, too?...Which is why we called one section of the line the intelligible and the other the visible. (7, 523e3–524c13)

The question is, how are crafts whose first principles are summoners then to proceed? How are they to deal with their first principles?

Here the mathematical crafts[8] are Socrates' primary exhibit:

> I think you know that students of geometry, calculation, and the like hypothesize the odd and the even, the various figures, the three kinds of angles, and other things akin to these in each of their investigations, regarding them as known. These they treat as hypotheses and do not think it necessary to give any account of them, either to themselves or to others, as if they were evident to everyone. And going from these first principles through the remaining steps, they arrive in full agreement at the point they set out to reach in their investigation... [T]hey use visible forms and make their arguments about them, although they are not thinking about them, but about those other things that they are like. They make their arguments with a view to the square itself and the diagonal itself, not the diagonal they draw, and similarly with the others. The very things they make and draw, of which shadows and reflections in water are images, they now in turn use as images, in seeking to see those other things themselves that one cannot see except by means of thought.... This, then, is the kind of thing that I said was intelligible. The soul is forced to use hypotheses in the investigation of it, not traveling up to a first principle, since it cannot escape or get above its hypotheses, but using as images those very things of which images were made by the things below them, and which, by comparison to their images, were thought to be clear and to be honored as such. (6, 510c2–511a9)

If mathematics were a perception-based craft, it could "get above its hypotheses," by means of visible paradigms in the way that it attempts to do by using these as images. It could present our perception with the very things it cannot give an account of. But because its first principles are summoners, this approach will not work. The distinction between nonsummoners and summoners thus tracks the distinction between perception-based and hypothesis-based crafts. Hence, having diagnosed in *Republic* 5 why ethical wisdom cannot be perception based, it is precisely to a comparable critique of hypothesis-based crafts that Socrates turns in *Republic* 6. It is at this point that his own human wisdom reenters the picture.

8. Calculation and geometry are crafts at *Chrm.* 165e5–6, arithmetic at *Tht.* 198a5.

Hypothesis-Based Crafts and Dialectic

Socrates' alternative to leaving first principles as unproven hypotheses is to employ the craft of dialectic (*Phdr.* 276e5–6) to render them unhypothetical:

> By the other subsection of the intelligible I mean what reason itself grasps by the power of dialectical discussion, treating its hypotheses not as first principles, but as genuine hypotheses (that is, stepping stones and links in a chain), in order to arrive at what is unhypothetical and the first principle of everything. Having grasped this principle, it reverses itself and, keeping hold of what follows from it, comes down to a conclusion, making no use of anything visible at all, but only of forms themselves, moving on through forms to forms, and ending in forms. (6, 511b3–c2)

So while mathematics treats its first principles as hypotheses, dialectic uses them as stepping stones to what is unhypothetical and then uses this to establish the other principles in an unhypothetical way.

Since the "unhypothetical first principle of everything" is the good itself, which, as "the final goal of the intelligible," is the pinnacle of dialectic's upward path (7, 535a5–b2), the first problem is to explain how the good itself can be reached from the first principles of *mathematics*.[9] Once the good itself is reached, the second problem is to explain how the first principles of mathematics are to be rendered unhypothetical by it. The third problem is to explain why the objection Socrates raises to mathematics cannot also be raised against dialectic itself.

To see how Socrates proposes to solve these problems, we naturally turn for assistance to the allegory of the sun, beginning with the part that deals with knowledge, since it provides our best clue to the nature of the good itself:

> You must say, then, that what gives truth to the things known and the power to know to the knower is the form of the good. And as the cause of knowledge and truth, you must think of it as an object of knowledge. Both knowledge and truth are beautiful things. But if you are to think correctly, you must think of the good as other and more beautiful than they. In the visible realm, light and sight are rightly thought to be sun-like, but wrongly thought to be the sun. So here it is right to think of knowledge and truth as good-like, but wrong to think that either of them is the good—for the state of the good is yet more honored. (6, 508e1–509a4)

9. Aristotle refers to this problem: "In mathematics nothing is proved by means of this kind of [final] cause, nor is there any demonstration [appealing to] 'because it is better (or worse),' indeed, no one ever mentions anything of this sort" (*Met.* 3.2, 996a29–32).

The good is like a self-illuminating object, then, that can shed the intelligible analogue of light on other objects of knowledge in such a way as to render them intelligible, too. It is an intelligible object that is somehow a condition of the intelligibility of other things. This suggests that the light it gives off is something like rational order or logical structure, and that it itself is a paradigm of such order.[10] Whereas beauty is literally incandescent, and so accessible to some extent to perception, goodness is only metaphorically so. For beauty is somewhat visible to the eye, but goodness, as an entirely intelligible object, is visible only to the eye of the mind.

To make this aspect of goodness a little less metaphorical, let's suppose that we have a true definition or account of a form F that tells us what *is* F, and that is a first principle of some craft or science. Because this account is true, and the craft's other principles follow from it, it must exhibit whatever pattern of rational order or logical structure is required to guarantee that it has these two features—at a minimum, it must be consistent. Because such an account is made true by a form, this form must, at a minimum, possess the level of rational order that is an ontological correlate of consistency. As the form or paradigm of rational order, the good itself is an object of knowledge like any other form, but since there would be no truth, and so no knowledge, without it, it is the cause of truth and knowledge, and so is "other…than they are." Furthermore, as the very paradigm of rational order, it is "the brightest thing that is" (7, 518c9–d1) and so is more beautiful than knowledge or truth.

Besides this epistemological side, the allegory of the sun also has a metaphysical side that attempts to capture the role of the good not just in explaining the truth or intelligibility of knowable objects but in explaining their very existence and being:

> The sun, I think you would say, not only gives visible things the power to be seen but also provides for their coming-to-be, growth, and nourishment—although it is not itself coming-to-be.…Therefore, you should also say that the objects of knowledge not only owe their being known to the good but their existence and being are also due to it, although the good is not being, but something yet beyond being, superior to it in rank and power. (6, 509b2–10)

Visible things—including the sun—are components of the visible realm, but the sun has a very special role therein: without it there would be no such realm. The same holds of the good considered as a paradigm of rational order.

10. See John M. Cooper, "The Psychology of Justice in Plato," in his *Reason and Emotion: Essays on Ancient Moral Psychology and Ethical Theory* (Princeton: Princeton University Press, 1999), pp. 138–150.

Like other forms it is a component of the intelligible realm, but, unlike them it is a condition of the existence or being of the realm itself, since if there were no rational order, nothing could be intelligible. That explains why the good is characterized as "beyond being, superior to it in rank and power."

"The natural aim of a craft is to consider and provide what is advantageous" for the things with which it naturally deals, such as human bodies in the case of medicine or sailors in the case of captaincy (1, 341d7–8). *Good-relatedness* is thus a defining feature of craft. But so, too, is *hierarchicalization*, which is the phenomenon of one craft, C_n, producing the raw materials for another, C_{n+1}, as the miller produces flour for the baker. As a user of the products of C_n, C_{n+1} has a role to play in it, specifying the kinds of products it needs as raw materials in order to produce good or high-quality products of its own:

> For each thing there are these three crafts, one that will use, one that will make, one that will imitate.... Then aren't the virtue, goodness, and correctness of each manufactured item, living creature, and activity related to nothing but the use for which each is made or naturally developed?... So it is entirely necessary, then, that the user of each thing has the most experience of it, and that he inform the maker about what the good and bad points are in actual use of the thing he uses. For example, it is the flute-player, I take it, who informs the flute-maker about which flutes respond well in actual playing, and prescribes how they should be made, while the maker obeys him.... Doesn't the one who knows give information, then, about good and bad flutes, whereas the other, by relying on him, makes them?... So, as regards the same manufactured item, its maker—through associating with the one who knows and having to listen to the one who knows—has correct belief about its good and bad qualities, while its user has knowledge. (10, 601d1–602a1)

Since a single craft may draw its raw materials from a variety of others, C_m may also stand to C_{n+1} in this sort of relationship. The idea of a master or superordinate craft that uses the products of all other subordinate crafts is naturally suggested.

But uses them to do what? That question is answered by good-relatedness: since all crafts aim at some good, the superordinate craft must aim at some sort of superordinate good. Notice how readily Aristotle makes the parallel assumption about practical and productive sciences, attributing both hierarchicalization and good-relatedness to craft in a single breath:

> Every craft... is believed to seek some good.... But since there are many sorts... of crafts and sciences, their ends turn out to be many as well; for health is the end of medicine, a ship of shipbuilding, victory of generalship, wealth of household

management. But some of these fall under some one capacity, as bridle making falls under horsemanship, along with all the others that produce equipment for horsemanship, and as it and every action in warfare fall under generalship—and, in the same way, others fall under different ones, and in all such cases the ends of the architectonic ones are more choiceworthy than the ones falling under them, since these are pursued for the sake also of the former. (*NE* 1.1, 1094a1–16)

On the admittedly controversial assumption that there is a single such hierarchy of crafts, and a single superordinate craft, as Aristotle also believes (*NE* 1.2, 1094a23–b7), we may speak of *the* craft hierarchy.

We see these ideas in operation throughout Plato's works, but their employment in the *Euthydemus* is particularly illuminating. Happiness or doing well, which is what all people want (278e3–6), consists in the possession and correct use of good things (279a2–282a4). Hence there is no "benefit to be gained from any of the...sciences—moneymaking, medicine, or whatever—unless it knows how to use what it makes" (289a4–7). Thus only the superordinate craft—the one that does not need to draw on another higher level craft in order to know how correctly to use its own products—really produces a benefit, really makes us happy. Could this craft be "the craft of making speeches"? Is *it* the craft "whose possession is bound to make us happy" (289c6–8)? No. For even though it is "superhuman and sublime" (289e3–4), it does not know how to use the speeches that it knows how to compose. Is, then, "generalship...the craft whose possession would bring happiness" (290b1–2)? No. For when generals have finished "hunting a city or an army, they make way for politicians, because they themselves do not know how to use their quarry" (290d1–3). Thus politics emerges as a candidate superordinate craft.

On the way to that candidate, a different hierarchy of crafts also emerges:

> Geometers, astronomers, and calculators...are [like generals] also hunters, for each of them is engaged not in making diagrams, but in discovering the things that *are*, and inasmuch as they do not know how to use them, but only how to hunt them down, they—at least, however many of them are not entirely without understanding—hand them over to dialecticians to use them to the full. (290b10–c6)

Socrates attributes the introduction of both hierarchies to Cleinias. But Crito, to whom he is reporting the conversation, is incredulous: "What are you saying, Socrates? Did that young man really assert all that?" (290e1–2). It is a challenge to Socrates' reliability that is unique in Plato. In response, Socrates acknowledges the uncertainty of his memory and tries a different answer: "Perhaps it was Ctesippus who said it" (290e7–8). That suggestion, too, is dismissed with incredulity. "Do you think," he asks in the end, "that some superior being was there to assert it?" (291a3–4). Though the phrase "superior being" usually refers to gods (*Sph.* 216b4; *Lg.* 4, 718a5), here it seems to be a joking reference to Plato himself (or the reformed Socrates as his representative), since—as we are about to see—the views expressed are apparently his own.

The mathematicians are not diagram-makers but hunters of the things that *are*—the things that their diagrams represent. But while they know how to hunt these things down, they do not know how "to use them to the full." That is why, if they are wise, they hand them over to dialecticians, who do know how to use them. Since the things that *are* are forms, however, the only way to hand them over is in an account. So it is the accounts of these forms that the dialectician effectively knows how to use:

> Who or what provides us with the names we use?...Don't you think that the law provides us with them?...So when an instructor uses a name, he is using the product of a lawgiver....It isn't every man who can give names...but only a name-maker, and he, it seems, is the lawgiver, the kind of craftsman most rarely (*spaniōtatos*) found among human beings....And who can best supervise the work of a lawgiver, whether here or abroad, and judge its products? Isn't it whoever will use them?...And isn't that the person who knows how to ask questions?...And he also knows how to answer them?...And what would you call someone who knows how to ask and answer questions? Wouldn't you call him a dialectician?...But it's the work of a lawmaker, it seems, to make a name. And if names are to be given well, a dialectician must supervise him. (*Cra.* 388d9–390d5)

Notice that this also suggests a way to integrate the two hierarchies that emerged in the *Euthydemus*. The lawgiver is a politician, but he must be supervised by the dialectician if he is do his work well. Consequently, the wise mathematicians and the general, in the end, hand over their captives to the same man—the one the *Republic* will identify as the philosopher-king.[11] The identification is hinted at even in the earlier dialogue, when the wisdom that ensures the correct use of good things is called *philosophia* (*Euthd.* 282c5–d3).

---

11. The adjective *spanios*, which is used to characterize the lawgivers at *Cra.* 389a2, and which is itself quite rare in Plato's works, is used twice in the *Republic* (5, 476b11; 6, 503d11); both times to refer to philosopher-kings.

In the *Euthydemus*, correct use is connected to happiness, since using a good thing correctly or to the full is using it to further happiness in the most effective way. In the *Cratylus*, use is—in one significant case, at least—a matter of being able to ask and answer questions correctly. But the one significant case has general repercussions. For even a craft like weaving will not be correctly practiced unless it is practiced as the superordinate craft of politics, and so of dialectic, requires. Even the correct use of so mundane an implement as a shuttle depends, therefore, on the correct use of words—on dialectic.

Just what dialectic is, though, must be inferred from descriptions that are not quite as explicit as we might wish. Here is the longest of them:

> Then isn't this at last...the theme itself that dialectical discussion sings? It itself is intelligible. But the power of sight imitates it. We said that sight tries at last to look at the animals themselves, the stars themselves, and, in the end, at the sun itself. In the same way, whenever someone tries by means of dialectical discussion, and without the aid of any sense-perceptions, to arrive through reason at the being of each thing itself, and does not give up until he grasps what good itself *is* with understanding itself, he reaches the end of the intelligible realm, just as the other reached the end of the visible one....Well, then, don't you call this journey (*poreia*) dialectic?...Then the release from bonds and the turning around from shadows to statues and the light, and then the ascent out of the cave to the sun, and there the continuing inability to look directly at the animals, the plants, and the light of the sun, but instead at divine reflections in water and shadows of the things that *are*, and not, as before, merely at shadows of statues thrown by another source of light that, when judged in relation to the sun, is as shadowy as they—all this practice of the crafts we mentioned has the power to lead the best part of the soul upwards until it sees the best among the things that *are*, just as before the clearest thing in the body was led to the brightest thing in the bodily and visible world....And mustn't we also insist that the power of dialectical discussion could reveal it only to someone experienced in the subjects we described, and cannot do so in any other way?...At the very least, no one will dispute our claim by arguing that there is another road of inquiry that tries to acquire a systematic and wholly general grasp of what each thing itself *is*. By contrast, all the other crafts are concerned with human beliefs and appetites, with growing or construction, or with the care of growing or constructed things. As for the rest, we described them as to some extent grasping what *is*—I mean, geometry and the subjects that follow it. For we saw that while they do dream about what *is*, they cannot see it wide-awake as long as they make use of hypotheses which they leave undisturbed, and of which

they cannot give any account. After all, when the first principle is unknown, and the conclusion and the steps in between are put together out of what is unknown, what mechanism could possibly turn any agreement reached in such cases into knowledge? (*R.* 7, 532a1–533d1)

Hence, though dialectic must pass through mathematics on its way to the good, it is not restricted in its origins to mathematics; its philosopher practitioner must also pass through the other uncontroversially good-related types of craft as well. There is no question of the philosopher reaching the good itself from mathematics alone—Socrates refers to "calculation, geometry, and *all the preparatory education* that serves as preparation for dialectic" (7, 536d4–5). Moreover, because the good itself is reached from these various origins, it must be of quite general application. It must serve as a measure of good proofs, but it must also serve as a measure of good laws, good political institutions, good poems, and good people. If one asks what sort of good this could be, one is bound to be led toward syncategorematic notions, such as unity, harmony, or—to use the notion we introduced earlier—rational order. But if rational order is the good, mathematics will itself emerge as good related, since it studies patterns of such order.

That Socrates is led in the same direction is clear. In the *Philebus*, the good itself is said to be found "somewhere in the area of measure" (66a6–7). In the *Timaeus*, the god "desiring that all things should be good, . . . took over all that is visible . . . and brought it from disorder into order, since he judged that order was in every way the better" (30a2–6). In the *Gorgias*, Callicles' immoral advocacy of "doing better (*pleonexia*)" is diagnosed as a consequence of his having neglected geometry, which would have shown him that it is "geometrical [or proportionate] equality," not doing better, that makes "this universe a world-*order* . . . and not a world-*disorder*" (507e6–508a8). In essence, this is the answer to the first problem we raised about how the good itself, as a paradigm or measure of goodness generally, could be reached from the first principles of mathematics.

This brings us to the third of the problems we discussed. To avoid being subject to the same criticism as mathematics and other hypothesis-based crafts, dialectic cannot leave the good itself unproven. Yet how can it avoid doing so, since the good itself is an elusive first principle? Socrates offers us a clue when he implies that the alternative to treating something as a hypothesis is to refute all the objections that can be raised against it: "in order to avoid going through all these objections one by one and taking a long time to prove them all untrue, let us hypothesize that this is correct and carry on" (4, 437a4–8). Moreover, being able to defend the good itself in this way is precisely what is required of a philosopher:

> Unless someone can give an account of the form of the good, distinguishing it from everything else, and can survive all examination (*elegchōn*) as if in a battle, striving to examine (*elegchein*) things not in accordance with belief, but in accordance with being, and can journey through all that with his account still intact, you will say that he does not know the good itself or any other good whatsoever. And if he does manage to grasp some image of it, you will say that it is through belief not knowledge that he grasps it, that he is dreaming and asleep throughout his present life, and that, before he wakes up here, he will arrive in Hades and go to sleep forever. (7, 534b8–d1)

What makes a first principle unhypothetical isn't a demonstration of it from something else, then, but a dialectical defense of it against all objections—something that can only be given if the principle itself is (at least) elenchus resistant. So it is the elenchus, or a descendant of it (notice the double use of *elegchein* in the passage), that proves to be the philosopher's distinctive craft.

A defense of this sort is not the same thing, obviously, as a demonstration *from* first principles of the sort that we find in Euclid's geometry. Aristotle tells us that Plato was well aware of this:

> We must not forget that arguments leading *from* first principles and arguments leading *to* first principles are different. Plato too was rightly puzzled about this: he would examine whether the road (*hodos*) was leading from first principles or to first principles, just as in a stadium that of the athletes may lead away from the starting-point toward the boundary or in the reverse direction. (*NE* 1.4, 1095a30–b1)

In discussing his own ultimate first principle, the principle of noncontradiction, Aristotle acknowledges that it cannot be *unconditionally* demonstrated, since no science can demonstrate its own first principles in that way (*Met.* 11.5, 1062a2–5), but it can, he claims, be demonstrated "by refutation (*elegktikōs*)" (*Met.* 4.4, 1006a12) or "against someone" (*Met.* 11.5, 1062a3). This, we might think, is the status we should accord to a dialectical defense of the good itself: it cannot be an unconditional demonstration, but it can be an elenctic one. Interestingly, it is the principle of noncontradiction that Socrates is discussing when he implies that the alternative to treating something as a hypothesis is to refute all objections to it (4, 436e7–437a8).

Crafts, whether hypothesis based or perception based, are all part of the craft hierarchy. Consequently, successful demonstrations of their first principles from the good itself must enable them to be consistently integrated into it. The very mark of a dialectician, indeed, is an ability to take such a unified view of things:

> The subjects they learned in no particular order in their education as children, they must now bring together into a unified vision of their kinship with one another and with the nature of what *is*. That, at any rate, is the only instruction that remains secure in those who receive it. . . . [This] is the greatest test of which nature is dialectical and which is not. For the person who can achieve a unified vision is dialectical, and the one who cannot isn't. (7, 537c1–7)

So we might think of rational order as itself being cashed out somewhat like this. The dialectician recasts the entire craft hierarchy as a formal system in which all accounts of first principles are assigned such logical forms (or patterns of rational order) as are determined by the rules of inference for the system. The good itself, as the very paradigm of logical form, will also exhibit it. It will, therefore, be consonant with all the subordinate goods that are the first principles of the subordinate crafts in the hierarchy. More particularly, they will all share in the very form—the very pattern of rational order—that makes the good itself unhypothetical, and so will themselves become unhypothetical principles, worthy sources not just of belief but of knowledge.

Desire and Pleasure

Because the good is an object of desire, not just of theoretical cognition, it cannot be an unhypothetical first principle unless it can be shown to be an unhypothetical object of desire—something desirable for its own sake and for whose sake other things are desired. If the good itself is specified as a paradigm good thing, or as the best good of all, this problem can be readily solved. For the analytic or conceptual connection holding between the possession of good things and being happy—a connection it would be stupid or simple minded to deny—ensures that the good itself, as both the best thing and a cognitively reliable paradigm of the goodness of everything else, must be an unhypothetical object of desire (*Euthd.* 278e3–279a4; *Smp.* 204e2–205a4; *R.* 6, 505d5–e4). What this connection does not do is admit of trivial extension to an actual candidate good itself that is specified in other terms. For example, it does not trivially extend to rational order.

Consequently, if those who were in the best position to judge found that the most rationally ordered life was less pleasant (say) than a less ordered one, that would seem to pose a serious challenge to the claim that the good just is rational order. For how could we accept something as the good life for us that we experienced as less than good from the inside?

Aware of the need to deal with this sort of challenge, Socrates undertakes to prove that the philosopher's characteristic pleasure—the pleasure of knowing the truth and so of knowing the good itself—is most pleasant of all. His argument has both a subjective side, based on experience, and an objective one, based on the nature of epistemic authority. The subjective side acknowledges that people disagree about what sort of life is most pleasant. Money-lovers, because of how their soul is ruled, think that a life focused on food, drink, sex, and the money needed to get them is "more pleasant and free from pain," whereas honor-lovers and philosophers, because of how their souls are ruled, think that lives devoted to victories and honors or to learning and knowing the truth have this status (9, 580d7–582a2). The resulting dispute seems impossible to settle, because it seems to hinge wholly on subjective claims. Not so, Socrates argues. Judgments about pleasure are no different from judgments about other things: the only criterion to use in making them is "experience, wisdom, and reason" (9, 582a5–6). Hence the philosopher's judgment should be trusted, since he is wise, ruled by reason, and has experienced appetitive and spirited pleasures since childhood, whereas "the pleasure pertaining to the sight of what is cannot be tasted by anyone except the philosopher" (9, 582c7–9). The problems with this argument are twofold. First, the philosopher cannot claim to know what appetitive or spirited pleasures feel like to true devotees who spend their lives exploring them. This weakens his authority. Moreover, the crucial claim that an appetitive or spirited person cannot know the philosopher's pleasure seems suspect. Glaucon concedes only that the former, "even if he were eager to taste it, could not *easily* do so" (9, 582b4–5).

This point is worth developing. A nonphilosopher, such as an appetitive or spirited person, can be just as intelligent as a philosopher (7, 519a1–b5). If he lives in a city where the highest rewards in money or honor go to the best dialecticians, he will have a powerful incentive to acquire an education of the sort provided to philosophers in Kallipolis, since it will be the best means to the money or honor he desires (9, 580e5–581a1). If he does acquire such an education, he can surely come to know the ideal of rational order the philosopher calls the good. (If not, why not?) Suppose he does. What is to ensure that he won't continue to think his favorite pleasures more pleasant than the philosophic ones? What is to ensure that he will not refuse to identify the ideal of rational order he has come to know with the good, since knowing or contemplating it does not provide him with the most pleasant pleasures? If the answer is "nothing," Socrates' claim that the philosopher's judgment about the relative pleasantness of pleasures will be undercut. For the nonphilosopher will have the same credentials as the philosopher but will disagree with him about which pleasures are most pleasant and so about what the good is. Thus Socrates must show that one cannot know the ideal of rational order without finding the knowledge of it both intrinsically pleasant and intrinsically more pleasant than anything else.[12] His account of pleasure, advertised as constituting "the greatest and most decisive of the overthrows" (9, 583b6–7) seems intended to show precisely this.

Desires, it familiarly claims, are kinds of states of emptiness of either the body or the soul (9, 585a8–b4), and pleasure is having those emptinesses appropriately filled (9, 585d11). One pleasure is more pleasant than another, or a truer pleasure, if it is a case of "being more filled with things that *are* more" (9, 585d12–e1). Thus, having the emptiness that is one's rational desire to know the good appropriately filled is more pleasant than having the emptiness that is one's appetitive desire for food appropriately filled. For the food, by being digested, will soon cease to fill that emptiness, whereas the good itself, since it is eternally and perfectly good, will suffer no such fate. Hence a nonphilosopher cannot both know the good itself and continue to find appetitive or spirited pleasures more pleasant than philosophic ones. The very nature of pleasure rules it out.

A question arises at this point that is analogous to the famous one raised in the *Euthyphro* about whether what is pious is pious because it is loved by the gods or loved by the gods because it is pious (10a5–11b5). We might put it like this: Is the good itself good because of the rational order of which it is the paradigm? Or is it good because of the pleasure that knowing or contemplating it involves? Is some form of rationalism or intellectualism the correct account of the good? Or some form of hedonism? In the *Philebus*, one of his latest works, Plato has Socrates confront this problem head on. The task is the Euthydemean one of showing "some possession or state of the soul to be the one that can render life happy for all human beings" (11d4–6). This possession or state will then be "the good...in human beings" (64a1). The contenders are, first, "pleasure, amusement, enjoyment, and whatever else is of that kind" (19c7–8); second, "understanding, knowledge, comprehension, craft, and everything that is akin to them" (19d4–5); and third, "a mixture of pleasure with understanding and wisdom" (22a1–3). Pleasure alone is ruled out, because without correct belief, you "wouldn't believe that you are enjoying yourself even when you are," and without the ability to rationally

12. See my *Philosopher-Kings*, pp. 95–100.

calculate, "you wouldn't be able to rationally calculate any future pleasures for yourself" (21c4–6). Similarly, knowledge alone cannot be the good in human beings, since no one "would choose to live in possession of every kind of wisdom, understanding, knowledge, and memory of all things, while having no part, whether large or small, of pleasure or pain" (21d9–e1). Hence neither the hedonism advocated by Philebus nor the intellectualism defended by Socrates yields a correct account of what the good in human beings is (22c1–4).

When we turn from this good to the good in the gods, there is much in the *Philebus* to encourage us to think that intellectualism is the correct account of it and that their life is a pleasureless one of understanding, wisdom, and knowledge alone.[13] At one point, for example, Socrates mentions with approval a life he describes as consisting of "neither pleasure nor pain, but of thinking wise thoughts (*phronein*) in the purest degree possible" (55a6–8). Earlier he says that it would be "unseemly (*aschēmon*)" for the gods to experience either pleasure or pain (33b10–11). Were these remarks best understood as positively excluding all pleasure from the life of the gods, however, it would be unsettling, to say the least. The gods, after all, are supposed to be the happiest of beings: "the divine paradigm is supremely happy" (*Tht.* 176e3–4). Yet few would think them so if their lives were pleasureless: it is a proof that the philosopher's life is most pleasant, remember, that provides the most decisive proof that his life is also the happiest (9, 583b6–7). Moreover, God is supremely just: "God is not at all or in any way unjust, but as just as can be, and there is nothing more like him than any one of us who becomes in his own turn as just as possible" (*Tht.* 176b8–c3). But if he could be supremely just without being supremely happy, as it seems he would be if his justice involved no pleasure, it is hard to see why the same could not be true of us. Socrates' response to Glaucon's challenge would then be undermined, and with it the entire argument of the *Republic* and the eudaimonistic conception of ethics that pervades it and the other dialogues.[14] Hence it is with some relief that we find pleasure being explicitly attributed to one divine being, namely, the demiurge responsible for the creation of the universe:

> Now when the father who had begotten the universe observed it set in motion and alive, a thing that had come into being as an image (*agalma*) of the

---

13. Dorothea Frede, *Plato: Philebus* (Indianapolis: Hackett, 1993), defends this view, writing that pleasure "is at best a remedial good, and…the state of pleasureless imperturbability is actually preferable" (xlii).

14. The threat to eudaimonism is generally overlooked by those who defend the view that the *Philebus* does exclude pleasure from the life of the gods.

everlasting gods, he was well pleased, and in his delight he thought of making it yet more like the paradigm he had copied in making it. (*Ti.* 37c6–d1)

It is with relief, too, that we find Socrates talking about the role of knowledge, pleasure, and their mixture not just in human life but in the lives of "gods and human beings" (*Phlb.* 65b1–2).

What has happened in the meantime to make this sort of talk intelligible is that the "tribe of pleasures" (65e2) has undergone much sorting out. Some of its members, such as appetitive ones, are indeed pleasures it would be unseemly to attribute to the gods. Others have emerged as not like that at all. Here is how wisdom and understanding—now personified and being questioned by Socrates—describe them:

> Will you have any need to associate with the strongest and most intense pleasures, we will say, in addition to the true ones? Why on earth should we need them, Socrates, they might reply. They are a tremendous impediment to us, since they infect the souls they dwell in with madness or even prevent our own development altogether. Furthermore, they totally destroy most of our offspring, since neglect leads to forgetfulness. But as to the true pleasures you mentioned, those we regard as our kin. And besides, also add the pleasure of health and of temperance and all those that commit themselves to virtue as to their god and follow it around everywhere. But to forge an association between understanding and those pleasures that are forever involved with lack of wisdom would be totally unreasonable for anyone who aims at the most stable mixture or blend. That is true particularly if he wants to discover in this mixture what the good is in man and in the universe and to get some hunch about the nature of the good itself. (63d1–64a3)

Apparently, then, the true pleasures, which are akin to wisdom and understanding and are "attached to the various sorts of knowledge" (66b5–6), should be included with these even in the lives of the gods. So when Socrates earlier divides off the pure pleasures—those unmixed with pain—from the impure ones, and the violent and intense ones from "the measured (*emmetrian*) ones" (52c4), he includes the pure and moderate ones in "the class of things that possess measurement (*emmetrōn*)" (52c1–d1). That is why it is only if these pleasures alone are included in the mixture that we will discover in it "some hunch" about the good itself, which is "somehow connected with measure (*metron*) and the measured (*metrion*)" (66a6–8). No doubt it is also why pleasure—at any rate, of the measured and true sort—is included on the list of genuinely good things with which the dialogue concludes (66b4–6).[15]

One other problem that the *Philebus* raises also stems in part from the account of pleasure that the *Republic* defends:

> Every process of generation...always takes place for the sake of some particular being, and...all generation taken together takes place for the sake of the existence of being as a whole....Now pleasure, if indeed it turns out to be a kind of generation, comes to be for the sake of some being....But that for whose sake something comes to be ought to be put into the class of good things, while that which comes to be for the sake of something else belongs in another class....So if pleasure is indeed a kind of generation, will we be placing it correctly, if we put it in a class different from that of the good?...We ought to be grateful, then, to the person who indicated to us that there is always only generation of pleasure and that it has no being whatsoever. And it is obvious that he will laugh at those who claim that pleasure is a good thing....But this same person will also laugh at those who find their fulfillment in processes of generation....I mean those who cure their hunger or anything else that is cured by a process of generation. They take delight in generation as a pleasure and proclaim that they would not want to live if they were not subject to hunger and thirst and if they could not experience all the other things one might want to mention in connection with such conditions. But would we not all say that destruction is the opposite of generation?...So whoever makes this choice would choose generation and destruction in preference to that third life, which consists of neither pleasure nor pain, but is a life of thinking wise thoughts (*phronein*) in the purest degree possible. (54c2–55a8)

If we take this passage to be about all pleasures, we will have to conclude that the third life, which we have already looked at briefly, is pleasure free. Yet its insistence on associating pleasure with hunger, thirst, and the like, and its carefully conditional formulation of the claim that pleasure is a process of becoming, suggest a more cautious reading. Pleasure as a whole includes pleasures, such as the appetitive ones of eating, drinking, and sexual intercourse, that are processes of becoming—of filling up and emptying. For in their case there is no state of being filled, since no sooner is a point of satiation reached than emptying begins. Hence someone like Philebus, who identifies the good with pleasure as a whole, can be shown mistaken by appeal to such pleasures, even if other pleasures

---

15. See Emily Fletcher, "Plato on Pure Pleasure and the Best Life," retrieved from http://utoronto.academia.edu/EmilyFletcher/Papers/1120938/Plato_on_Pure_Pleasure_and_the_Best_Life.

are not like that. The third life—that of the purest kind of thinking wise thoughts—need not be devoid of all pleasure, therefore, but only of those pleasures that are processes of filling and emptying again. And this is what the identification of one measured, pure, and true pleasure as akin to and accompanying the exercise of wisdom seems to require. For that pleasure, apparently, is intrinsic to wisdom and inseparable from it. The question is, how can such a pleasure be a thing that *is* and its possessor avoid being enmeshed in becoming by enjoying it?

In another late dialogue, the *Sophist*, Plato raises a cognate question. The speaker is the Eleatic Visitor:

> If knowing is doing something, then necessarily what is known has something done to it. When being is known by knowledge...insofar as it is known it is changed by having something done to it—which we say couldn't happen to something that is at rest....But for heaven's sake, are we going to be convinced that it is true that change, life, soul, and wisdom are not present in that which completely *is* (*tō[i] pantelōs onti*) and that it neither lives nor thinks wise thoughts (*phronein*) but stays changeless, solemn, and holy, without any understanding?...Then are we going to say that it has understanding but doesn't have life?...Then are we saying that it has both these things while denying that it has them in its soul?...And are we saying that it has understanding, life, and soul but that it is at rest and completely changeless even though it is alive?...Then both what changes and change as well have to be admitted to be things that *are*. (248d10–249b3)

Consequently, there must be a kind of change or process—of which living, knowing, understanding, and thinking wise thoughts are examples—that something can undergo without jeopardizing its status as a being, a thing that *is*. Just what sort of process this could be needn't detain us, since Plato himself leaves its nature as a problem for his readers.[16] We need only note that it is precisely the sort of process that the pleasure of thinking wise thoughts would have to be in order to be included in a life that is itself a thing that *is*.

The good in human beings, as in the gods, seems to consist in the mixture of knowledge and pleasure that the *Republic* defends when it argues that the pleasure of knowing the truth is the best sort of happiness. The *cause* of the mixture's goodness (*Phlb.* 22c8–d4), on the other hand, the

16. See my "Motion, Rest, and Dialectic in the *Sophist*," *Archiv für Geschichte der Philosophie* 67 (1985): 47–64.

element whose "goodness makes the mixture itself a good one" (65a4–5), the "ingredient in the mixture that we ought to regard as most valuable and at the same time as the cause that makes it valuable to us" (64c5–7), is something else:

> Any kind of mixture that does not in some way or other possess measure or the nature of proportion will necessarily corrupt its ingredients and most of all itself. For there would be no blending at all in such cases but really an unconnected medley, the ruin of whatever happens to be contained in it. (64d9–e3)

Hence the good itself, as the cause of goodness, and the good of "the first rank," is what is "somehow connected with measure, and the measured, and the timely, and whatever else is to be considered similar to them" (66a6–8). For it is this that makes not only the mixture good but those pleasures that, because they are orderly, have a place in it.

The elusiveness of the good—to remind ourselves of that—was dramatized by the fact that the masses believe that pleasure is the good, but admit that there are bad pleasures, while the more refined believe the good is wisdom or knowledge but identify the wisdom in question as knowledge of the good. Rational order turns out to be the common element in the two accounts, uniting the masses and the more refined—the many and the wise. For rational order is at once what distinguishes good pleasures from bad ones, and what makes the good the first principle of knowledge and its primary object.

CHAPTER 9

✦

The Happiness of the Philosopher-Kings

Aided by Adeimantus, Glaucon challenges Socrates to show that justice pays higher eudaimonistic dividends to the individual who has it in his soul than does injustice. He later worries, however, that precisely because philosophers have just souls, they will consent to rule Kallipolis, even though they will "live a worse life when they could lead a better one" (7, 519d8–9) as a result. Unless we can persuade ourselves that his worry is baseless, we must either revise our understanding of his challenge or conclude that the entire project of the *Republic* is (wittingly or unwittingly) compromised or undermined. Since our earlier account of the challenge makes revision untenable, it is the worry we must confront.

Ships of State

The so-called ship-of-state simile in *Republic* 6 is the place to begin our investigation, though students of Glaucon's challenge seldom see it as relevant to their topic:

> Imagine that the following sort of thing happens either on one ship or on many. The ship-owner is taller (*megethei*) and stronger (*hrōmē*) than everyone else on board. But he is hard of hearing, a bit shortsighted, and his knowledge of seafaring is correspondingly deficient. The sailors are quarreling with one another about the captaincy. Each of them thinks that he should captain the ship, even though he has not yet learned the craft and cannot name his teacher or a time when he was learning it. Indeed, they go further and claim that it cannot be taught at all and are even ready to cut to pieces anyone who says it can. They are

always crowding around the ship-owner himself, pleading with him, and doing everything possible to get him to turn the rudder over to them. And sometimes, if they fail to persuade him, and others succeed, they execute those others or throw them overboard. Then, having disabled their noble (*gennaion*) ship-owner with mandragora or drink or in some other way, they rule the ship, use up its cargo drinking and feasting, and make the sort of voyage you would expect of such people. In addition, they praise anyone who is clever at persuading or forcing the ship-owner to let them rule, calling him a sailor, a skilled captain, and an expert about ships, while dismissing anyone else as good-for-nothing. They do not understand that a true captain must pay attention to the seasons of the year, the sky, the stars, the winds, and all that pertains to his craft, if he is really going to be expert at ruling a ship. As for *how* he is going to captain the ship, whether people want him to or not, they do not think it possible to acquire this craft or practice at the same time as the craft of captaincy. When that is what is happening on board ships, don't you think that a true captain would be sure to be called a stargazer, a useless babbler, and a good-for-nothing by those who sail in ships so governed? (6, 488a7–489a1)

James Adam tells us that the key to decoding the simile is this: "The *nauklēros* is the Demos [the masses], as Aristotle observed (*Rh.* III 4. 1406b35)....As the *nauklēros* owned his own ship..., it is right that the Demos should be *nauklēros* in a democracy....It is the *dēmagōgoi* (in the widest sense of the term, including demagogues, sophists etc.), and not the *dēmos* who are here attacked. With *megethei...kai hrōmē* compare *megalou kai ischurou* 493A."[1] Although Adam's proposal does go back to Aristotle and is widely enough accepted to be called the standard interpretation, it cannot be quite right.[2] The *dēmos* —the democratic masses— may be one analogue of the shipowner, but they cannot be the only one.

The first reason for this is that Socrates' expressed purpose is to convey what "the best philosophers experience in relation to *cities*" (6, 488a3), not what they experience in Athens or specifically democratic cities alone. The simile may be particularly apt as applied to democratic Athens, where the majority of philosophers were, in fact, found, but its application is clearly much broader.

---

1. Adam, *The Republic of Plato*, p. 9. I have transliterated the Greek in the quotation.
2. Two recent defenders are Giovanni Ferrari, *Plato: The Republic* (Cambridge: Cambridge University Press, 2000), p. 191 n. 4, and David Keyt, "Plato and the Ship of State," in *The Blackwell Guide to Plato's Republic*, ed. Gerasimos Santas (Oxford: Blackwell, 2006), pp. 189–213.

Second, the shipowner is *gennaios* (6, 488c4), noble or well-born, which is something the masses could be only in an ironical sense, as when Socrates refers to antilogic as a "noble (*gennaia*) power" (5, 454a1), or to "noble (*gennaia*) tyranny" (8, 544c6).[3] The people who are truly *gennaios* in the *Republic* are "the very small group" in actual cities, who "associate with philosophy in a way that is worthy of her," and who, because they possess "a noble and well brought-up character" (6, 496a10–b2), have the potential to become philosopher-kings (7, 535a9–b3). Similarly the "noble captain (*gennaion kubērnēton*)" mentioned in the *Statesman* is an image of "our kingly rulers" (279e9–11). The *gennaios* shipowner could be an analogue of the masses, then, but it needn't be an analogue of only them.

Third, the ruler in any city, whether democratic, oligarchic, or tyrannical, is always the stronger there (1, 338d9–10; compare *Lg.* 3, 690b4–8). Hence the descriptions Socrates gives of the shipowner, interpreted in Adam's way, are almost certain to fit any ruler or ruling group in any city or constitution. The fact that the masses are characterized as "the largest and most powerful class" in a democracy (8, 565a2–3) is not by itself conclusive evidence, therefore, that the shipowner, who is "taller (bigger) and stronger" than everyone else on board, is always just the democratic masses in disguise.

The fourth reason is that the *megalou kai ischurou*—the "huge, strong beast"—that Adam likens to the shipowner is not just the democratic masses considered as a specifically political entity, such as the Athenian assembly, but any gathering of a "mass of people in public," whether "in assemblies, courts, theaters, or army camps" (6, 492b5–7). Some of these gatherings certainly sound Athenian or democratic, but army camps have a distinctively Spartan ring. Besides, what is being described is not the specifically political power of the masses to captain or steer the ship of state, but the moral influence of public opinion (6, 492a1–c2). Socrates' point, as he puts it himself, is simply that there "is not now, never has been, or ever will be, a character whose view of virtue goes contrary to the education these people provide" (6, 492e3–4).

So much for preliminary criticism of the standard interpretation. Consider now the description of the young man with a philosophical nature:

> Right from the start, then, won't someone like that be first among the children in everything, especially if his body's nature matches that of his soul? . . . So as

---

3. In the *Apology*, Socrates famously likens himself to a gadfly on "a large and noble (*megalō[i] men kai gennai[ō]*) horse" (30e4), but here the horse is Athens, not the democratic masses as opposed to the aristocrats or oligarchs. Socrates is willing to examine almost anyone "alien or fellow citizen" (*Ap.* 23b5–6).

he gets older, I imagine his family and fellow citizens will want to make use of him in connection with their own affairs....They will get down on their knees, begging favors from him and honoring him, flattering ahead of time the power that is going to be his, so as to secure it for themselves....What do you think someone like that will do in such circumstances—especially if he happens to be from a great city where he is rich and well-born (*gennaios*) and is good-looking and tall (*megas*) as well? Won't he be filled with impractical expectations and think himself capable of managing the affairs not only of the Greeks but of the barbarians too? And won't he exalt himself to great heights, as a result, and be brimming with pretension and empty, senseless pride?...Now, suppose someone gently approaches a young man in that state of mind and tells him the truth, that he has no sense, although he needs it, and that it can't be acquired unless he works like a slave to attain it. Do you think it will be easy for him to hear that message through the evils that surround him?...And suppose that, because of his noble nature and his natural affinity with the arguments offered to him, a young man of that sort somehow sees the point and is turned around and drawn towards philosophy. What do you think those people will do, if they believe that they are losing his services and companionship? Is there anything they won't do or say in his regard to prevent him from being persuaded? Or anything they won't do or say in regard to his persuader to prevent him from succeeding, whether it is in private plots or public court cases?[4] (6, 494b5–e7)

"It has long been admitted that this picture is drawn chiefly from Alcibiades...Plato is portraying the type, although Alcibiades sits for the portrait."[5] For Alcibiades is "both the most beautiful and the tallest (*megistos*) man around" and from Athens' "leading family" (*Alc.* 104a5–7). Tall, nonironically well-born, courted by those who want to make use of him and who will destroy anyone who suggests that ruling is a craft that requires expertise and training—he is surely just as good an analogue of the shipowner as the masses are.

Why, then, it might be asked, is the shipowner described as "hard of hearing, a bit shortsighted," and with a knowledge of seafaring that is "correspondingly deficient"?[6] The answer is that these defects are part of the simile. They refer not to deafness, blindness, and deficient seafaring (which are genuine defects in a real ship's captain), but to their analogues in a political leader. Moreover, they are the results not of a noble

---

4. The trial of Socrates is the obvious case in point.
5. Adam, *The Republic of Plato*, p. 25.
6. See Mark L. McPherran, "Commentary on Reeve," *Proceedings of the Boston Area Colloquium in Ancient Philosophy* 22 (2006): 212–214.

nature, but of a noble nature corrupted by a bad upbringing. Alcibiades may think he knows how to captain the ship of Athens, but, in fact, he is a like a deaf, shortsighted ship's captain with deficient knowledge of how to steer a ship.

Goat-Stags

In the preamble to the simile, Socrates issues the following warning:

> What the best philosophers experience in relation to cities is so difficult to bear that there is no other single experience like it. On the contrary, one must construct one's simile, and one's defense of them, from *many* sources, just as painters paint goat-stags by combining the features of different things. (6, 488a2–7)

We might wonder why he bothers. For the simile doesn't seem to be remotely like a painting of a goat-stag. Yet the warning is important, precisely for that very reason: if the simile were obviously like a goat-stag, we wouldn't need it.[7] Now when painters paint goat-stags, what they do is combine (representations of) features that stags have with (representations of) features that goats have to produce a (composite representation of) a mythical animal of a new kind.[8] So we would expect the simile (the painting) to combine (analogues of) a sort of experience one type of philosopher has in relation to cities with (analogues of) a sort of experience another type of philosopher has in relation to cities, so as to produce (a composite analogue of) a sort of experience philosophers in general have in relation to cities in general. Just as the goat-stag painting as a whole represents no one actual sort of real animal, we would expect the ship simile as a whole to represent no one sort of real experience. Rather, as with the painting, parts of it should represent one sort, parts of it, another.

---

7. In *Plato and the Traditions of Ancient Literature* (Cambridge: Cambridge University Press, 2012), pp. 67–89, Richard Hunter looks at the possible historical sources of the simile, noticing the many other complex mythical beasts we find in Plato's dialogues, but he does not explain how the simile is like one of these beasts or why it has to be that way to represent what philosophers experience in cities.

8. Aristotle (*APr.* 1.38, 49a24; *APo.* 2.7, 92b7) follows Plato in treating goat-stags as mythical. Kenneth J. Dover, *Aristophanes: Frogs* (Oxford: Clarendon Press, 1993), p. 309, notes that the name also applies to a real genus "represented by several species in Europe and the Middle East."

Once the simile is complete, Socrates makes explicit use of it to characterize just one of these sorts of experience:

> I don't think that you need to examine the simile to see the resemblance to cities and their attitude towards true philosophers, but you already understand what I mean.... First tell this simile, then, to the person who is surprised that philosophers are not honored in cities, and try to persuade him that it would be far more surprising if they were honored.... And tell him that what you say is true, that the best among the philosophers are useless to the masses. But tell him to blame their uselessness on those who don't make use of them, not on those good philosophers. You see, it isn't natural for the captain to beg the sailors to be ruled by him, nor for the wise to knock at the doors of the rich. The man who came up with that bit of sophistry was lying.[9] What is truly natural is for the sick person, rich or poor, to knock at the doctor's door, and for anyone who needs to be ruled to knock at the door of the one who can rule him. It isn't for the ruler—if he is truly any use—to beg the subjects to accept his rule. Tell him he will make no mistake if he likens our present political rulers to the sailors we mentioned a moment ago, and those who are called useless stargazers to the true ship's captains. (6, 489a4–7)

This obvious reading is intended to explain why true philosophers are nonculpably useless to their cities, and succeeds in doing so once we see (or are told) that the sailors are the analogues of our present political rulers, while the ones they call useless star-gazers are the true ships' captains. We may conclude that to convey just this sort of experience, we really do not need to interpret—or find a particular analogue for—the shipowner at all. He simply represents the power on board the ship that determines where it will sail—a power usurped by the sailors when they take over the helm.

Socrates then turns to another sort of experience: "Do you next want us to discuss," he asks Adeimantus, "why it is inevitable that the greater number [of so-called philosophers] are bad, and try to show, if we can, that philosophy isn't responsible for this either?" (6, 489d10–e1). Here the shipowner *is* a functioning part of the simile. He represents the promising, young, naturally equipped philosopher who gets corrupted by the appetitive values of those citizens whose praise and blame shape his character, with the result that he will "call the same things beautiful or

9. When Simonides was asked whether it was better to be rich or wise, he replied: "Rich—because the wise spend their time at the doors of the rich" (Aristotle, *Rh.* 2.16, 1391a7–12).

ugly as these people, practice what they practice, and become like them"
(6, 492c7–9). When he achieves political power, he will steer the ship as
those values and their representatives direct, so that they—the sailors—
will determine where the ship should go.

Though shipowner and captain were typically different figures on board
Greek ships,[10] in the simile no captain is initially present (though the
sailors do eventually usurp the role). This absence is important. It allows
Plato to use the shipowner in a way that would otherwise lead to problems. In the first case we looked at, in which the shipowner has no specific
symbolic role, the true ships' captains are the true political rulers—the
philosophers. In the second, the shipowner stands for someone with a
philosophical nature—that is to say, for the person who, in the first case,
is the natural (but not the actual) captain.

Because Plato's ship is like this, and because his simile is intended to
convey the complex experience of philosophers in cities and not as ship-
of-state similes often are, to say something general and contentious about
political authority, it is immune to the kinds of objections commonly
made to it.[11] Critics are right that a captain does not set the goal or destination of the voyage but steers to where the shipowner decides; but they
are wrong to think that it should follow that true rulers do not set goals
for their city. All we are entitled to infer is that what such rulers experience at the hands of cities resembles what true captains experience at the
hands of people on relevantly similar ships. It follows, too, that we cannot
infer that Plato's true captain, "were he to win the helm of the unruly ship,
would sail, not for a destination of his own choosing, but for the very one
the shipowner wishes to reach."[12] Plato has simply encoded nothing whatever of that sort in his simile. Why, given his purposes, should he? Besides,
in his view, the true ship's captain—the philosopher—is steersman and
shipowner combined, determining both the ship's goal or destination and
how to sail there. Put another way, he steers only in cities he, so to speak,
owns or rules (4, 419a3–4 with 9, 592a7–8).

In the first case Plato describes, we see what happens to true captains at
the hands of those who sail on ships like the one in the simile. In the second, we see what happens to young men with a philosophical nature in the
cities that resemble such ships. In the third (if it is separate from the second), which we have not discussed, we see what happens when such men do

---

10. Keyt "Plato and the Ship of State," pp. 191–193.
11. For example, Michael Walzer, *Spheres of Justice* (New York: Basic Books, 1983),
pp. 286–287.
12. Keyt, "Plato and the Ship of State," p. 200.

not take up philosophy, but leave it "desolate and unwed" (6, 495c1): others take it up instead and bring disgrace on it. In the fourth, to which I now come, we discover what a different group of philosophers experiences:

> There remains, Adeimantus, only a very small group who associate with philosophy in a way that is worthy of her: a noble and well brought up character, perhaps, kept down by exile, who stays true to his nature and remains with philosophy because there is no one to corrupt him; or a great soul living in a small city who disdains the city's affairs and looks beyond them.[13] A very few are perhaps drawn to philosophy from other crafts that they rightly despise because they have good natures. And some might be held back by the bridle that restrains our friend Theages—you see, he meets all the other conditions needed to make him fall away from philosophy, but his physical illness keeps him out of politics and prevents it. Finally, my own case is hardly worth mentioning— my daimonic sign—since I don't suppose it has happened to anyone else or to only a few before. Now, those who have become members of this little group have tasted how sweet and blessed a possession philosophy is. At the same time, they have also seen the insanity of the masses and realized that there is nothing healthy, so to speak, in public affairs, and that there is no ally with whose aid the champion of justice can survive; that instead he would perish before he could profit either his city or his friends, and be useless both to himself and to others—like a man who has fallen among wild animals and is neither willing to join them in doing injustice nor sufficiently strong to oppose the general savagery alone. Taking all this into his calculations, he keeps quiet and does his own work, like someone who takes refuge under a little wall from a storm of dust or hail driven by the wind. Seeing others filled with lawlessness, the philosopher is satisfied if he can somehow lead his present life pure of injustice and unholy acts, and depart from it with good hope, blameless and content. (6, 496a11–e2)

The representative of these philosophers in the simile is not the reviled true captain, who, like Socrates but also like other philosophers (*Ap.* 23d4–7), is called a stargazer and idle babbler. Instead, it is someone who only may be on board—someone who suggests that the craft of captaincy (politics) is teachable; someone the sailors are ready to cut to pieces and cities ready to destroy by private intrigues or public court cases (6, 494b4–d3).

Even if shipowner and captain are different, the Socrates-figure in the simile implies that a truly philosophical captain will combine both roles.

---

13. This is not a description, notice, that could easily be applied to a philosopher in nonsmall city like democratic Athens.

Like the owner, he will know the best destination for the ship's voyage (the overall good for the ship or city). Like the captain, he will know how best to steer it there. This, I think, is the import of the obscure sentence: "As for *how* he is going to captain the ship, whether people want him to or not, they do not think it possible to acquire this craft or its practice at the same time as the craft of captaincy" (6, 488d8–e2).[14] While the sailors or citizens object to the existence of an end-neutral craft of captaincy or ruling—an analogue of what Aristotle calls "cleverness" (*NE* 6.12, 1144a23)—they are yet more skeptical about its including a component that determines ends. They think that even if a craft of politics did exist, it could never include both the effective capacity to rule and the ability to determine the goal or end the state should aim to achieve.

Philosophers in Actual Cities

The costs to this final group of naturally equipped philosophers of living in a city other than Kallipolis are variously characterized. In a suitable constitution, Socrates says, such a philosopher's "growth will be fuller and he will save the community as well as himself" (6, 497a3–5). His assessment a few lines later is similar: "no city, no constitution, and no individual man will ever become perfect until some chance event compels those few philosophers who are not vicious (the ones who are now called useless) to take care of a city, whether they are willing to or not, and compels the city to obey them" (6, 499b2–6). If we had just these texts to go on, we might infer that the costs involved are moderate—less than full growth, something short of perfection. In a third passage, which appears between them, we get the basis for a different estimation. "Which of our present constitutions," Adeimantus asks, "do you think is suitable for philosophy?" Socrates replies:

> None of them. But that is exactly my complaint. There is not one city today with a constitution worthy of the philosophic nature. That is precisely why it is turned around and altered. It is like foreign seed sown in alien ground: it tends to be overpowered and to fade away into the native species. Similarly, the philosophic species does not maintain its own power at present but declines into a different character. But if it were to find the best constitution, as it is itself the best, it would be clear that it is really divine and that other natures and pursuits are merely human. (6, 497b1–c4)

14. The sentence is difficult. Adam, *The Republic of Plato*, pp. 74–76, explores alternative interpretations and the problems they generate. On "whether people want him to or not," see *Plt.* 293a6–d2.

In all actual cities, not just democratic ones, the philosophic nature is turned around into one that is merely human, when in Kallipolis it could develop into one that is really divine—or as divine as it is possible for such a nature to be (6, 500c9–d2). Since the difference between the divine and the merely human is enormous for Socrates, the price paid by the philosopher in any city besides Kallipolis must surely be substantial.

In the *Apology*, when Socrates finally homes in on the meaning of the Delphic oracle's message to him, it turns out to be familiarly deflationary: the god alone is really wise; human wisdom, by comparison, is worth little or nothing (*Ap.* 23a5–b4). Yet it is the craftlike divine wisdom that true virtue requires: "wisdom is clearly virtue, either the whole of it or a part" (*Men.* 89a3–4). Becoming godlike, in consequence, is a matter of becoming virtuous and wise:

> It is mortal nature and our vicinity that are haunted by evils. And that is why we should also try to escape from here…as quickly as we can. To escape is to become like god so far as is possible, and to become like god is to become just and holy accompanied by wisdom. (*Tht.* 176a7–b3; compare *Phd.* 69a6–c3)[15]

Putting it the other way around, failure to become godlike is failure to become virtuous, which is a catastrophic failure indeed.

That it is an ethical catastrophe is obvious. That it is also a prudential one is guaranteed by the argument of the *Republic*, since its aim—as we are assuming until forced to think otherwise—is to show that psychic justice (justice considered as a state of the soul) pays higher eudaimonistic dividends than psychic injustice. The *Timaeus* makes this point in the most immediately pertinent terms:

> If someone has committed himself entirely to learning and to true wisdom, and it is these among the things at his disposal that he has most practiced, he must have immortal and divine wisdom, provided that he gets a grasp on truth. And so far as it is possible for human nature to have a share in immortality, he will not in any degree lack this. And because he always takes care of that which is divine, and has the daimon that lives with him well ordered, he will be outstandingly happy. (90b6–c6)

Divine wisdom, and so outstanding happiness, are available to the philosopher provided he has the opportunity afforded to him in Kallipolis

---

15. See David Sedley, "The Ideal of Godlikeness," in *Plato 2: Ethics, Politics, Religion, and the Soul*, ed. Gail Fine (Oxford: Oxford University Press, 2000), p. 312.

to develop his love of learning and grasp the truth. Life for a Kallipolian philosopher should be as close to life in the heavens, therefore, as life in any earthly city can be:

> Until philosophers rule as kings in their cities or those who are nowadays called kings and leading men become genuine and adequate philosophers, so that political power and philosophy become thoroughly blended together, while the numerous natures that now pursue either one exclusively are forcibly prevented from doing so, cities will have no rest from evils, my dear Glaucon, nor, I think, will the human race, nor will the same constitution (*politeia*) that we have now described in our discussion ever be born, to the extent that it can, or see the light of the sun. It is this claim that has made me hesitate to speak for so long; I saw how very unbelievable it would sound, since it is difficult to accept that *ouk an* [1] *allē* or [2] *allē(i) tis eudaimonēsein oute idia(i) oute dēmosia(i)*. (5, 473c11–e4)

About the claim that made Socrates hesitate to speak there can be no credible skepticism. It is that only rule by philosophers will bring certain desirable consequences—prominent among which is that the constitution of Kallipolis will be "born to the extent that it can." True, this constitution can exist in an individual soul as well as in a city (9, 590e4, 591e1; 10, 605b7–8, 608b1); nonetheless, it cannot be born fully *in either* unless philosophers rule a city. If we keep this firmly in mind, there will be less at stake in the interpretation of the final clause. If we accept (1) with the manuscripts, we will read *allē* as an adjective qualifying *politeia*, understood from the previous sentence. Socrates will then be claiming that what is difficult to accept is that there "can be no happiness, public or private, in any other constitution." And that could mean either that there can be no individual happiness outside Kallipolis, or outside a soul with a Kallipolis-like constitution. If, on the other hand, we follow the vast majority of editors and accept (2), we will read *allē(i)* as an adverb of manner or place. Socrates will then be claiming that it is difficult to accept that there "can be no happiness, public or private, in any other way (manner)" or "in any other constitution (place)."

When Socrates returns to the topic, however, there is no misinterpreting his intent:

> When the masses realize that what we are saying about him [the philosopher] is true, will they be harsh with philosophers or mistrust us when we say that there is no way a city can ever find happiness unless its plan is drawn by painters who use the divine model? (6, 500a11–e3)

What goes for cities, he tells us in a closely preceding passage, goes also for individuals:

> Neither city nor constitution and likewise no man either will become perfect until some lucky event compels those few philosophers who are not vicious (the ones who are now called useless) to take care of a city, whether they want to or not, and compels the city to obey them—or until a true passion for true philosophy flows by some divine inspiration into the sons of the men now wielding dynastic power or sovereignty or into the men themselves. (6, 499b3–c1; also 492e6–493a2)

That is why a naturally equipped philosopher in a city other than Kallipolis must be satisfied "if he can somehow lead his present life pure of injustice and unholy acts, and depart from it with good hope, blameless and content" (6, 496d9–e2). We are reminded, as we are intended to be, of Socrates, who, because he lived not in Kallipolis but in Athens, goes to his death with "good hope" (*Ap.* 41c8–9; also 40c4), confident only that he has never intentionally committed injustice against anyone (37a5–6).

A philosopher will be "willing" to rule in Kallipolis, Socrates says, but "he may not be willing to do so in his fatherland, *barring some stroke of divine luck*" (9, 592a5–8). The italicized clause—initially enigmatic—is explained by the two texts we have just discussed. The second (6, 499b3–c1) identifies the divine luck in question with whatever gets philosophers to rule (or rulers to become philosophers) "whether they want to or not"; the continuation of the first (6, 500a11–e3) specifies the sole condition under which they will want to:

> They would take the city and people's characters as their sketching slate but first they would wipe it clean, which is not at all an easy thing to do. And you should be aware that this is an immediate difference between them and others: that they refuse to take either a private individual or a city in hand, or to write laws, unless they receive a clean slate or are allowed to clean it themselves. (6, 501a2–7)

Hence the stroke of divine luck that makes philosophers willing to rule is being given a clean slate to work with or an opportunity to clean the one they have. The salient point for us, though, is that it could not be a stroke of *luck*, divine or otherwise, at any rate for the philosophers, if they would be better off not ruling a city at all.

Philosophers in Kallipolis

We are in a position now to reflect on the shape of the argument Plato is developing. Its core is this: to live in any actual city is (divine luck aside) an ethical and prudential—a eudaimonistic—disaster for anyone with a philosophical nature. So if a naturally gifted philosopher is to fulfill his nature, become truly virtuous, and achieve true happiness, it cannot be in any actual city, whether tyranny, democracy, oligarchy, or timocracy. Is he then to live outside a city altogether? It is a presupposition of the entire argument of the *Republic* that this cannot be the most prudent option. We all have needs we cannot satisfy by ourselves and so must live in a community with others (2, 369b5–c4). So when we turn to the immediately following discussion of the life of the natural philosopher in Kallipolis, it must be with the expectation that it will continue in the same prudentialist, eudaimonist vein. Such a philosopher will be happier there—we are being set up to conclude—than in any other city, and that means than anywhere else on earth.

If we ask what in particular about Kallipolis enables it alone of cities to have such a profound positive effect on those with a philosophic nature, we can give a brief answer. It is only there that everyone, including the future philosophers, has the enormous benefit of being ruled by reason from the very moment of his birth (if not before—remember eugenics):

> It is better for everyone to be ruled by a divine and wise ruler, preferably one that is his own and that he has inside himself, otherwise one imposed on him from outside, so that we may all be as alike and as friendly as possible, because we are all *captained* by the same thing....This is clearly the aim of the law as well, which is the ally of everyone in the city. It is also our aim in ruling our children. We do not allow them to be free until we establish a constitution in them as in a city. That is to say, we take care of their best part with the similar one in ourselves and equip them with a guardian and ruler similar to our own to take our place. Only then do we set them free. (9, 590d3–591a3)

The true captain, whether of a ship or a city, is thus the rational part of the soul—the wise and divine element within it, which alone knows and desires what is good both for each of the soul's three parts and for the complex whole they constitute, and so can steer them toward genuine happiness (4, 442b6–7, c5–8).

That the philosopher is supposed to have excellent prudential reasons to prefer Kallipolis to other cities, we may accept as Platonic doctrine.

The question is, does he really have them? Already in *Republic* 1 Socrates claims that ruling is a craft that benefits not its practitioners but its subjects, so that wages "must be provided to a person if he is going to be willing to rule, whether they are in the form of money or honor or a penalty if he refuses" (347a3–5). When Glaucon fails to understand what this penalty is or how it could be a wage, Socrates responds that the "best people" will not rule for money or honor, since lovers of these things are rightly despised (1, 347b1–4):

> So, if they are going to be willing to rule, some compulsion or punishment must be brought to bear on them.... Now the greatest punishment for being unwilling to rule is being ruled by someone worse than oneself. And I think it is fear of this that makes good people rule, when they do rule. They approach ruling not as though they were going to something good or as though they were going to enjoy themselves in it, but as something compulsory, since it cannot be entrusted to anyone better than—or even as good as—themselves. In a city of good men, if it came into being, the citizens would fight in order *not to rule*, just as they now do in order to rule. There it would be quite clear that anyone who is really and truly a ruler does not naturally seek what is advantageous for himself, but what is so for his subject. As a result, anyone with any sense would prefer to be benefited by another than to go to the trouble of benefiting him. (1, 347b9–e2)

But just as in the case of money-lovers and honor-lovers, what compels the best people to rule is reason in the form of rational self-interest: that is precisely why the compulsion is compatible both with voluntariness and with reluctance or lack of desire.[16] I desire (that is, anticipate with pleasure and as something good) listening to the Beaux Arts Trio playing Haydn this evening. I want (though do not desire in that full-blooded way) to have—and am willing to have—beneficial, but excruciatingly painful, root-canal surgery tomorrow morning. Similarly, the best people want to rule, rule willingly, but do not desire to rule. What is most salient about their motive for ruling, however, is that it is entirely negative: they rule out of fear of the worse, rather than desire for the good or better. For while they see ruling only as compulsory, money-lovers and honor-lovers—Socrates suggests by implicit contrast—see it as good or enjoyable.

---

16. David Sedley, "Philosophy, the Forms, and the Art of Ruling," in *The Cambridge Companion to Plato's Republic*, ed. G. R. F. Ferrari (Cambridge: Cambridge University Press, 2007), helped me to appreciate this.

In *Republic* 7, this argument (like others) from *Republic* 1 is redeployed in a subtly revamped form. First, we have "the best natures," rather than the best people, compelled to rule by the laws enacted by Socrates and Glaucon as "legislating founders" of Kallipolis (7, 519c8, e1). Second, we are given a different explanation of the motives such natures have to rule:

> Both *for your own sakes* and for the rest of the city, we have bred you to be leaders and kings in the hive, so to speak. You are better and more-completely educated than the others and better able to share in both types of life. So each of you in turn must go down to live in the common dwelling place of the other citizens and grow accustomed to seeing in the dark. For, when you are used to it, you will see infinitely better than the people there and know precisely what each image is and also what it is an image of, because you have seen the truth about fine, just, and good things. So the city will be awake, governed by us and by you, not dreaming like the majority of cities nowadays, governed by men who fight against one another over shadows and form factions in order to rule—as if that were a great good. No, the truth of the matter is surely this: A city in which those who are going to rule are least eager to rule is necessarily best and freest from faction, whereas a city with the opposite kind of rulers is governed in the opposite way. (7, 520b5–d4)

Unlike the best people, the best natures do not rule simply out of fear of the bad but to achieve the best not simply for their subjects but for themselves, too.[17]

Third, we learn that it is not enough that the best natures rule for these reasons they must, in addition, have something else to do that is better than ruling:

> If you can find a way of life that is better than ruling for those who are going to rule, your well-governed city will become a possibility. You see, in it alone the truly rich will rule—not those who are rich in gold, but in the wealth the happy must have, namely, a good and rational life. But if beggars—people hungry for private goods of their own—go into public life, thinking that the good is there for the seizing, then such a city is impossible. For when ruling is something fought over, such civil and domestic war destroys these men and the rest of the city as well. (7, 520e4–521a8)

---

17. This is what makes them truly just and virtuous. Compare *Phd.* 68d11–13: "It is through being afraid (*dedienai*; notice *deisantes* at *R.* 1, 347c5), then—that is, though fear—that all except philosophers are brave. And yet it is quite irrational to think that anyone could be brave through fear and cowardice."

Fourth, we have a new argument to explain why in Kallipolis the best natures should rule:

> Observe, then, Glaucon, that we won't be unjustly treating those who have become philosophers in our city, but that what we will say to them, when we compel them to take care of the others and guard them, will be just. We will say: When people like you come to exist in other cities, they are justified in not sharing in the others' labors. After all, they have grown there spontaneously, against the will of the constitution in each of them. And when something grows of its own accord, and owes no debt for its upbringing, it has justice on its side when it is not keen to pay anyone for its upbringing. (7, 520a6–b4)

In Kallipolis, it is implied, philosophers have a motive of justice to rule: they owe a debt to the city for an upbringing that has made them virtuous and godlike. Our reading of the ship-of-state simile has revealed the basis for this claim.

Fifth, we are told that the philosophers rule both willingly and out of compulsion[18]:

> [Socrates] Do you think the people we have nurtured will disobey us when they hear these things, and be unwilling to share the labors of the city, each in turn, and wish while living the greater part of their time with one another in the pure realm? [Glaucon] No, they couldn't possibly. After all, we will be giving just orders to just people. However, each of them will certainly go to rule as to something compulsory, which is exactly the opposite of what is done by those who now rule in each city. (7, 520e1–3)

Sixth, and finally, we learn that the best natures are the philosophers, who alone have "different honors and a better life than the political," namely, "the life of true philosophy" (7, 521b1–10). This is the life philosophers lead when they are not ruling down in the cave or city. Hence Socrates characterizes them as sharing "the labors of the city, each in turn, while living the greater part of their time with one another in the pure realm" (7, 520d7–8);[19] as

---

18. As is invariably the case when this topic is under discussion: 1, 347c1, d1; 2, 360c7; 4, 421b9; 5, 464e6; 6, 499b2, 5, c7, 500d4; 7, 519e4, 520e2, 521b7, 539e4, 540a7, b4, e2; 8, 556a9; 9, 579c7, d2, 592a1–10; 10, 617e3.

19. Compare: "They will spend the greater part of their time practicing philosophy, but, when his turn comes, each must labor in politics and rule for the city's sake, not as something fine, but rather *as something compulsory*" (7, 540b2–5). Since these men and women are mature philosophers, not mere trainees, it is not open to us to suppose that compulsion disappears, so to speak, once training is completed.

better able "to share both" (7, 520b7–c1)—that is, both life in the cave and life in the pure realm—than the other citizens; and as thinking, were they permitted to stay forever in that realm, that they "had emigrated, while still alive, to the Isles of the Blessed" (7, 519c5–6). The life of philosophy is where the philosophers find the good, and not, as in the case of money-lovers and honor-lovers, in the life of ruling. It is this that guarantees that they are not "lovers of ruling" (7, 531b4).

The major reason for these differences between *Republic* 1 and 7 lies in the differences we have already explored between Kallipolis and other cities. In Kallipolis, we have fully developed godlike philosophers, who will serve as its rulers. In other cities, we have good people who may be naturally equipped to be philosophers, but if so, two things will be true of them. Their natures will have been "turned around and altered" by the upbringing and hostile treatment they have received, and they will not rule willingly, unless (as is very unlikely) they have a clean slate to work with.

Compulsion, Persuasion, and Voluntariness

In the case of the best people, the nature of the compulsion to rule and the explanation of its compatibility with voluntariness are both clear: the compulsion is that of reason in the shape of rational prudence. In the case of the best philosophical natures, it is less clear, since it apparently involves not just considerations of prudence but of laws and justice.[20] If these laws and the justice they embody were being conceived deontically or non-eudaimonistically, there would indeed be a real issue here. As Socrates reminds us more than once, however, the aim of his laws is the outstanding happiness or well-being of the entire city (4, 421b3–5; 7, 519e1–3; compare *Lg.* 9, 858d6–9). The sort of compulsion they exert, therefore, the basis of their normative authority or grip, is simply that exerted by (laws of) rational prudence. This explains (to repeat) why such compulsion is compatible with voluntariness, even when it goes against desire.

Compulsion and persuasion certainly can come apart (7, 536d9–e3; 8, 554d1–3), but they can also work together—"compel and persuade"

---

20. It is a great virtue of Eric Brown, "Justice and Compulsion for Plato's Philosopher-Rulers," *Ancient Philosophy* 20 (2000): 1–17, to have more adequately appreciated than others the importance of the fact that the philosophers are compelled *by a legal requirement*, even though he misconstrues the nature of the normative authority of that requirement.

(4, 421b9), "persuasion and compulsion" (7, 519e4)—when what is necessary and compelled is good and conduces to well-being (8, 558d8–559c1).[21] This explains why compulsion continues to be compulsive even when it accords with desire: the law compels us not to harm others even when that is what we desire anyway. Similarly, learning is something that philosophers absolutely love (5, 475b11–c2), yet they are compelled, nonetheless, to learn, to ascend out of the cave and come to see the good itself (7, 519c9, 540a7). Lastly, the fact that the compulsion is rational explains why understanding can itself be compelled to do such things as sort out the muddles about bigness and smallness caused by perception (7, 524c7): it must avoid contradiction in order to obey its own rational laws.

In the *Laws*, too, good laws are presented (4, 719e8–720a3, 722b5–c2; 9, 858d6–9) as needing to mix force (*bia*) or threat of sanctions with persuasion (*peithein*) or prudential considerations.[22] But force and compulsion are not the same: "against necessity or compulsion (*anagkēn*) it is said not even a god can use force (*biazesthai*)" (5, 741a4–5; also 7, 818b2–3). That is why laws compel even when they do not force.[23] In some cases, indeed, the compulsive element is also missing, since the laws "advise (*sumbouleutikos*) but do not compel (*ouk anagkastikos*)" (11, 930b5). As in the *Republic*, then, compulsion and voluntariness remain compatible: poets, for example, are referred to as people "in a way compelled to sing voluntarily" (2, 670c8–d1).[24]

In one respect, the philosophers in Kallipolis are like the weak people Glaucon describes. These, he says, are not strong enough either to commit injustice with impunity (which they think would be the best thing, if only they could pull it off) or to avoid suffering it without taking revenge (which they think is the worst thing), so they agree with one another to enact and obey just laws—laws requiring them not to do injustice in

---

21. Though Socrates is discussing necessary and unnecessary appetites in this passage, it shows him again bringing together what is compulsory or necessary and what is beneficial.

22. As Christopher Bobonich, *Plato's Utopia Recast* (Oxford: Clarendon Press, 2002), pp. 97–106, has argued. In claiming that this "contrast between compulsion and persuasion is not made with the word *anagkē*," Brown, "Justice and Compulsion," p. 13 n. 35, overlooks *Lg.* 2, 660a4–5: "The correct lawgiver will persuade—or, if he cannot persuade, compel (*peisei te, kai anagkasei mē peithōn*)."

23. See *Lg.* 1, 648b8; 2, 660e1, 661c6; 6, 757e6, 764b1, 767e1, 780b7; 7, 789e4, 798a3; 8, 847b1; 9, 862d2, 866b6, 868b4; 11, 937c1; 12, 951d6, 965c9.

24. It is irrelevant that in these texts the *Laws* is talking about "the relationship between laws and ordinary citizens" (Brown, "Justice and Compulsion," p. 13 n. 35). The compulsion exerted on the philosophers in the *Republic* to rule is that of law full stop. There is something special about philosophers, to be sure, but not about the kind of compulsion they are under.

return for not suffering it. As a result, he says, they practice justice "as something compulsory, not as something good" (2, 358c3–4). That is the respect in which they are like the best natures (7, 520e2). Glaucon also says that they are just "unwillingly" (2, 358c3) and "only when compelled" (2, 360c6–7). For them, justice belongs in the class of instrumental goods, which consists of things "burdensome but beneficial to us"—things we would not "choose for their own sake, but for the sake of the wages and other things that are their consequences" (2, 357c8–d2). If we are compelled to do good things of that sort, apparently, we do not merely do them against our desires, we do them also against our will.

This way of looking at justice is one Socrates correctly attributes to Thrasymachus (2, 358a7–9; 8, 545a5–b2; 9, 590d1–6). Someone like that, he says, "calls everything he is compelled to do just and fine, never having seen how much the natures of compulsion and goodness really differ, and being unable to explain it to anyone" (6, 493c4–6). For possessing only a knack based on "the convictions the masses hold" about virtue, he lacks craft knowledge of the soul, and of the real effects of different practices on it (6, 493a6–c3; compare 10, 618c1–619a1). Hence he cannot teach virtue itself in the way an expert in a craft would, since he cannot explain why what are nominally virtues are genuine ones (if indeed they are), or why genuine virtues are choiceworthy not just because they are compulsory (socially legislated and backed by rewards and punishments), but because they are good things that make their possessors happy. So if justice is choiceworthy also for its own sake, the philosophers should choose it voluntarily and not simply because they are compelled—by law or anything else—to do so.

What exactly is it that they are then choosing? In their elaborate description of how they want Socrates to respond to Thrasymachus, Glaucon and Adeimantus say repeatedly that they want him to focus on justice itself as a force for happiness when it is unobserved in the soul (2, 367b3–d3). Thus Socrates' focus is required to be on justice as a psychological state or state of character, not on just actions. But a state might well be choiceworthy for its own sake, as we saw, even though not all the actions it causes or motivates its possessor to do are themselves choiceworthy in that way. Character choice, of the sort imagined to occur at the spindle of Necessity in *Republic* 10, is not the same, or constrained by the same considerations, as action choice. Justice may be choiceworthy as a good thing that is crucial for blessed happiness, even though some of the actions it requires of its possessor are of a sort that involve choosing to do what is not desirable for its own sake.

Ruling is something that philosophers in Kallipolis do not consider to be a "great good" (7, 520d1) or enjoy doing for its own sake (1, 347c5–7). It is not something they desire to do in a way that involves looking on it with pleasure. But that, as we have repeatedly seen, does not entail that they do not want or will to do it or do it involuntarily. It does not entail, either, that they do not see justice—the state of character—as one of the finest goods, choiceworthy for its consequences, certainly, but "much more so" (2, 367c8) for its own sake. It does not even entail that ruling cannot be something they consider choiceworthy for its own sake when—as supposedly in Kallipolis—justice in the shape of a just law requires it (7, 520a6–9, e1).[25]

Would philosophers rule Kallipolis if there were no law compelling them to do so?[26] There is only one reason available now to think that they would not, namely, that they lacked access to the considerations that lead its legislators to enact the laws they do so that the laws would introduce a new and otherwise inaccessible element into their practical, prudential calculation. But that reason we can exclude. For Socrates is explicit that the philosophers must have such access. "There must always be some people in the city," he says to Adeimantus, "who have a rational account of the constitution, the very same one that you, the lawgiver, also had when you made the laws" (6, 497c7–d2). The bottom line is that each philosopher in Kallipolis can construct for himself an analogue of the legislators' argument for why he should rule, whether there is a law requiring him to do so or not.

As what justice demands of philosophers in Kallipolis differs from what it demands of them in other cities, so, too, do the wages of ruling. In other cities a naturally equipped philosopher would get freedom from being ruled by people worse than himself as his sole wage. For these cities, to put it mildly, have made no provision for the training and education of philosophers or for their leisure. In Kallipolis, by contrast, philosophers, like other guardians, receive their upkeep "as a wage for their guardianship" (3, 416e2). Wages of ruling as such are not mentioned explicitly in *Republic* 7, but they are surely presupposed both when Socrates speaks of "harmonizing the citizens together through persuasion or compulsion, and making them share with one another the benefits they can confer on the community" (7, 519e3–520a2), and when he reminds the philosophers that, though they do have to rule, they nonetheless get to spend "the greater part of their time" in the pure

---

25. This is a friendly amendment to the somewhat different proposal defended in Richard Kraut, "Return to the Cave: *Republic* 519–521," in *Plato 2: Ethics, Politics, Religion, and the Soul*, ed. Gail Fine (Oxford: Oxford University Press, 2000), pp. 247–251.

26. Compare Brown, "Justice and Compulsion," p. 9: "If the founders were not to legislate that the philosophers must rule, the philosophers would not rule."

realm, doing philosophy (7, 520d8, 540b2). In any case, when the con-
clusions reached in *Republic* 3 about the upkeep and lifestyle of the
guardians are repeated in *Republic* 8, the philosopher-kings are clearly
included among those who "receive their minimum yearly upkeep from
the other citizens as a wage for their guardianship, and take care of
themselves and the rest of the city" (8, 543c1–3).

It is this fact, in all likelihood, that explains why Socrates is so insistent that the constitution of Kallipolis will include laws compelling
philosophers to rule—although the force and point of the laws and
their compulsion is based on considerations quite other than those that
explain that insistence.[27] For the producers and guardians in Kallipolis
will need to see what the philosophers are required to do to earn
their security and upkeep. Like Glaucon (7, 520a5) and Adeimantus
(4, 419a1–420a1), they will need to be reassured that Kallipolis is not
a Thrasymachean exploitation machine set up to benefit its rulers at
the expense of the other citizens. How better to reassure them—or us,
for that matter—than to point out that the appropriate requirement
is actually embodied in the constitution? It is a nice irony that recent
readers of the *Republic* have been more concerned about the *rulers* being
the ones exploited!

The picture presented in *Republic* 1 of a "city of good men" in which "the
citizens would fight in order not to rule, just as they now do in order to
rule" (347d1–4), needs to be counterpoised to another: "in all constitutions, change originates in the ruling element itself when faction breaks
out within it" (8, 545d1–2). So it must be that whatever fighting, literal
or figurative, breaks out among the philosophers in Kallipolis is somehow guaranteed to avoid becoming faction. Socrates does not explicitly
address the question of the basis of this guarantee except to remind us
that the philosopher's distinctive craft—dialectic—is never to be practiced in a competitive manner for the sake of victory but always for the
sake of truth (7, 537e1–539d1) and to say that each philosopher must
rule "when his turn comes" (7, 520d8, 540b2). What we are to imagine,
surely, is that justice demands that the philosophers share the task of
ruling equally and that they, as just people, act accordingly. Their treatment of each other is thus a special case of the "debt for . . . upbringing"

---

27. We may agree with Brown, "Justice and Compulsion," p. 6 n. 15, that if "all
Socrates is doing with his appeals to *anagkē*" is emphasizing that Kallipolis is not a
Thrasymachean exploitation machine, "then he is employing mere rhetorical trick-
ery." Even *Philosopher-Kings*, p. 203, however, which Brown is tentatively criticizing,
does not make that silly claim. It is Socrates' emphasis and insistence that is being
explained, not the normative status of his laws.

(7, 520b4) that each of them owes to Kallipolis. A philosopher rules producers in exchange for upkeep, guardians in exchange for protection, and his fellow philosophers in exchange for being ruled, so that, having been taught philosophy, he has the leisure to practice it.

Should the Philosophers Rule Kallipolis?

Even with all these matters appropriately clear, a philosopher might still feel uncertain about whether the law requiring him to rule in Kallipolis really does promote his outstanding happiness. Such uncertainty is bound to grow when he reflects that, though Kallipolis may have many rulers, it may also have only one (4, 445d3–6; 7, 540d3–5). For Socrates' claim that philosophers in Kallipolis spend "the greater part of their time" doing philosophy (7, 520d8, 540b2) will then seem especially tendentious.

What such a philosopher is worried about are the costs in Kallipolis that psychic justice imposes on him. His worry thus has three potential foci. First, psychic justice itself: should he have it? Second, Kallipolis: is it where he should live? Third, contemplating the good (philosophic happiness): can he get more of it than, as a just person, he gets in Kallipolis? If the philosopher approaches these questions as Socrates does, he will think as follows: Happiness is what I will have when good things have become mine forever—or for the closest mortal equivalent thereof (*Smp.* 204e1–6, 206a9–13). Since, like everyone else, I want things that are objectively and not merely apparently good (6, 505d5–9), I must not use a "broken yardstick" or "blank measuring tape" as my paradigm of goodness (*Chrm.* 154b9). Instead, I must use the form of the good. As something akin to an ideal of rational order, this tells me that a rationally ordered soul is best and that, for an embodied soul like mine, with three constitutive elements, psychic justice is part and parcel of such rational order. Similarly, it tells me that the best, because rationally ruled and ordered city, is Kallipolis. Since I am not self-sufficient, and cannot satisfy all of my needs myself, I have no alternative but to live together with others in some sort of city or community. So these two bests, the one psychological, the other political, lead to a third: the best life for me is that of the best human being in the best city, since only there am I ruled both internally and externally by reason.

Persuaded by these arguments and equipped now with a rationally ruled and so just soul, there our philosopher is in Kallipolis. It is his turn to stop contemplating the good and go down into the city to rule. It flashes into his mind—we may for the sake of argument imagine—that he should cheat, play the free-rider, and get more contemplation time. What will he do? He will rule, of course, since he will act—how else?—out of his acquired and firmly fixed states of character (4, 429e6–430a5; 10, 618b3–4). Is what he will do what he should do, what reason would have him do? Does rational prudence prescribe for him as it does for Kallipolis itself? That is a live issue only if we are doubtful about whether self-interested practical reason, when directed to the question not of what a person should do, but at the prior question of what sort of person he should be, would recommend not the virtue of justice but something else—something more like opportunism.

If a philosopher inside or outside Kallipolis is convinced by Socrates' argument, he will think that practical reason has done all it can do by way of ensuring happiness when it has made him and his world as just as possible. Socrates says as much himself:

> If we are making genuine guardians, the sort least likely to do the city evil, and if our critic is making pseudo-farmers—feasters happy at a festival, so to speak, not in a city—he is not talking about a city, but about something else. What we have to consider, then, is whether our aim in establishing the guardians is the greatest possible happiness for them, or whether—since our aim is to see this happiness develop for the whole city—we should compel or persuade the auxiliaries and guardians to ensure that they, and all the others as well, are the best possible craftsmen at their own work; and then, with the whole city developing and being governed well, *leave it to nature to provide each group with its share of happiness.* (4, 421a8–c6)

How big a share of happiness that will be depends on nature. Reason cannot ensure that a plague or tsunami will not wipe out most of the philosophers or that hostile neighbors will not keep the city in a perpetual state of war. It cannot, for that matter, rule out the possibility that some "necessity" will force those who are "foremost in philosophy to take charge of a city," so that Kallipolis will come into existence even though no one plans on it (6, 499c7–d6).

Luck, especially bad luck, is the goad we kick against. That practical reason, even when given its largest scope, still leaves us prey to it is hard for us to accept. Like the guardian in the following passage, we are inclined to want more:

> If a guardian tries to become happy in such a way that he is no longer a guardian at all, and is not satisfied with a life that is moderate, stable, and (we claim)

best, but is seized by a foolish, adolescent belief about happiness, which incites him to use his power to take everything in the city for himself—he will come to realize the true wisdom of Hesiod's saying that in a sense the half is worth more than the whole. (5, 466b5–c3)

Wanting more, in other words, means getting less.

INDEX OF PASSAGES

INDEX